Lecture Notes in Computer Science 12326

Founding Editors

Gerhard Goos
Karlsruhe Institute of Technology, Karlsruhe, Germany
Juris Hartmanis
Cornell University, Ithaca, NY, USA

Editorial Board Members

Elisa Bertino
Purdue University, West Lafayette, IN, USA
Wen Gao
Peking University, Beijing, China
Bernhard Steffen ⓘ
TU Dortmund University, Dortmund, Germany
Gerhard Woeginger ⓘ
RWTH Aachen, Aachen, Germany
Moti Yung
Columbia University, New York, NY, USA

More information about this series at http://www.springer.com/series/7407

Dalibor Klusáček · Walfredo Cirne ·
Narayan Desai (Eds.)

Job Scheduling Strategies for Parallel Processing

23rd International Workshop, JSSPP 2020
New Orleans, LA, USA, May 22, 2020
Revised Selected Papers

 Springer

Editors
Dalibor Klusáček
CESNET
Prague, Czech Republic

Walfredo Cirne
Google
Mountain View, CA, USA

Narayan Desai
Google
Seattle, WA, USA

ISSN 0302-9743   ISSN 1611-3349   (electronic)
Lecture Notes in Computer Science
ISBN 978-3-030-63170-3   ISBN 978-3-030-63171-0   (eBook)
https://doi.org/10.1007/978-3-030-63171-0

LNCS Sublibrary: SL1 – Theoretical Computer Science and General Issues

© Springer Nature Switzerland AG 2020
This work is subject to copyright. All rights are reserved by the Publisher, whether the whole or part of the material is concerned, specifically the rights of translation, reprinting, reuse of illustrations, recitation, broadcasting, reproduction on microfilms or in any other physical way, and transmission or information storage and retrieval, electronic adaptation, computer software, or by similar or dissimilar methodology now known or hereafter developed.
The use of general descriptive names, registered names, trademarks, service marks, etc. in this publication does not imply, even in the absence of a specific statement, that such names are exempt from the relevant protective laws and regulations and therefore free for general use.
The publisher, the authors and the editors are safe to assume that the advice and information in this book are believed to be true and accurate at the date of publication. Neither the publisher nor the authors or the editors give a warranty, expressed or implied, with respect to the material contained herein or for any errors or omissions that may have been made. The publisher remains neutral with regard to jurisdictional claims in published maps and institutional affiliations.

This Springer imprint is published by the registered company Springer Nature Switzerland AG
The registered company address is: Gewerbestrasse 11, 6330 Cham, Switzerland

Preface

This volume contains the papers presented at the 23rd workshop on Job Scheduling Strategies for Parallel Processing (JSSPP 2020) that was held on May 22, 2020, in conjunction with the 34th IEEE International Parallel and Distributed Processing Symposium (IPDPS 2020). The proceedings of previous workshops are also available from Springer as LNCS volumes 949, 1162, 1291, 1459, 1659, 1911, 2221, 2537, 2862, 3277, 3834, 4376, 4942, 5798, 6253, 7698, 8429, 8828, 10353, 10773, and 11332.

This year eight papers were submitted to the workshop, of which we accepted six. All submitted papers went through a complete review process, with the full version being read and evaluated by an average of four reviewers. Additionally, one invited paper and one keynote were included in the workshop. We would like to especially thank our Program Committee members and additional reviewers for their willingness to participate in this effort and their excellent, detailed, and thoughtful reviews.

For the first time in its history the JSSPP workshop was held fully online due to the worldwide COVID-19 pandemic. Despite the obvious logistic problems, all talks were presented live, allowing for the participants to interact with the authors of the papers. We are very thankful to the presenters of accepted papers for their participation in the live workshop session. Recordings from all talks at the 2020 edition can be found at the JSSPP's YouTube channel: https://bit.ly/3mXyT8F.

This year, the workshop opened with a keynote delivered by César De Rose from the PUCRS, School of Technology, Brazil. De Rose discussed interference-aware scheduling in virtualized environments, where multiple applications contending for shared resources are susceptible to cross-application interference, thus leading to possible significant performance degradation and consequently an increase in the number of broken SLAs. Therefore, interference-aware scheduling has gained traction, with the investigation of ways to classify applications regarding their interference levels and the proposal of static cost models and policies for scheduling co-hosted applications. The keynote was concluded with a demonstration of how interference-aware scheduling can improve resource usage while reducing SLA violations, with further opportunities for improvement in the areas of application classification and pro-active dynamic scheduling strategies.

Papers accepted for this year's JSSPP focused on several interesting problems within the resource management and scheduling domains. The first two papers focused on the problem of resource contention and workload interference. Yoonsung et al. discussed the performance degradation due to the contention for shared resources, such as cache and memory bandwidth. In this paper, the trade-offs between software and hardware isolation techniques were illustrated. Also, authors showed the benefit of coordinated enforcement of multiple isolation techniques.

Thiyyakat et al. presented a new scheduling policy that improves the performance of critical workload that is co-located with less important batch workloads. The authors showed that their policy decreases the slowdown for critical workloads compared to a solution that used standard Control Groups (cgroups).

In their invited paper, Jaroš et al. discussed the problems related to scheduling ultrasound simulation workflows. They described how therapeutic ultrasound plays an increasing role in modern medicine. To optimize its benefits, the treatment procedures must be adapted carefully to patients needs by computing various DAG-like workflows that refine the parameters needed for the actual ultrasound machine. In their paper, authors discussed several scheduling problems that must be solved in order to execute these workflows efficiently.

Cavicchioli et al. approached the problem of under-utilizing available memory bandwidth when avoiding memory interference in systems that feature high-performance multi-core CPUs tightly integrated with data-parallel accelerators. They performed a set of experiments where they showed that the standard conservative approach that relies on exclusive use of shared main memory can be extended by injecting controlled amounts of memory requests coming from other tasks than the one currently granted exclusive DRAM access, thus using the available bandwidth more efficiently.

Nobre et al. proposed a highly optimized GPU+CPU based approach for epistasis detection. Epistasis (multiple interacting variations in DNA) detection is an important research topic in the field of DNA analysis as it allows to better understand various DNA variations that may cause, e.g., Alzheimer's disease, breast cancer, or Crohn's disease. As such, epistasis detection represents a computationally intensive optimization problem.

The sixth paper focused on walltime prediction and its impact on job scheduling performance and predictability. Job walltimes estimates, usually specified by users, are known to be very imprecise which causes problems both to the users and to the scheduling policies. Klusáček et al. presented an experimental analysis that demonstrated how the use of walltime predictors impacts the actual performance of a job scheduler as well its ability to provide accurate predictions concerning future job execution.

Last but not least, Geng et al. presented PDAWL, a novel dynamic approach for scheduling tasks that are capable of running simultaneously on both CPUs and general-purpose accelerators. It uses machine learning to build communication and computation performance estimation model of the workload with respect to the actual CPU and GPU performance. The online scheduler then adaptively adjusts the workload allocation based on the runtime situation.

We hope you can join us at the next JSSPP workshop, this time in Portland, Oregon, USA, on May 21, 2021. Enjoy your reading!

September 2020

Dalibor Klusáček
Walfredo Cirne
Narayan Desai

Organization

Workshop Organizers

Dalibor Klusáček	CESNET, Czech Republic
Walfredo Cirne	Google, USA
Narayan Desai	Google, USA

Program Committee

Ashvin Agrawal	Microsoft, USA
Amaya Booker	Facebook, USA
Julita Corbalan	Barcelona Supercomputing Center, Spain
Stratos Dimopoulos	Apple, USA
Hyeonsang Eom	Seoul National University, South Korea
Dror Feitelson	Hebrew University, Israel
Liana Fong	IBM T. J. Watson Research Center, USA
Eitan Frachtenberg	Facebook, USA
Alfredo Goldman	University of São Paulo, Brazil
Allan Gottlieb	New York University, USA
Zhiling Lan	Illinois Institute of Technology, USA
Bill Nitzberg	Altair, USA
P-O. Östberg	Umeå University, Sweden
Gonzalo P. Rodrigo	Apple, USA
Larry Rudolph	Two Sigma, USA
Uwe Schwiegelshohn	TU Dortmund, Germany
Yingchong Situ	Google, USA
Leonel Sousa	Universidade de Lisboa, Portugal
Ramin Yahyapour	University of Göttingen, Germany

Additional Reviewers

Diogo Marques
Ricardo Nobre

Contents

Towards Interference-Aware Dynamic Scheduling in Virtualized Environments

Vinícius Meyer, Uillian L. Ludwig, Miguel G. Xavier, Dionatrã F. Kirchoff, and Cesar A. F. De Rose

School of Technology, Pontifical Catholic University of Rio Grande do Sul (PUCRS), 6681 Ipiranga Ave, Building 32, Porto Alegre, Brazil
{vinicius.meyer,uillian.ludwig,dionatra.kirchoff}@edu.pucrs.br
{miguel.xavier,cesar.derose}@pucrs.br

Abstract. Our previous work shows that multiple applications contending for shared resources in virtualized environments are susceptible to cross-application interference, which can lead to significant performance degradation and consequently an increase in the number of broken SLAs. Nevertheless, state of the art in resource scheduling in virtualized environments still relies mainly on resource capacity, adopting heuristics such as bin packing, overlooking this source of overhead. However, in recent years interference-aware scheduling has gained traction, with the investigation of ways to classify applications regarding their interference levels and the proposal of static cost models and policies for scheduling co-hosted cloud applications. Preliminary results in this area already show a considerable improvement on resource usage and in the reduction of broken SLAs, but we strongly believe that there are still opportunities for improvement in the areas of application classification and pro-active dynamic scheduling strategies. This paper presents the state of the art in interference-aware scheduling for virtualized environments and the challenges and advantages of a dynamic scheme.

Keywords: Resource management · Interference-aware scheduling · Dynamic scheduling · Virtualized environments

1 Introduction

In order to allow virtualized platforms to deliver SLA guarantees for high user satisfaction, efficient and automatic resource scheduling strategies are essential. Resource scheduling is a core function and a central component to coordinate all the other platform components to deliver performance-oriented solutions [18].

Typically, in large data centers, resource scheduling is accomplished through heuristics such as bin packing, which considers only resource capacity aspects [29], overlooking other sources of overhead [1]. However, related work [34] shows that several applications contending for shared resources in such environments can generate cross-application interference, which may lead to significant

© Springer Nature Switzerland AG 2020
D. Klusáček et al. (Eds.): JSSPP 2020, LNCS 12326, pp. 1–24, 2020.
https://doi.org/10.1007/978-3-030-63171-0_1

performance degradation and consequently to an increase in the number of broken Service Level Agreements (SLAs) [19].

Looking for alternatives, in previous work we have explored scheduling policies based also on interference generated by co-allocated applications [16]. We proposed an attraction/repulsion model built upon the workload profile of each application, beyond the traditional concept of just observing resource usage and capacity. In that work, web applications were investigated since they are a category that presents workload variations at run time resulting in an hard to predict resource utilization due to users' different request patterns and periodicity [5]. Dynamic service demands and workload profiles further raise the challenges for service providers in managing resources on-demand to satisfy SLAs while minimizing the costs [36]. Therefore, any solution to address these challenges should account for workload variability and performance interference due to the dynamic nature of the problem [24].

Although our preliminary results in this area already show a considerable improvement on resource usage and in the reduction of broken SLAs, but we strongly believe that there are still opportunities for improvement in the areas of application classification and pro-active dynamic scheduling strategies. This paper presents the state of the art in interference-aware scheduling for virtualized environments and the challenges and advantages of a dynamic scheme.

2   Background

This section outlines the concepts intrinsic to this work.

2.1   Resource Management and Virtualization

In data centers, orchestration systems need highly elastic and scalable infrastructures that allow the dynamic allocation of different resources (such as compute, storage, networking, software, or a service) in the right location and with minimal delays, enabling the deployment of applications [30]. The elasticity in such environments is obtained abstracting physical resources from an underlying layer through virtualization. There are different virtualization technologies, but the two most relevant in this landscape are *Hardware virtualization* and *System-level virtualization*:

- *Hardware virtualization* (Hypervisors) abstracts the underlying hardware layers to enable complete operating systems to run inside the hypervisor as if they were an application. Paravirtualization solutions (Xen[1]) and hardware virtualization solutions (KVM[2]), in combination with hardware-specific support, integrated into modern CPU (Intel VT-x and AMD-V), can achieve a low level of overhead due to the new layer added between the virtual instance and the hardware.

---

[1] https://xenproject.org/.
[2] https://www.linux-kvm.org/.

– *System-level virtualization* (Containers) is based on fast and lightweight process virtualization and allows to tie up an entire application with its dependencies in a virtual container that can run on every Linux distribution. It provides its users an environment as close as possible to a standard Linux distribution. Due to the fact that containers are more lightweight than VMs, the same host can achieve higher densities with containers than with VMs. This approach has radically decreased both the start-up time of instances and the processing and storage overhead, which are typical drawbacks of Hypervisor-based virtualization [21].

Containerization is the state-of-art virtualization solution for provisioning platforms and its virtual instances only need seconds to initiate, versus minutes for a regular VM [35]. By encapsulating run time contexts of software components and services, containers improve portability and efficiency for cloud application deployment. In addition, one container can be scaled out/in within a minute, and consequently can react immediately when encountering possible unforeseen crash. Therefore, containers are capable of tolerating fluctuating stress and reducing overhead [22], features which auto scaling solutions rely on. There are many well known container solutions, such as: Docker[3], Linux LXC[4], OpenVZ[5] and Linux-VServer[6].

2.2   Resource Sharing and Performance Interference

With the advent of resource sharing techniques, physical machines host multiple applications. Even though the use of resource sharing methods, such as virtualization or containerization, provide techniques to fairly share resource between co-hosted applications, when multiple services intensively use a resource at the same time, resource contention may happen. This problem is known as performance interference, and it may lead to severe performance degradation [1].

Virtualization technologies and server consolidation are the main drivers of high resource utilization in modern Data Centers. Combining virtual machines into the same server may lead to severe performance degradation. This performance degradation is known as virtual machine interference. Supporting a higher virtual machine interference may result in a higher consolidation, while strict low interference requirements may demand more resources. Jersark and Ferreto [7] claim that applications are affected by other virtual machines, which use the same resource intensively in the same physical machine. Furthermore, each resource is affected differently. CPU intensive applications led to performance degradation of 14%. Memory and disk I/O intensive applications, performance degradation may be as high as 90%. Therefore, it is clear that performance interference is a problem, and performance degradation varies depending on the stressed resource.

---

[3] http://www.docker.com.

[4] https://linuxcontainers.org/.

[5] https://openvz.org/.

[6] http://www.linux-vserver.org.

Performance interference affects container-based environments as well. Disk-intensive applications running over containers promote performance degradation that uses different resources intensively. Xavier et al. [34] have tested several combinations of co-hosted workloads. While some of these combinations led to performance degradation up to 38%, they could also combine the workloads with no interference. Cluster systems usually run several applications-often from different users-concurrently, with individual applications competing for access to shared resources such as the file system or the network. Low application performance may be caused by interference from different sources. Shah et al. [23] state that mapping performance data related to shared resources onto time slices can establish the simultaneity of application usage across jobs, which can be indicative of inter-application interference. In some cases, inter-application interference causes performance degradation by up to 50%.

2.3   Service Level Agreements

Service Level Agreements (SLAs) have been proposed for cloud services as contracts used to record the rights and obligations of service providers and their customers [15]. At the end of the negotiation process, provider and consumer commit to an agreement. This agreement is referred to as a SLA. This SLA serves as the foundation for the expected level of service between the consumer and the provider. The Quality-of-Service (QoS) attributes that are generally part of an SLA (such as response time and throughput) however change constantly and to enforce the agreement, these parameters need to be closely monitored [8].

3   State of the Art

Scheduling tasks in virtualized environments in a way that minimizes the performance interference effect from co-located applications is referred to as interference-aware scheduling [34]. This section will present the state of the art in the following areas related to this work: interference profiling, interference classification and interference-aware scheduling algorithms.

3.1   Interference Profiling

Modern high-performance computer systems continue to increase in size and complexity. Tools to measure application performance in these increasingly complex environments must also increase the richness of their measurements to provide insights into the increasingly intricate ways in which software and hardware interact [28]. Interference profiling is essential in this work, since dealing with dynamic workloads and evaluating the impact of interference over time requires a tool that captures such metrics at run time.

To help advanced users to utilize their hardware more efficiently, the Linux trace toolkit [14] was developed. It is a suite of tools designed to extract program execution details from the Linux operating system and interpret them. Specifically, it enables its users to extract processor utilization rates and allocation information for a certain period. It is possible to perform various calculations on this data and dump it to a text file. The toolkit provides flexible, low-overhead mechanisms to trace a variety of kernel events such as system call invocations, process, memory, file system and network operations.

Urgaonkar et al. [31] used kernel-based profiling mechanisms in the context of shared hosting platforms to profile applications execution. The advantage of this approach is that it works with any application and requires no changes to the application at the source or binary levels. This is especially important in hosting environments where the platform provider may have little or no access to third-party applications.

Terpstra et al. [28] proposed PAPI (the Performance API), a tool that provides a consistent interface and methodology to use performance counters found in most major microprocessors. PAPI enables software engineers to see, in near real-time, the relation between software performance and processor events. In addition, PAPI provides access to a collection of components that expose performance measurement opportunities across the hardware and software stack.

3.2 Interference Classification

Classification is a necessary step in the identification of tasks that can be scheduled on the same virtual instance. An accurate interference classification allows a manager or a scheduler to better select which tasks will share resources, minimizing interference among them which could cause overhead and adversely affect their performance.

Javadi and Gandhi [6] presents DIAL, an interference-aware load balancer for cloud environments. The interference detection is accomplished using decision tree-based classifier to find the dominant source of resource contention. It monitors the impact of interference on user metrics such as CPU utilization, I/O wait time, etc. The model is trained and the decision tree can classify the source of interference, even for unseen workloads, based on the observed metric values.

Kumar and Setia [13] introduce an interference-free scheduling algorithm with better performance for cloud computing applications. A random forest technique is used to classify applications into class labels: CPU, network and memory intensive. When recognized by the system each task is immediately classified and scheduled on the desired VM to better use the available resource.

In order to avoid cross-application I/O interference, Kougkas et al. [10] explore the negative effects of interference at the burst buffer layer. In their study, a code-block classifier is applied that categorizes the nodes into two classes: compute or I/O blocks. As a result, they claim that, through better I/O scheduling, their work can outperform existing state-of-the-art buffering management solutions by three times and can lead to better resource utilization.

3.3   Interference-Aware Scheduling Algorithms

In virtualized ecosystems, consolidating multiple user applications onto multi-core servers generates interference between co-hosted applications, which impacts application performance. To minimize interference effects and overcome those issues, a common solution is to apply resource scheduling policies [1,19,33].

The cloud scheduler proposed by [19] makes this decision based upon the resource requirements of workloads. To determine resource requirements, VMs are first profiled on a staging server to determine the amount of resources needed to attain a desired level of QoS in an interference-free environment. To incorporate performance interference relationships between VMs that are consolidated onto a server, they have adopted a multi-input, multi-output (MIMO) model approach which captures performance interference interactions. It is considered a discrete-time MIMO model of the platform with its inputs and outputs in order to design a model predictive control framework. The inputs are defined as the actuators used by the platform controller to manage resource allocations at particular time step. The outputs are the predicted QoS values.

In [1] strategy, all newly created VMs are assigned to a PM by a load balancing scheduler that is generally based on a heuristic such as bin packing. After that, the scheduler decides whether to trigger migration by comparing the slowdown factor among all potential PMs and migrates VMs to the PM with the smallest slowdown factor. The algorithm greedily finds the most suitable PM for each VM by picking the PM with the smallest slowdown when assigned the new VM. It requires the loading vectors from each VM as input. The processing step of a VM request within a PM uses a discrete-time Markov chain in which the states represent the hypervisor layer and physical resources.

To minimize interference and job execution time in Apache Spark jobs, [33] designs and implements a scheduler that automatically schedules and executes submitted Spark jobs leveraging a performance prediction framework. When a new job arrives in the system the scheduler locates available servers that can execute the job. If existing jobs are running in the system with possibly more jobs waiting in the queue, the scheduler calculates the waiting time of the new job and readjusts the waiting time of the jobs that are already in the queue to determine the best scheduling plan and updates the scheduling file accordingly.

4   Measuring Performance Interference

Uncontrolled access to shared resources can cause performance variations that lead applications to fail or run unsteadily. The friction generated by the competition to access RAM, disk storage, cache or internal busses is called resource contention. Many efforts have been made to alleviate contention at the operating system level, ranging from better scheduling techniques in multi-core architectures [38] to dynamically addressing mapping to minimize memory contention [20]. The steady growth of virtual data centers has raised a concern about resource contention, and the impact it might cause in environments where performance is crucial and SLA cannot be violated, such as clouds. I/O contention, for instance, occurs when multiple tasks compete for a portion of disk bandwidth in a scenario where the demand is higher than the available resources.

On the other hand, performance interference may also arise due to isolation issues in the virtualization layer, which occurs when a virtual instance exceeds the amount of allocated resources. Because resource limit settings are capacity-driven (e.g. GB, VCores, etc.) and not throughput-driven (e.g. bandwidth, IPC, etc.), even though a virtual instance receives a limited portion of resource, there is nonetheless leakage due to uncontrolled access to operating system queues and uncore hardware components. Data center administrators have been exaggerated the amount of allocated resources to sidestep contentious scenarios, making the data center underutilized.

4.1   Interference Profiler Tool (IntP)

In this section we present IntP [34], a tool for the quantification of per application resource sensitivity. By using instrumentation techniques to infer application behaviors during runtime, IntP gives users information about how their applications are sensitive to hardware components and OS layers. Results provided by IntP can assist data center administrators in scheduling strategies to place applications that cause more noise between each other onto different machines. In addition, the infrastructure becomes more balanced, since applications with different characteristics can be interleaved, making the data center resource efficient.

4.2   System-Level Resource Contentious Instrumentation

Unlike current solutions, IntP is composed of a set of modules running in the operating system level, which collects metrics from different hardware subsystems and operating system levels. Once started, the modules consist of hooks that probe operating system functions and apply a filter on every instruction that comes from tasks to the hardware. For the case of storage block and network stack, interference may come from scheduling queues, and the dispatch rate is governed by the synchronism between the operating system and an external timer clock. This synchronism is architecture-dependent and comes from an external hardware timer that fires interrupts (jiffies) in time intervals of $1/HZ$, where HZ is a compile-time constant that varies from 100 to 1000 in modern operating systems. Hence, the variables analyzed by IntP to assess interference in scheduling queues are defined in Table 1.

The service time per unit of time is defined by:

$$f(t) = \frac{\upsilon * \gamma}{t} \tag{1}$$

Considering that the operating system performs scheduling decisions at intervals denoted by HZ, we divided the service time by HZ and integrate it from the instant t_0 to t_1:

$$I_{queue} = \int_{t_0}^{t_1} f(t)/HZDt \tag{2}$$

Table 1. Queue instrumentation variables

Variable	Description
v	Average service time
γ	Arrival rate
t	Elapsed time
HZ	Timer interrupt rate

It means that each time the operating system looks at a scheduling queue, a job may or not be in progress. This assumption gives us the level of stress that an application is putting on queues over the operating system level at instant time t. The next subsections describe IntP instrumentation points that collect above mentioned variables and other interference perspectives that IntP is capable of infer.

4.3   Block Layer Points

Although many optimization techniques have been developed, such as page caches for Writeback operations, the performance of block devices has a big impact on overall system performance. When a block request arrives into elevator scheduling queues, the scheduler does optimization functions (sorting, merging) in request queues to get efficient I/O. It means that requests are merged with others if either request ever grows large enough that they become contiguous. Afterward, they are sorted, not allowing a read to be moved ahead of a write or vice-versa. These optimization algorithms allow more contiguous read/write operations dispatched to disks, reducing seeks and head movements in hard drives per unit of time. However, the higher the number of requests arriving at the elevator queues, the less efficient the general operation becomes, since the disk handles incoming requests at lower rates than CPU. This overload increases the queue depth (number of pending requests), and becomes even more noticeable in SMP machines, on which multiple tasks contend for a single disk.

A good metric to assess performance is defined by the time the disk takes to handle a request (i.e. service time). In order to infer the service time, we measured the delta-time from the *block_rq_complete* to *block_rq_issue* kernel functions. Theses points are called whenever a block segment is added and removed from the scheduling queue after the optimizations have taken place. Based on this, we measured the average service time v (in milliseconds) for I/O requests and the arrival rate γ to quantify interference in elevator queue. This interference metric is referred to as I_{disk} in the IntP.

4.4   Network Stack Points

We focused on analyzing the network packet path from the network device (ring buffer) to the application buffer (socket's receive buffer) or vice-versa, so that an application can be classified by its level of pressure placed on hardware device (throughput) and operating system's network stack (latency). The latency is meant as the average service time v. Since the OS's network stack controls two-ways communications (send/recv) using different queues, the IntP should instrument the scheduler functions in isolation. The average service time of the sending queue is obtained by the delta-time from the *net_dev_xmit* to *__dev_queue_xmit* functions. And the average service time of the receiving queue is obtained by the delta-time from the *napi_complete_done* to *__napi_schedule_irqoff* functions. The average service time v is given by the sum of both metrics. The arrival rate γ is given by the total of send and receive packets per unit of time. This interference metric is referred to as $I_{netstack}$ in the IntP.

On the other hand, IntP aims to measure the interference sourced from contention in the network card, which occurs when the bandwidth is not enough for multiple tasks to carry all the data that is needed (i.e. capacity overflow). The bandwidth consumed per tasks is obtained using the probes as above, but accumulating the length of each packet dispatched and received per unit of time. Hence, the interference from the hardware device is given by:

$$I_{netc.apacity} = \int_{t_0}^{t_1} \frac{SUM(length)}{bandwidth} \tag{3}$$

Where bandwidth is the nominal limit of the network card capacity.

4.5 Memory Points

IntP aims to assess the level of interference an application causes during memory accesses. The IntP's memory module collects counters from the memory controller, which is a digital circuit that manages the flow of data going to and from the main memory. It is usually called integrated memory controller (IMC). The first approach was to use LLC_MISS (last level cache miss) * 64 Bytes (size of cache line). However, the problem with this approach is that he LLC_MISS counter would not include prefetch misses. This can be a huge issue when there are a lot of prefetching activities involved (for example, when there is streaming access involved in the program). Recent CPU architectures made available counters that can be fetched from the uncore IMC, allowing more precise observations. Hence, the level of interference an application puts on memory access is given by:

$$\gamma_{th} = \int_{t_0}^{t_1} (MRC + MWC) * CLDt \tag{4}$$

Where MRC and MWC denote the number of reads and memory writes, respectively. And CL is the size of cache line (commonly 64). Finally, the integration of application's threads is summed as follows:

$$I_{mem} = \sum \gamma_{th}, \forall_{th} \in S \tag{5}$$

By normalizing I_{mem}, IntP outputs a metric (0..1), which ranges from lowest to highest interference degree, of which is possible to infer the behavior of the application's threads while they are accessing the main memory.

4.6   LLC Points

The last level cache is a key resource to manage, since multi-threaded architectures and multicore platforms are constantly arise. The chip industry has been introducing a new feature in the hardware that allows an OS to determine the usage of cache by applications running on the platform. This is the case of Intel Cache Monitoring Technology (CMT) [3]. CMT provides mechanisms for an OS to indicate a software-defined ID for each of the threads that are scheduled to run on a core. This ID is called the Resource Monitoring ID (RMID). Since there are associations between threads and RMIDs, they are programmed via a thread-specific model-specific register called MSR, and can be read by system software at any time through an MSR interface. The built-in cache module of IntP takes advantages of this feature and begins mapping application's threads to RMIDs during run time to infer per-application cache usage, thus cache interference can be denoted by;

$$\theta_{th} = \int_{t_0}^{t_1} MSR(rmid_{th})Dt \tag{6}$$

Where MSR is the interface that read the thread-specific $rmid$ from the CPU register during the instant time t. Finally, the total of cache occupancy of an application is given by:

$$I_{cache} = \sum \theta_{th}, \forall_{th} \in S \tag{7}$$

4.7   Use Case: IntP-Assisted Job Scheduling for Big Data

This section demonstrates the use of IntP for better BigData-centric application scheduling. IntP was used to assess interference metrics of heterogeneous applications that put stress on different hardware components and OS's subsystems. We selected popular benchmarks from HiBench Benchmark Suite [4], which are well-known representatives for the field of data analytics. The applications were chosen and classified by their resource intensity levels, such as cache intensive, compute intensive, and disk-/network-intensive. Such classification covers contention scenarios that IntP proposes to instrument. The applications we choose are presented in Table 2.

We implemented an interference-aware task scheduling in Apache Hadoop YARN [32]. YARN is the architectural center of Hadoop that allows multiple data processing engines such as interactive SQL, real-time streaming, data science and batch processing to handle data, as such that applications we have used during our analysis. We selected a set of applications from different frameworks and programming engines to extend heterogeneity, including Hadoop, Spark, and Storm. In addition, we chose the YARN's Fair policy (default installed) to compare it with the proposed interference policy. We used a carefully-crafted external script to connect to the YARN's client API and work like the dispatcher moving

Table 2. Workload characteristics

App	Type	Workload
App01	Machine learning	LLC
App02	Machine learning	LLC
App03	Machine learning	LLC
App04	Streaming	LLC/memory
App05	Streaming	LLC/memory
App06	Ordering	Memory
App07	Ordering	Memory
App08	Classification	CPU/memory
App09	Classification	CPU/memory
App10	Search engine	CPU
App11	Sort	Network
App12	Sort	Network
App13	Query/scan	Disk
App14	Query/join	Disk
App15	Query/merge	disk

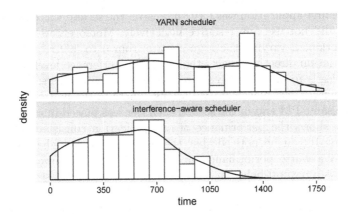

Fig. 1. Comparison between intp-based scheduler and YARN's scheduler. Density represents the number of jobs completed per time slice.

jobs every 5 s on the 10-in-10 order (no job completion waiting). The experiment aims to evaluate the jobs' turnaround times (makespan) and total completion times. The performance evaluation, as well as the comparison with the default YARN scheduler is presented in Fig. 1.

The graph shows that the reduced job turnaround times reflected on the total completion time, and also improved the efficiency (density), expected when evaluating performance in scheduling. We observed a performance optimization up to 35%, This is because applications have been better balanced according to their interference level, so that they compete less for resources.

5   Static Interference-Aware Scheduling

After better understanding on how to measure interference we developed a static interference-aware scheduling scheme based on the IntP tool described in the previous Section.

5.1   Placement Policies

The first step towards a static interference-aware scheduling model was the creation of policies to make efficient placement decisions. To achieve that, we analyzed the performance of applications that use CPU and Disk I/O intensively, and, then, generate the placement policies based on such analysis.

For the performance analysis, we use the node-tiers[7] benchmark, considering three multi-tier applications with two tiers each, where both tiers stress the same resource. The first application was CPU-intensive, the second was disk-intensive, and the last did not use any resource intensively. Moreover, we generated an increasing workload, varying the request rate from 0 to 300 requests per second. This variation directly impacts the resource interference levels since higher request rate leads to more resources used to answer the requests. Furthermore, we have considered two placement variations, where in the first both tiers were placed in the same PM and in the second each tier was placed in a different PM.

Figure 2a shows the performance of an application consisted of two CPU intensive tiers. It can be noticed that the execution with higher request size (512 KB) had a worse performance as compared with the lower request size (1 KB). This is a natural behavior since the higher the request size is, the more pressure it puts on both operating system and network. Additionally, while the request rate was low, the performance for all executions remained stable. However, as the request rate increased, the execution with high network usage running in different PMs suffered performance degradation. In this case, the network becomes flooded with many requests, and as the network bottleneck is reached, the response time increases exponentially. On the other hand, while running with same request size, but in the same PM, there is no impact on the performance.

Figure 2b presents the response time of the application that had two disk I/O intensive tiers. The response time kept acceptable while the workload was low. However, as the workload increased, the application presents a different behavior from the one seen in the CPU intensive application. All four executions of this application have performance degradation, but this degradation comes

---

[7] https://github.com/uillianluiz/node-tiers.

earlier in the executions that run the tiers on the same PM. As a conclusion of this execution, disk I/O intensive applications tend to suffer more from the interference of co-hosted tiers.

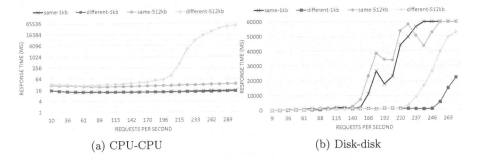

(a) CPU-CPU   (b) Disk-disk

Fig. 2. Response time of the applications while varying the workload.

5.2   Classification Based on Thresholds and Static Model

Even though the aforementioned insights are useful for optimizing the placement, it would be important to consider other resources, such as memory and cache, and also to consider the levels of interference from each one. For these reasons, we present an interference classification based on thresholds for deciding the best placement of web applications.

As already mentioned, each resource may suffer from interference in different ways. A high level of disk interference may be much more prejudicial to an application than a high level of CPU interference. For this reason, we are not going to use the interference levels by themselves, but rather the performance degradation a given interference level generates. Hence, we classified interference levels into four classes for simplification: **Absent, Low, Moderate**, and **High**. Even though this classification reduces the breadth of the problem, it is still an improvement to the state-of-the-art works, which most of them consider only two levels (absent and present). Each class covers different interference levels that go from 0 to 100% as follows: Absent (0–0%), Low (1–20%), Moderate (21–50%), and High (51–100%).

Based on this classification, we analyzed performance interference for co-hosted applications using the node-tiers benchmark and response time as performance metric. Initially, we prepared synthetic workloads that fit an application into each of the interference classes. For the Absent class, there is no performance degradation, i.e., it increases the response time in 1.0 time. For other classes, we conducted experiments running a two-tiers application, and put a load stress using the stressing tool Artillery [25] to find out the workload necessary to fit the application into the Absent, Low, Moderate, and High classes.

The interference-related performance degradation was obtained using a simulated one-tier application deployed by node-tiers. Artillery was configured with 50 concurrent threads producing HTTP's request bursts to the application during the 40-min run time. We collected the average response time while the application was running in isolation. Afterwards, we inserted Low, Moderate, and High applications in the same PM, and calculated the performance degradation using the equation $perf_{class}/perf_{absent}$, where $perf_{class}$ is the average response time for each interference class, and $perf_{absent}$ is the average response time while running in isolation. Furthermore, based on this methodology, the characterization of interference performance degradation is shown in Table 3.

Table 3. Performance degradation generated by resource interference.

Level	CPU	Memory	Disk	Cache	Network
Absent	1.00	1.00	1.00	1.00	1.00
Low	1.03	1.07	1.12	1.07	1.05
Moderate	1.15	1.62	1.82	1.18	1.32
High	1.33	1.74	2.25	1.26	1.57

Placement algorithms aim to put a set of applications in the smallest number of PMs to make the data center resource efficient. In order to minimize the performance degradation generated by resource interference, we have created CIAPA[8]. This is a scheduling analysis tool that uses an interference cost function.

All resource interference metrics are measured and allocated into an interval. Depending on the interval which they are set, the cost value varies according Table 3. CIAPA tries to minimize the total cost by testing all possible combinations of applications per host.

To evaluate and analyze the quality of CIAPAs placement algorithms, first, we define two scenarios that will serve as workload in this section: (I) set of two multi-tier applications with high conflict between resource interference. The first application has two CPU moderate-intensive tiers, while the second has two disk I/O high-intensive tiers; (II) set of three multi-tier application with less conflict in the same application, but high affinity levels and resource interference between tiers from different applications. Medium workload to emulate a private cloud and to allow the execution in our real test bed.

In order to validate if cost is actually correlated with performance, we verify how CIAPA performs when compared to related work, so that we have run both scenarios with CIAPA and in a real environment. We executed the placement algorithms for both cases, comparing CIAPA again with the interference [26] and affinity [27] strategies, and after reproducing them in our experimental environment. Figure 3 shows the cost generated by each placement as well as the average response time achieved by the multi-tier applications for both cases. Also here,

---

[8] https://github.com/uillianluiz/ciapa.

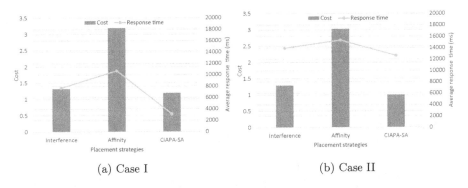

(a) Case I   (b) Case II

Fig. 3. Cost and average response time comparison of CIAPA against Interference and Affinity aware placement strategies for Cases I (a) and II (b).

we can see that CIAPA was not only able to generate a placement with lower cost, but this cost also led to the best overall application's performance. In Case II, a more representative workload, we can observe a reduction in response time of 10% when compared to Interference strategies, and up to 18% when considering only affinity strategies.

6 Dynamic Scheduling Scheme

In the last section, we presented an interference-aware scheduling schema based on a static classification of applications, that was fixed over their entire execution. In this section, we begin to experiment with a dynamic scheme, to better react to workload changes during the execution of these applications, and consequently improve resource usage even more.

6.1 Exploring Dynamic Interference Profiles

To explore a dynamic interference-aware profile, we had to use an application that has variations in its workload. So, a QoS-oriented e-commerce benchmark, called Bench4Q[9], has been elected. First, we created an increasing workload, starting with a low load and gradually going to a high load, and profiled it with IntP. Figure 4 shows interference suffered by each resource in this experiment. The top chart presents the classification method seen in Sect. 5, with one label per profiled resource over the entire application execution. After observing the interference behavior change, a question came up: what if this method were executed more than once over curse of the application execution in a segmented way? Would these labels change? So, we executed the static classification multiple times. Since we do not know what would be the best number of intervals to perform it, we arbitrarily divided the execution into four parts and ran the classification method for each part again. Results are shown at the bottom chart, in the same figure.

---

[9] https://projects.ow2.org/view/bench4q.

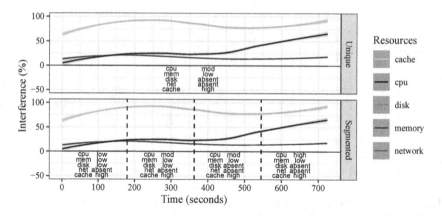

Fig. 4. Unique (top) and Segmented (bottom) Interference Classification. *To facilitate the visualization, a Loess function was applied to smooth short-term variations. **Resources that suffered classification changes are shown in bold.

It is possible to notice that there are resources that do not change their labels, for instance, memory, cache, and network. Since they keep their interference metrics at the same level, on average, with no expressive variation, their labels are maintained. On the other hand, some resources do change their labels, namely CPU and disk. Disk has a smooth decrease in its behavior, moving from low to absent label, at the execution halfway. But CPU has the biggest behavior change, starting with low, going to moderate levels, and ending with a high interference level. This highlights that, due to their dynamic workload nature, each application should be handled differently.

6.2   AI-driven Interference-Aware Application Classifier with Preliminary Results

As we showed in the previous experiment applying a static classification method over some applications with high workload variations will lead to an unrepresentative classification estimate. Thus, this approach may disfavor the placement of different types of applications that have dynamic workload patterns. To tackle this issue, we created an interference-aware application classifier based on machine learning techniques. The proposed classifier receives monitored metrics from applications and automatically outcomes their interference levels without setting its thresholds.

To implement the classifier, two machine learning algorithms have been chosen: SVM for classification and K-Means for clustering. Initially, SVM receives interference metrics collected from the target application. Then those metrics are separated into main resource classes: Memory, CPU, Disk, Network, and Cache. Subsequently, K-Means quantifies them and returns their interference levels. Both machine learning algorithms use a training dataset, previously defined, to

assist their decisions. Figure 5 illustrates an overview of how the classifier works
with more details.

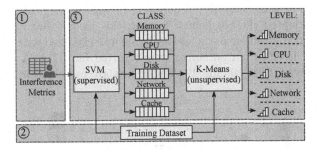

Fig. 5. Classifier Architecture Overview: (1) collecting of interference metrics; (2) training dataset assisting ML algorithms; (3) classification process [17].

The target application is monitored with the IntP tool, every second. When
the defined monitoring period is over, the classifier gathers interference metrics
collected and utilizes it as input data. After, the SVM algorithm trains its model
supported by the data set and turns back the classification results. After classi-
fying a given application into target classes (Memory, CPU, Disk, Network, and
Cache), they are stored in classes queues and become K-Means input data. We
have set four possible levels: absent, low, moderate, and high. When there is no
incidence of interference from some class, the classifier interprets it as Absent.
When any class produces interference activity, it is sent to K-Means that determines the interference levels of each resource class.

To evaluate the proposed classifier, we verify how it performs when compared
to state-of-the-art studies. Since few related works optimize interference at levels
similar to ours, three approaches have been chosen, as follows:

– **Even** implements the *EvenScheduler*, the Apache Storm[10] default scheduler;
– **Ludwig et al.** [16] evaluates the profile of the application workloads and
  uses an static interference classification at levels;
– **Proportional** categorizes the interference from each resource through a proportional division of the ranges of interference levels. This strategy is commonly adopted in the resource management field [11].

Even uses an "in order" scheduling strategy, so, it does not take interference
classification aspects into account. *Ludwig et al.* and *Proportional* are similar
approaches that utilize interference classification based on fixed thresholds. The
difference between them lies in how their intervals are delimited: *Ludwig et al.*
defines them empirically, and *Proportional* applies a fair division. To perform the
comparison, we used three applications: Bench4Q, TPC-H[11], and LinkBench[12].

---

[10] https://storm.apache.org/.
[11] http://www.tpc.org/tpch/.
[12] https://github.com/facebookarchive/linkbench.

For each application, we have created four workload patterns: increasing, periodic, decreasing, and constant.

A classification scheme, that better represents workload variations, tends to use resources more efficiently [17]. Therefore, in this experiment, all classification methods adopted the Segmented format, this means that all interference traces were divided into four parts and each one was classified with all classification methods. Classification outcomes were inserted into CIAPA over different numbers of hosts: 4, 6, 8, 10, and 12. The results are presented in Fig. 6.

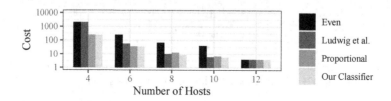

Fig. 6. Comparison of Scheduling Costs with State-of-the-Art.

It is possible to observe that, in all executions, the *Even* method presented the worst results (higher costs), which was already expected since this method is not interference-aware driven. In general, our solution demonstrated the best placement costs, presenting an improvement in the scheduling efficiency by 27%, on average, compared to the other strategies from related work. The only exception appears with 12 hosts. In this case, each host handles only one application, producing no interference and generating the lowest possible scheduling costs. As the number of hosts decreases, scheduling costs become higher. Therefore, the resource concurrency among co-hosted applications tends to increase as well. With 4 hosts, the highest costs occurred, revealing the case with more cross-application interference incidence and greater performance degradation.

Preliminary results, with different workloads, have confirmed that resource interference may result in overhead that has a high impact on application performance, which was already demonstrated by related work. These experiments enforce that an AI-driven interference-aware fine-grained classification scheme, which represents better the variability of workloads over time, can improve results even more, executing efficient scheduling decisions while enhancing the performance of applications and reducing SLA violations.

6.3   Challenges of a Dynamic Scenario

Although the proposed static methods already deliver better scheduling decisions and improve resource usage than state of the art, we have shown that by performing a dynamic classification, it is possible to reach even better resource scheduling results. After analyzing the experiments' outcomes, we have noticed that this idea presents great research potential. However, changing the scheduling architecture from static to dynamic is a challenging task and we believe some modifications should be done in order to adjust the system due to the following issues:

– Since dynamic workloads present variations over time, it is mandatory to have a method that analyzes time-series information to find the right moments to perform scheduling decisions;
– It is essential to build a manager module that coordinates and schedules all resources and application executions at runtime;
– Implementing all these features will probably generate system overhead. Smart policies are needed to keep this overhead low to not consume the benefits of a improved dynamic scheduling.

6.4   Prediction Models for Proactive Scheduling

As previously stated, the workload may fluctuate a lot in certain environments, and to avoid QoS drops that may result in SLA violations providers usually resort to over-provisioning. But this leads to increasing provisioning costs and energy consumption. Predicting the future workload is one of the strategies by which the efficiency and operational cost can be improved. This strategy allows the previous allocation of sufficient resources to maintain QoS and avoid SLA violations.

Several works in this area explored strategies to better adapt environments to applications fluctuating demands using machine learning algorithms by tracing high and low level data (e.g., HTTP requests, disk, cache, CPU, throughput) [12]. They mentioned predictive models could be applied over past workload traces to accurately allocate the resources that are necessary to satisfy QoS in advance.

In this context, the prediction models solve a regression problem, which means that variables are estimated over time, and the target is the amount of workload in a future period (e.g., seconds, minutes, hours, days) [2].

We evaluated the most popular machine learning-driven models that are broadly adopted in related work [9]: ARIMA, MLP, and GRU. We used short-term predictions that allow flexibility for scheduling strategies. Thus, our preliminary results compare the models under different time intervals of workload predictions following the distribution order of 5 min in a 60 min interval. The NASA HTTP traces[13] were used as workload in our experiments.

Figure 7 shows a more detailed view of the predictions for 15 min confirming that all three techniques coped with the dynamics of the proposed workload. As previously stated, our experiments show that short-term predictions achieved good predictions. A disadvantage of ARIMA is that the time series are recalculated for each prediction. This can be time consuming and compromises its application in certain environments. ARIMA laso showed to be more dependent on the number of workload samples and the definition of its parameters than MLP

---

[13] http://ita.ee.lbl.gov/html/contrib/.

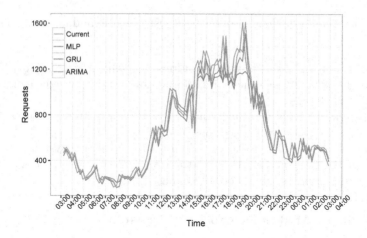

Fig. 7. Predictions with 15-min

and GRU. Both MLP and GRU models need fewer samples to give precise forecasts in all experiments. Based on the accuracy metrics, GRU achieved slightly better results for workload characteristics in our preliminary experiments.

7   Related Work

Many studies have been previously conducted on building interference-aware scheduling strategies, and the challenge is to have fast and scalable tools for addressing real-world applications. Furthermore, with virtualization technology, it has become possible to consolidate easily and quickly adapt resource allocation. In this section, we only discuss those works that are most closely related to interference-aware classification and scheduling aspects.

Zang et al. [37] propose two schedulers: one in the virtualization layer to minimize interference, and one in the Hadoop framework that helps batch processing jobs meet their own performance deadlines. The combination of these schedulers allows data center administrators to safely mix resource-intensive Hadoop jobs with latency-sensitive web applications, and still achieve predictable performance for both. The evaluation shows that both schedulers allow a mixed cluster to reduce web response times by more than ten fold while meeting more Hadoop deadlines and lowering total task execution times by 6.5%.

Chen et al. [1] present CloudScope, a system for diagnosing interference for multi-tenant cloud systems. It employs a discrete-time Markov Chain model for the online prediction of performance interference of co-resident VMs. It uses the results to optimally (re)assign VMs to physical machines and to optimize the hypervisor configuration, e.g. the CPU share it can use, for different workloads. The authors have implemented CloudScope on top of the Xen hypervisor and conducted experiments using a set of CPU, disk, and network-intensive workloads and a real system (MapReduce). The interference-aware scheduler improves virtual machine performance by up to 10% compared to the default scheduler, achieving an average error of 9%. The authors claim that the hypervisor reconfiguration can improve network throughput by up to 30%.

To address latency-sensitive application issues, such as QoS impact, and overcome limitations in existing offline approaches, Shekhar et al. [24] present an online, data-driven approach that utilizes Gaussian Processes-based machine learning techniques to build predictive run time models of the performance of the system under different levels of interference. The predictive online models are then used in dynamically adapting to the workload variability by vertically auto-scaling co-located applications such that performance interference is minimized, and QoS properties of latency-sensitive applications are met. A comparison with a representative latency-sensitive application reveals up to 39.46% lower tail latency than reactive approaches.

Wang et al. [33] developed data-driven analytical models to estimate the effect of interference among multiple Apache Spark jobs on job execution time in virtualized cloud environments. Next, they present the design of an interference aware job scheduling algorithm leveraging the developed analytical framework. The evaluation of model accuracy was measured using real-life applications on a 6 node cluster while running up to four jobs concurrently. Experimental results show that the scheduling algorithm reduces the average execution time of individual jobs and the total execution time significantly and ranges between 47 and 26% for individual jobs and 2 to 13% for total execution time, respectively.

8   Conclusions

Virtualized environments have been heavily applied by the IT community due to their flexibility and efficacy to manage resources, allowing also their efficient sharing to improve utilization rates and reduce energy consumption. However, multiple services contending for shared resources may generate cross-application interference and this can lead to severe performance degradation. There is strong evidence showing that this kind of interference can have a significant impact on application performance and consequently break service level agreements. It is also dependent on the type of the shared resource and workload variations.

In this paper we presented the state of the art in interference-aware scheduling for virtualized environments, our main contributions to this area and the challenges and advantages of applying a dynamic scheduling scheme to this problem.

After more than a decade investigating ways to better understand and avoid cross-application interference we strong believe that, due to its sensitivity to workload variations, this is the way to go. Nevertheless, there are still opportunities for improvement in the areas of application classification and pro-active dynamic scheduling strategies.

Acknowledgements. This work was partially supported by the Coordenação de Aperfeiçoamento de Pessoal de Nível Superior - CAPES Brazil and also by the Green-Cloud project (#16/2551-0000 488-9), from FAPERGS and CNPq Brazil, PRONEX 12/2014 program.

References

1. Chen, X., et al.: CloudScope: diagnosing and managing performance interference in multi-tenant clouds. In: IEEE 23rd International Symposium on Modeling, Analysis, and Simulation of Computer and Telecommunication Systems, pp. 164–173 (2015)
2. Gollapudi, S.: Practical Machine Learning. Packt Publishing Ltd., Birmingham (2016)
3. Herdrich, A.: Cache Qos: from concept to reality in the intel® xeon® processor e5–2600 v3 product family. In: 2016 IEEE International Symposium on High Performance Computer Architecture (HPCA), pp. 657–668. IEEE (2016)
4. Huang, S., Huang, J., Dai, J., Xie, T., Huang, B.: The HiBench benchmark suite: characterization of the MapReduce-based data analysis. In: Agrawal, D., Candan, K.S., Li, W.-S. (eds.) New Frontiers in Information and Software as Services. LNBIP, vol. 74, pp. 209–228. Springer, Heidelberg (2011). https://doi.org/10.1007/978-3-642-19294-4_9
5. Iqbal, W., Erradi, A., Mahmood, A.: Dynamic workload patterns prediction for proactive auto-scaling of web applications. J. Netw. Comput. Appl. **124**, 94–107 (2018)
6. Javadi, S.A., Gandhi, A.: Dial: reducing tail latencies for cloud applications via dynamic interference-aware load balancing. In: IEEE International Conference on Autonomic Computing (ICAC), pp. 135–144 (2017)
7. Jersak, L.C., Ferreto, T.: Performance-aware server consolidation with adjustable interference levels. In: 31st ACM Symposium on Applied Computing, pp. 420–425 (2016)
8. Keller, A., Ludwig, H.: The WSLA framework: specifying and monitoring service level agreements for web services. J. Netw. Syst. Manag. **11**, 57–81 (2003)
9. Kirchoff, F.D., Xavier, M.G., Mastella, J., De Rose, C.A.: A preliminary study of machine learning workload prediction techniques for cloud applications. In: 27th Euromicro International Conference on Parallel, Distributed, and Network-Based Processing, pp. 253–260 (2019)
10. Kougkas, A., Devarajan, H., Sun, X., Lofstead, J.: Harmonia: an interference-aware dynamic I/O scheduler for shared non-volatile burst buffers. In: IEEE International Conference on Cluster Computing (CLUSTER), pp. 290–301 (2018)
11. Krzywda, J., et al.: Modeling and simulation of QoS-aware power budgeting in cloud data centers. In: 28th Euromicro International Conference on Parallel, Distributed and Network-Based Processing (PDP), pp. 88–93 (2020)
12. Kumar, J., Singh, A.K.: Workload prediction in cloud using artificial neural network and adaptive differential evolution. Future Gener. Comput. Syst. **81**, 41–52 (2018)
13. Kumar, R., Setia, S.: Interface aware scheduling of tasks on cloud. In: 4th International Conference on Signal Processing, Computing and Control (ISPCC), pp. 654–658 (2017)
14. LTT: Linux trace toolkit. https://opersys.com/LTT/. Accessed 01 June 2020
15. Lu, K., et al.: Fault-tolerant service level agreement lifecycle management in clouds using actor system. Future Gener. Comput. Syst. **54**, 247–259 (2016)
16. Ludwig, U.L., Xavier, M.G., Kirchoff, D.F., Cezar, I.B., De Rose, C.A.F.: Optimizing multi-tier application performance with interference and affinity-aware placement algorithms. Concurr. Comput. Pract. Exper. **31**, e5098 (2019)

17. Meyer, V., Kirchoff, D.F., Da Silva, M.L., De Rose, C.A.F.: An interference-aware application classifier based on machine learning to improve scheduling in clouds. In: 28th Euromicro International Conference on Parallel, Distributed and Network-Based Processing (PDP), pp. 80–87 (2020)

18. Meyer, V., Xavier, M.G., Kirchoff, D.F., da R. Righi, R., De Rose, C.A.F.: Performance and cost analysis between elasticity strategies over pipeline-structured applications. In: International Conference on Cloud Computing and Services Science (CLOSER), pp. 404–411 (2019)

19. Nathuji, R., Kansal, A., Ghaffarkhah, A.: Q-clouds: managing performance interference effects for QoS-aware clouds. In: Proceedings of the 5th European Conference on Computer Systems, pp. 237–250 (2010)

20. Potter, K.H.: Dynamic addressing mapping to eliminate memory resource contention in a symmetric multiprocessor system, uS Patent 6,505,269, 7 January 2003

21. Rosen, R.: Linux containers and the future cloud (2014). https://www.linuxjournal.com/content/linux-containers-and-future-cloud

22. Scheepers, M.J.: Virtualization and containerization of application infrastructure: a comparison. In: 21st Twente Student Conference on IT, pp. 1–7 (2014)

23. Shah, A., Wolf, F., Zhumatiy, S., Voevodin, V.: Capturing inter-application interference on clusters. In: IEEE International Conference on Cluster Computing, pp. 1–5 (2013)

24. Shekhar, S., Abdel-Aziz, H., Bhattacharjee, A., Gokhale, A., Koutsoukos, X.: Performance interference-aware vertical elasticity for cloud-hosted latency-sensitive applications. In: 2018 IEEE 11th International Conference on Cloud Computing, pp. 82–89 (2018)

25. Shoreditch, O.L.: Artillery (2020). https://artillery.io/. Accessed 05 June 2020

26. Somani, G., Khandelwal, P., Phatnani, K.: VUPIC: virtual machine usage based placement in IaaS cloud. arXiv preprint arXiv:1212.0085 (2012)

27. Su, K., Xu, L., Chen, C., Chen, W., Wang, Z.: Affinity and conflict-aware placement of virtual machines in heterogeneous data centers. In: IEEE Twelfth International Symposium on Autonomous Decentralized Systems (ISADS), pp. 289–294 (2015)

28. Terpstra, D., Jagode, H., You, H., Dongarra, J.: Collecting performance data with PAPI-C. In: Müller, M.S., Resch, M.M., Schulz, A., Nagel, W.E. (eds.) Tools for High Performance Computing 2009, pp. 157–173 (2010)

29. Thamsen, L., et al.: Hugo: a cluster scheduler that efficiently learns to select complementary data-parallel jobs. In: Schwardmann, U., et al. (eds.) Euro-Par 2019. LNCS, vol. 11997, pp. 519–530. Springer, Cham (2020). https://doi.org/10.1007/978-3-030-48340-1_40

30. Tosatto, A., Ruiu, P., Attanasio, A.: Container-based orchestration in cloud: state of the art and challenges. In: 2015 Ninth International Conference on Complex, Intelligent, and Software Intensive Systems, pp. 70–75 (2015)

31. Urgaonkar, B., Shenoy, P., Roscoe, T.: Resource overbooking and application profiling in shared hosting platforms. SIGOPS Oper. Syst. Rev. **36**, 239–254 (2003)

32. Vavilapalli, V.K., et al.: Apache hadoop yarn: yet another resource negotiator. In: 4th Symposium on Cloud Computing (2013)

33. Wang, K., Khan, M.M.H., Nguyen, N., Gokhale, S.: Design and implementation of an analytical framework for interference aware job scheduling on apache spark platform. Cluster Comput. **22**, 2223–2237 (2019). https://doi.org/10.1007/s10586-017-1466-3

34. Xavier, M.G.: Data processing with cross-application interference control via system-level instrumentation. Ph.D. thesis, Pontifical Catholic University of Rio Grande do Sul, Porto Alegre, Brazil (2019)

35. Zhang, F., Tang, X., Li, X., Khan, S.U., Li, Z.: Quantifying cloud elasticity with container-based autoscaling. Future Gener. Comput. Syst. **98**, 672–681 (2019)

36. Zhang, Q., Cheng, L., Boutaba, R.: Cloud computing: state-of-the-art and research challenges. J. Internet Serv. Appl. **1**(1), 7–18 (2010). https://doi.org/10.1007/s13174-010-0007-6

37. Zhang, W., Rajasekaran, S., Wood, T., Zhu, M.: MIMP: deadline and interference aware scheduling of Hadoop virtual machines. In: 2014 14th IEEE/ACM International Symposium on Cluster, Cloud and Grid Computing, pp. 394–403 (2014)

38. Zhuravlev, S., Blagodurov, S., Fedorova, A.: Addressing shared resource contention in multicore processors via scheduling. ACM SIGARCH Comput. Architect. News **45**, 129–142 (2010)

Towards Hybrid Isolation for Shared Multicore Systems

Yoonsung Nam[1(✉)], Byeonghun Yoo[1], Yongjun Choi[1], Yongseok Son[2], and Hyeonsang Eom[1]

[1] Department of Computer Science and Engineering, Seoul National University, 1 Gwanak-ro, Gwanak-gu, Seoul, Korea
{yoonsung.nam,isac322,drgnjoon,hseom}@snu.ac.kr
[2] Department of Computer Science and Engineering, Chung-Ang University, 84 Heukseok-ro, Dongjak-gu, Seoul, Korea
sysganda@cau.ac.kr

Abstract. Co-locating and running multiple applications on a multicore system is inevitable for data centers to achieve high resource efficiency. However, it causes performance degradation due to the contention for shared resources, such as cache and memory bandwidth. Several approaches use software or hardware isolation techniques to mitigate resource contentions. Nevertheless, the existing approaches have not fully exploited differences in isolation techniques by the characteristics of applications to maximize the performance. Software techniques bring more flexibility than hardware ones in terms of performance while sacrificing strictness and responsiveness. In contrast, hardware techniques provide more strict and faster isolations compared to software ones. In this paper, we illustrate the trade-offs between software and hardware isolation techniques and also show the benefit of coordinated enforcement of multiple isolation techniques. Also, we propose *HIS*, a hybrid isolation system that dynamically uses either the software or hardware isolation technique. Our preliminary results show that *HIS* can improve the performance of foreground applications by from 1.7–2.14× compared with static isolations for the selected benchmarks.

1 Introduction

A variety of applications from the simple web server to the complicated machine learning are running in the modern data centers. In the data centers, these applications are typically running on the multicore servers, sharing the computing resources such as CPUs and memory to improve resource efficiency. Sharing resources on a machine is essential to reduce the total cost of ownership (TCO) of the data center; however, it causes contentions for the shared resources leading to performance degradation [13]. The performance degradation may result in user complaints and tremendous revenue loss [14]. To meet the service level objectives (SLOs) of multiple applications while improving resource efficiency

© Springer Nature Switzerland AG 2020
D. Klusáček et al. (Eds.): JSSPP 2020, LNCS 12326, pp. 25–44, 2020.
https://doi.org/10.1007/978-3-030-63171-0_2

in a machine, it is necessary to enforce isolation techniques appropriately to mitigate resource contentions.

There are two types of isolation techniques for multicore systems, that is, software and hardware ones. Software techniques are isolation techniques that allocate resources such as CPU and memory by controlling interactions among threads and resources in a software manner. They are broadly used in various platforms because it is relatively easy to adopt software isolation techniques [8, 21]. Moreover, software techniques are flexible in terms of performance, allowing multiple configurations for maximizing performance [6, 17]. On the other hand, software techniques are relatively loose isolation than hardware ones since they do not directly segregate or manipulate resources contrary to hardware ones. It makes software isolations less strict and less responsive than hardware ones, which may result in relatively slow isolation enforcement and high-performance variations [23]. Further, compared with hardware isolation, software one may have a larger search space for configurations due to considerable available combinations. For example, hardware cache partitioning provides strict isolation for last-level cache, and per-core dynamic voltage frequency scaling (DVFS) is useful when boosting latency-critical operations [9, 23].

Several research works have utilized software and hardware isolation techniques. First, some works use software techniques, such as core allocation, cycle throttling, and thread placement [6, 17, 20, 21]. Software approaches focus on efficient, portable, and flexible isolation. However, their approach is less strict in terms of providing predictable performance, and less responsive in that latency to isolation may be relatively high. Second, a few works utilize hardware techniques, such as hardware cache partitioning and per-core DVFS [9, 23]. Hardware approaches are strict and fast because they directly control the hardware feature for performance isolation. Their approach allows stable performance for workloads by segregating resources completely or quick response time for rapid changes in workloads. However, the approach may use a few hardware configurations that may not be enough for achieving maximum performance. Third, some research works use both hardware and software techniques for the isolation of multiple resources [4, 15]. Their works are in line with ours in terms of using multiple types of isolation techniques. However, we focus on the tradeoffs in hardware and software techniques, which they have not fully explored.

In this paper, we investigate the characteristics of isolation techniques in terms of strictness, responsiveness, and flexibility. We explore the tradeoffs lying between hardware and software techniques and further evaluate a prototype that combines software and hardware isolation techniques to overcome the shortcomings of each isolation technique. The proposed scheme considers the tradeoffs mainly caused by the isolation mechanism which is either strict and low-latency hardware techniques or loose but flexible software ones to mitigate the contentions dynamically according to the workloads' resource demands and execution patterns. To realize the hybrid isolation scheme, we developed a profiler and a user-level scheduler that uses four isolation techniques. It uses two hardware isolations, which are hardware cache partitioning and per-core DVFS, and two software isolations that allocate cores and perform thread placement. Using these techniques, the scheduler can perform isolation strictly, fast, and flexibly to consolidated workloads. We have evaluated our prototype with the two types of foreground workloads, such as latency-sensitive and batch one, while the batch workload runs in the background. Our preliminary results show that the proposed scheduler can improve the performance of foreground workloads by from 1.7–2.14× compared with static software isolations.

The contributions of our work as follows:

- We have explored the tradeoffs between hardware isolation techniques and software ones in terms of the strictness, responsiveness, and flexibility.
- We have designed and implemented a hybrid isolation system which adaptively isolates workloads considering the characteristics of workloads and tradeoffs in the isolation techniques.
- We have evaluated preliminarily that our system can improve the performance compared with static isolations for the selected benchmarks.

The rest of this paper is organized as follows: Section 2 briefly presents the background for isolation techniques. Section 3 describes the tradeoff between hardware and software techniques, and Sect. 4 shows problem of ineffective isolations. Section 5 describes the design and implementation of our prototype. Section 6 shows the preliminary evaluation. Section 7 covers the related work. Finally, Sect. 8 concludes this paper.

2 Background

This section briefly describes the existing software and hardware isolation techniques and illustrates tradeoffs between these isolation techniques.

2.1 Existing Isolation Techniques

Table 1 shows the existing hardware and software isolation techniques. Most schedulers utilizes the software isolation techniques and hardware isolation techniques in the table. All isolation techniques can be categorized by three types; Throttling, Scheduling, and Partitioning.

2.1.1 Software Isolation Techniques

Software techniques reduce contentions among workloads by using software interfaces. Throttling and Scheduling are the representative types of software isolation techniques. Throttling is a broadly used to minimize performance interference by controlling the execution rates of contentious workloads among co-located ones. For example, Google CPI^2 throttles CPUs of background workloads to protect the performance of co-located production workloads [21]. Memguard restricts the memory accesses of the memory-intensive workloads based on assigned memory budget throttling CPU cycles [20]. Limiting CPU cycles is an efficient software isolation technique which throttle the execution of specific workloads [8, 20, 21]. The technique mitigates the contention for shared resources by limiting the number of cycles to *quota* within the configured *periods*. If the assigned cycles are exhausted during a period, the core will remain idle until the new period begins.

Another technique is mitigating contentions via `Scheduling`. Two techniques are mostly used for `Scheduling`. One is *CPU allocation*, and the other is *thread migration*. *CPU allocation* is simple, yet the effective software technique to isolate workloads. It works purely in software manner, and easily reduces the contention of shared resources. It allocates dedicated CPU cores to each workload to minimize resource contention among workloads. When allocating cores to workloads, it is critical to consider which workloads will be colocated with each other [6, 11, 16, 17, 24]. Because resource contention among workloads can grow or not depending on which workloads are co-located. When resource contentions can not be resolved by other isolations in a socket, *thread migration* can be helpful by migrating the most suffered workload to the less contentious socket (or machine). This can be helpful where exist severe contentions that `Throttling` can not mitigate. In contrast, in the cases of all the possible schedule pairs can not relax the contention, `Scheduling` may result in poor performance due to the unnecessary overheads as it would fail to find better workload pairs.

Table 1. Comparison of the existing hardware and software isolation techniques

	Hardware isolation techniques		Software isolation techniques		
	Intel CAT [10]	Per-core DVFS [19]	CPU cycle limit [18]	CPU allocation [7]	Thread migration [7]
Type	Partitioning	Throttling	Throttling	Scheduling	Scheduling
Latency (ms)	3	2	40–50	3	90
Configurations (Xeon E5-2683v4)	# of ways (20 per LLC)	# of available freq. (10 per core)	Quota/period (100)	# of cores (16)	# of sockets (2)
Strictness	High	High	Medium	Medium	Low
Responsiveness	High	High	Medium	High	Low
Flexibility	Low	Low	High	High	High

2.1.2 Hardware Isolation Techniques

Hardware techniques physically allocate resources to mitigate contentions among workloads or exploits specific hardware features equipped on recent multi-core machines. Hardware techniques can provide fast and strict isolation compared with the software ones, because they directly control hardware interfaces. Besides, hardware techniques have lower latency than software ones. Because they have a fewer number of available configurations, which makes configuration search faster when enforcing isolations. There are two types of hardware isolation techniques; `Partitioning` and `Throttling`. `Partitioning` is a representative hardware isolation technique which strictly segregates resources for multiple workloads. For hardware partitioning, there are Intel Cache Allocation Technology (Intel CAT) for LLC way-partitioning [10] and Intel Running Average Power Limits (Intel RAPL) for limiting power consumption [5].

Another hardware isolation technique is `Throttling`-type one using dynamic voltage frequency scaling (DVFS). DVFS is originally designed to perform power management, however, owing to the advance of DVFS, voltage regulators on recent CPUs can adjust a voltage of each core in the CPUs. This enables faster and low-overhead controls for specific operations [9], thus this can enable fine-grained isolation for latency-sensitive workloads [23].

3   Trade-Offs Between Hardware and Software Techniques

In this section, we describe the trade-offs between hardware and software isolation techniques. Also, we present the effects of isolation techniques by the characteristics of workloads such as resource demands.

To describe the trade-offs, we ran two workloads, each is a multi-threaded process and ran on a single socket while enforcing performance isolation. The test machine has 32 GB of RAM, and its CPU is a Xeon E5-2683v4 (2.1 GHz, 16-cores). We turned off the hyper-threading feature. For baseline, we used static software isolation (i.e., *Core Allocation*). We used `cgroups cpuset` [7] to allocate 8 cores (16 cores) of one socket equally to each workload and allocate local memory. We chose several benchmarks for foreground workloads that show a diverse range of memory and LLC access pattern; `streamcluster` and `canneal` of PARSEC [2], and `kmeans` and `nn` of Rodinia [3], and Apache benchmark (`ab`). For background workloads, we used `SP` of the NASA parallel benchmark [1] because it shows high LLC and memory bandwidth usage enough to stress memory subsystem.

Strictness. To show the strictness of hardware techniques and software ones, we compared *hardware cache-partitioning* and *software cycle-limiting* by running two workloads concurrently on a socket. We ran `canneal` as a foreground and `SP` as a background by allocating the equal number of dedicated cores. For hardware isolation, we allocated the equal amount of LLC to each workload, and for software isolation, we limited the CPU cycles of a background workload to use only 50% of assigned CPU cycles to restrict LLC accesses to its half.

Figure 1 shows the changes in LLC usage and instructions per cycle (IPC) of foreground and background workloads. As shown in Fig. 1a and 1b, when using the hardware isolation technique, the LLC allocations are equally divided all the time due to the direct and strict segregation of hardware isolation. On the other hand, when using the software isolation technique, the LLC allocations are changed dramatically over times, because the software isolation does not guarantee the physical segregation of resources.

The difference between isolation techniques makes the performance of workloads unpredictable. Figure 1c and 1d show the performance variations of the software isolation. Software CPU cycle limiting shows a larger variation compared with the hardware cache partitioning in the case of foreground workload.

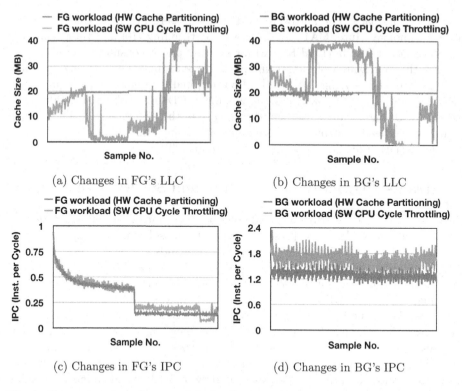

(a) Changes in FG's LLC   (b) Changes in BG's LLC

(c) Changes in FG's IPC   (d) Changes in BG's IPC

Fig. 1. Comparing the strictness of the hardware and software isolations, necessary for predictable performance, the software one shows high variation of performance. Workloads are `canneal` (foreground) and `SP` (background). *x-axis* represents the number of samples and *y-axis* represents LLC allocation and IPC of workloads.

Even worse, in the case of background workload, those variations are getting much bigger, showing more unpredictable IPCs when software cycle limiting. As a result, we find that the hardware isolation technique provides better predictable performance than the software isolation technique by enforcing strict isolation.

Responsiveness. We also compared responsiveness of the hardware and software technique to find which technique can provide more fine-grained contention control by performing isolation quickly. We define responsiveness of isolation technique as the latency to its effect. We chose per-core DVFS as a hardware isolation technique and CPU cycle limiting as a software one to demonstrate the difference in terms of the responsiveness. Per-core DVFS can adjust the core frequencies at 0.1 GHz granularity. On the other hand, CPU cycle limiting can change the cycle at 1% granularity. Even though the control granularity of software is more fine-grained, the speed of enforcing isolation is faster when enforcing hardware isolation. Enforcing core frequency takes a couple of milliseconds.

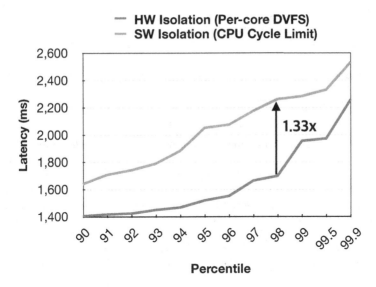

Fig. 2. Comparing the responsiveness of the hardware and software isolations. The graph shows the responsiveness can affect the performance. Workloads are apache web server (**ab**) (foreground) and SP (background). *x-axis* represents the percentile of web server request and *y-axis* represents the latency of web server

Meanwhile, enforcement of cycle limiting takes 40–50 ms which is 13–25× longer than DVFS as shown in Table 1.

To illustrate the responsiveness of the hardware and software isolation technique, we ran two workloads in a socket, and each runs on the eight dedicated cores; one is apache web server and the other is SP that shows high LLC and memory bandwidth demands. We evaluated the responsiveness of isolation techniques by running the apache benchmark (**ab**) which sends the requests to the web server. While running two workloads, we increased the request load of the web server, and also throttled the execution of the background workload. To compare hardware and software techniques, we conducted the experiments twice; first with per-core DVFS, and second with CPU cycle limiting. In both experiments, we throttled the CPU cores of the background workload by increasing the degree of isolation by a step at every 200 ms, and we increased ten steps. For per-core DVFS, we changed the CPU frequency of the background workload from 2.1 GHz to 1.2 GHz by 0.1 GHz. In the same way, for CPU cycle limiting, we also changed the allowed CPU cycle percentage from 100% to 57%, which is the same degree as DVFS. Figure 2 presents how the hardware isolation technique responds more quickly. When performing the software isolation, 98th percentile latency can be 1.33× higher than hardware isolation. This latency difference in tail-latency comes from fast isolation speed thanks to low overhead of hardware technique. The effect of fast isolation may be more important where the resource

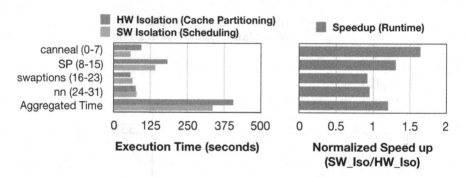

Fig. 3. Benefits of the flexible software isolation. `canneal` and `SP` show high LLC and memory contentions. However, `swaptions` and `nn` are relatively not. In case of performing the hardware isolation, the contention is still high. On the other hand, the software isolation can effectively mitigate the contention significantly. *x-axis* shows the runtime and speedup of workloads and *y-axis* shows their name and CPU affinities. The ranges in parenthesis indicate the range of CPU IDs where workloads runs.

contention changes frequently or fine-grained control matters. Consequently, we find that the hardware isolation technique is more responsive than software one.

Flexibility. We investigated the flexibility of the hardware and software isolation technique. Flexibility means the ability to choose better scheduling options by mapping threads to resources (e.g., CPU cores and memory nodes) or grouping workloads which minimize the contentions and improve the throughput for the workloads. To describe the effectiveness of flexibility, we grouped four workloads, which shows high LLC-intensity or memory bandwidth intensity, into two groups. And, two workloads are paired in each group, and scheduled each group to the separate sockets. We performed different isolations to the same four workloads; the first with the hardware cache partitioning and the second with scheduling by regrouping the background workloads. Figure 3 shows scheduling is more effective than hardware cache partitioning, so that the performance of `canneal` and `SP` improves by up to 1.6× and 1.3× than the hardware one. Some workloads show performance degradations, but their performance loss is reasonable considering the other workloads' performance benefit. The results indicate that software isolation can be useful when the resource contention can not be reduced by the hardware isolation, which have a few isolation options. In this experiment, hardware cache partitioning can only solve resource contention in a socket. However, software isolations such as migration enable more options for enhancing performance and improving resource efficiency.

4   Ineffective Isolations

In addition to the trade-offs between isolation techniques, the isolation effects depend on the characteristics of workloads such as resource demands. The same isolation technique can deliver different impacts according to the workloads. We

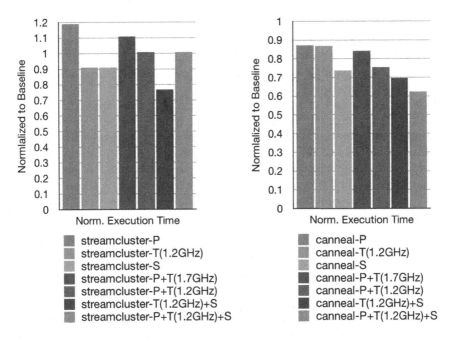

Fig. 4. Enforcing multiple isolations to `streamcluster` and `canneal`, each colocated with SP. The execution time is normalized to the performance of a workload running on the dedicated cores on the default system (P: `Partitioning`, T: `Throttling`, and S: `Scheduling`).

present a simple example of multiple isolations are performed on the different foreground under the high LLC and memory contention.

To demonstrate the effectiveness of each isolation, we tested all isolation techniques which are `Partitioning`, `Throttling`, and `Scheduling`. We manually divided LLCs evenly to workloads using Intel CAT for `Partitioning`. We also changed the execution rate of background workload by setting the frequency of core as the highest frequency (2.1 GHz), the middle frequency (1.7 GHz), and the lowest frequency (1.2 GHz) for `Throttling`. Finally, we changed the number of cores of the background workload to the half of allocated cores, which is four cores, to describe the effect of mitigating memory contention via `Scheduling`. The baseline is the case of when two workloads are running on its dedicated cores without performing any isolation.

As shown in Fig. 4, the performances of foregrounds vary according to the different isolation techniques. This is because the resource demands of the foregrounds are different from each other, and also isolation effects are different depending on the isolation techniques as well. In the case of `streamcluster`, partitioning LLC increased the execution time by 20% compared with the baseline, but `Throttling` or `Scheduling` reduced the execution time by 10% compared to the baseline. This is because the `streamcluster` is a memory bandwidth intensive workload, so restricting LLC makes its performance worsen.

However, `Throttling` or `Scheduling` could increase the memory bandwidth of `streamcluster` by reducing background's memory access. In the case of `canneal`, it uses less memory bandwidth than `streamcluster`, but it is an LLC intensive workload with high LLC hit ratio. For `canneal`, all three isolations can reduce the execution time significantly.

However, in the case of `streamcluster`, when both techniques (`Throttling` and `Scheduling`) are used, the execution time is reduced by 24% compared with the baseline configuration. On the other hand, in case of `canneal`, the execution time is reduced by up to 38%, which is the highest performance improvement. In this way, we find that effective isolation techniques can be different according to the characteristics of the workload. Moreover, we realize that it is necessary and important to enforce appropriate isolation techniques adaptively considering the changed contentions.

5   HIS: Hybrid Isolation System

This section briefly describes the overview of how our proposed system can deal with the trade-offs between multiple isolation techniques depending on the characteristics of workloads. To achieve this goal, we propose *HIS*, a hybrid isolation system that leverages hardware and software isolation techniques to mitigate contentions and improve the performance of workloads.

Figure 5 illustrates our *HIS* architecture. As described in the figure, our system consists of a profiler, isolation techniques, and a scheduler. We divide workloads as foreground workloads and background workloads. The foreground is a latency-critical or high-priority batch workload and the background is the best-effort workload. *HIS* groups these two types of workloads and performs isolations on *workload group*s and places a group on a socket to improve resource efficiency. We also assume there is one foreground workload in the workload group like other clouds do [15].

The profiler collects the performance counters from workloads, and then profiles resource contentions from the collected counters. To profile resource contention online, the profiler performs *solo-run mode*, which enables for a foreground workload to run alone, to obtain the performance counters of each workload when no contention exists. After profiling *solo-run* data, the profiler collects performance counters of consolidated workloads to estimate how contentions affect resource usages. We define the performance counters of workloads when workloads co-executes as *co-run* data. Note that, we currently consider the *solo-run* data for the foreground workloads. We will describe more detail of *solo-run* mode at the Sect. 5.1. Both the obtained *solo-run* data and the *co-run* data are used to calculate the resource contention. After that, it sends the information of resource contention to the scheduler. Then, the scheduler checks which resource contention is the most contentious and decides an isolation technique considering the types of isolation technique and resource contention. Once an isolation technique is selected, the scheduler searches for a configuration of isolation and enforces isolations until the contention is minimized to below the

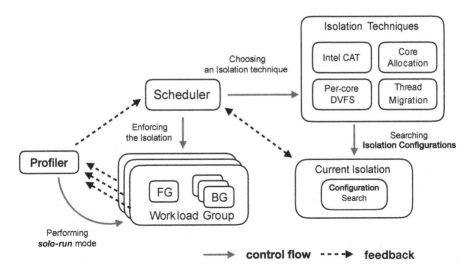

Fig. 5. *HIS* architecture. It consists of a *profiler, isolation techniques,* and a *scheduler.* The redline shows control flow and black dotted line shows the feedback of workload profiles, performances, and isolation decisions. The scheduler uses four isolation techniques; two hardware isolations (i.e., Intel CAT and per-core DVFS) and two software isolations (i.e., core allocation and thread migration).

pre-tuned threshold (i.e., 5% for each contention). In other words, the scheduler adjusts isolations to reduce the resource contention for a foreground workload close to when the workload runs alone. The scheduler repeats this procedure until the foreground workload finishes.

For isolations, *HIS* checks which isolation technique is the most appropriate one among multiple isolation ones; *HIS* considers multiple hardware and software isolations, and applies isolation techniques incrementally to improve the performance of a foreground workload while maximizing that of background one. This approach is useful because the scheduler reflects the subsequent resource contention and can enforce the corresponding isolation technique. For enforcing a proper isolation, the scheduler should know the dominant contention and decide appropriate isolations. Following sections will describe how the profiler profiles contention and how scheduler chooses isolation configurations in detail.

5.1   Profiling Contention

Profiling contention is essential for performance isolation. Our scheduler receives the resource usages of workloads from the profiler to estimate the contention on the system. To profile the contention, the profiler measures the per-workload performance counters such as LLC misses and LLC references in every profile interval (i.e., 200 ms). It calculates the resource contention by the difference of resource usages between when all workloads run concurrently (*co-run*) and when a workload runs alone (*solo-run*). We used the differences of *co-run* and *solo-run* data, because it presents resource sensitivity of a workload that how much the performance of workloads is degraded by the contention compared with no contention exists [11,22,23].

The profiler maintains the *solo-run* data for each foreground workload to calculate the resource contention, thus the scheduler checks whether the *solo-run* data exists or the execution phase has changed at every scheduling interval using already sampled data. If there is no data to calculate resource contention or the profile sample data is outdated, then the scheduler dictates to collect the new samples for *solo-run* data by stopping other background workloads. We call this procedure *solo-run mode*. We used two signals to enable *solo-run mode*; SIGSTOP for stop running workloads and SIGCONT for resume stopped workloads. To enable the *solo-run mode*, the profiler stops all current isolations and also pauses other background workloads during the successive profile intervals (e.g., one or two seconds). During the *solo-run mode*, only a foreground workload runs alone, and after finishing, the profiler stores all collected performance counters during the mode and resumes all previously paused isolations and background workloads.

The profiler classifies the workloads by their mostly used resources and also classify them by the type of the workload provided by users (e.g., FG and BG). We focused on the LLC and memory bandwidth to mitigate the contention on the memory subsystem. To measure the LLC contention, we used the LLC misses and LLC references, obtained by performance counters, and calculate the LLC hit ratio reflecting how much workload reuses the LLC. In addition, local_mem_bytes, obtained by Intel *Resctrl*, is used to estimate the memory bandwidth contention. The metrics can be added to consider more contentions and complicated execution patterns. With these metrics, the profiler can determine the dominant resource by comparing them, and also classify a workload as one of which CPU-intensive, LLC-intensive, or memory bandwidth intensive at every scheduling interval.

5.2   Hybrid Isolation

In this section, we will detail the trade-offs of isolation techniques and describe how our scheduler leverages them to mitigate the contention.

5.2.1   Isolation Mechanisms

HIS considers four isolations to mitigate contentions. In Table 1 of Sect. 2.1.1, HIS uses four techniques, which are hardware cache partitioning, per-core DVFS, core allocation, and thread migration, in hybrid isolation system.

Hardware Isolations. For hardware isolations, we used the Intel Cache Allocation Technology (Intel CAT) and per-core dynamic voltage frequency scaling (DVFS). With Intel CAT, *HIS* can allocate a LLC by the unit of a way. In our machine (i.e., Xeon E5-2683v4, 16-cores per socket), a socket has 40 MB of

LLCs and each consists of 20 ways. Intel CAT provides strict isolation for the LLC in a socket, because it partitions LLCs physically by masking the ways in *Resctrl*. We also used the per-core DVFS to throttle the execution of workload. Per-core DVFS is used to improve power efficiency of processors as well as mitigate the contentions and enable fine-grained control to improve performance of workloads. Using per-core DVFS, the scheduler can rapidly mitigate the memory contention, generated from contentious background workloads by adjusting the frequencies of cores running backgrounds. For enforcing core frequencies, we used the `CPUFreq Governor` of Linux.

The hardware isolations perform strict and quick isolation compared with the software isolations. Hardware cache partitioning provides the strict isolation which affects more predictable performance for the workloads. They generally take few milliseconds to reflect their effects to the workloads' performance. As shown in Table 1 (in Sect. 2.1.1), we observed 2–3 ms of latencies, and this low latency is beneficial to meet the SLOs of the latency-sensitive workload when the execution patterns of workloads changed frequently or the load of latency-sensitive workload shows high variation.

Software Isolations. For software isolations, we used the `cgroups cpuset` to allocate CPUs and memory nodes to workloads. To mitigate the contentions on the multicore systems, two software isolations are used in scheduling; core allocation and thread migration. Core allocation performs the allocation of CPU cores for workloads to isolate core resources by their CPU demands. For example, latency-sensitive workloads such as the web server can show high load variation by the user patterns, so the CPU demands can vary by their loads. Therefore, core allocation should be performed according to the CPU demands to improve resource efficiency and meet the SLO of foreground workloads.

Unlike core allocation which manages the contention of a workload group, thread migration detects the performance imbalance between workload groups, then it regroups those workloads by migrating workloads to the other socket. The thread migration is effective when the contention on a workload group is too large to be mitigated by other isolations (e.g., hardware isolations) on the single socket. However, too frequent thread migrations may be harmful to the performance because the cost of the memory migration over the sockets is expensive [12]. Therefore, we designed that thread migration is triggered only (1) if the performance benefit is estimated to exceed the threshold or (2) if the phase changes in a workload group is detected.

The software isolations provide flexibility compared with the hardware isolations. Core allocation treats CPU demands as well as mitigates memory contention according to the type of contention of workloads. They typically take more times than the hardware isolations to reflect isolation impacts on the workloads' performance (e.g., tens to hundreds of milliseconds).

5.2.2 Hybrid Scheduler

The hybrid scheduler periodically (1) chooses a proper isolation technique and (2) searches isolation configurations to improve the performance of foreground workloads within the workload groups. Before the hybrid scheduler initiates isolations, the profiler sends the information about current active workload groups, such as pid, workload type (FG or BG), and profiled resource contention to the scheduler. By using the workload group information, the scheduler initiates the isolations for the workload groups in parallel. While performing isolations, the scheduler checks whether the workloads in the group need *solo-run* data to calculate contentions, and if yes, requests for the profiler to perform *solo-run mode* to collect the new *solo-run* data.

Choosing an Isolation Technique. The hybrid scheduler chooses an isolation technique based on the mostly contentious resource, identified by the profiler. For the resource contention, at first, the scheduler checks whether the hardware isolation is available for the resource or not, and chooses the isolation if the isolation is possible and has not been tried. Between software and hardware isolations, the scheduler prioritizes hardware isolations for the strict and fast isolation. If all hardware isolation has tried before, the scheduler checks whether the software isolation technique are available for the resource or not and if it is possible then chooses the software isolation. If all the hardware and software isolations are used, the scheduler reconsider all techniques to reuse them. We implemented our policy to consider hardware isolation as much as possible. However, the policy for choosing an isolation technique can be changed to meet SLOs of the workloads.

There are two cases that the software isolations are chosen rather than hardware one. The first case is wrong invocation for an isolation technique. The scheduler often fails to search a better configuration due to the a few errors of profile data. For instance, the profiler may identify CPU contention as major factor when the actual contention is LLC contention. In this situation, the scheduler may perform hardware cache partitioning by its profile results. To minimize this case, we may choose isolation techniques more conservatively by not changing techniques until successive contentions are detected. The second case is when the scheduler exploits all hardware techniques, but still fails to reduce the contention because of their lower number of available configurations. For example, while the per-core DVFS may be not enough for mitigating severe memory contention due to its small configuration ranges, restricting the number of cores may be more beneficial to mitigate memory contention.

Enforcing Isolation. After choosing the isolation, the scheduler searches isolation configurations that minimize the resource contention by enforcing the various configurations repeatedly and incrementally. Whenever before enforcing isolation, the scheduler decides whether it allocates more resources to the foreground workload or not, based on resource contention. For example, if the dominant resource contention for the foreground workload is LLC contention, and also if the LLC hit ratio of the foreground one during *co-run* is lower than that of *solo-run*, the scheduler allocates more LLC ways to foreground workload. Because lower LLC hit ratio than the *solo-run* typically means that foreground workload can be improved if the workload is assigned more LLC ways.

Once the isolation is performed, the scheduler waits until the effect of enforcing an isolation is reflected, and then it repeatedly checks the degree of the contention. We empirically find that 200 ms is the most effective time to feedback contentions, yet the wait time can be tuned depending the target workloads. The scheduler finds there is no severe contention, or it can not perform the isolations further (e.g.., searching all possible configurations), then the configuration search ends. Finally, the scheduler enforces the configuration for chosen isolation.

6   Preliminary Evaluation

This section describes the preliminary experimental setup and results. We evaluated the hybrid isolation system for the batch and latency-sensitive workloads compared with the default Linux system using static software isolations. Here, we define the baseline as the case of *co-run* where the foreground and the background runs together on a socket. Both workloads share memory subsystem such as an LLC and a memory controller, but have their own dedicated CPU cores.

6.1   Experimental Setup

We evaluated the *HIS* on a dual 16-core Intel Xeon E5-2683 v4 server. The LLC size of the server processor is 40 MB and can be allocated to the workload in 2 MB units (per a way) using Intel CAT. The nominal frequency is 2.1 GHz and the configurable core frequencies are 10 steps from 1.2 GHz to 2.1 GHz. We turned off Turbo-boost and Hyper-threading. Our test machine is equipped 32 GB of RAM with each socket. The maximum bandwidth of the socket is measured to 68 GB/s by Intel *VTune* and we used Linux kernel 4.19.0.

We used various benchmark applications from four different suites. For batch foregrounds, we used PARSEC (`bodytrack`, `canneal`, `streamcluster`, `dedup`, `facesim`, `ferret`, `fluidanimate`, `swaptions`, and `vips`) and Rodinia (`cfd`, `nn`, `kmeans`, and `bfs`). For latency-sensitive foregrounds, we used the apache web server and `ab` (apache benchmark). In the case of latency-sensitive foreground, the scheduler should respond quickly to deal with the load spikes of the web server. We chose the `SP` from NPB as the background, because SP shows high memory bandwidth and LLC usage than other benchmarks.

6.2   Preliminary Results

6.2.1   Batch Workloads

We show the performance results for the batch workloads running as the foreground in Fig. 6. In the figure, *HIS* isolates foreground workload effectively, so that the performance of batch workloads are improved significantly compared to the *co-run*. In case of *canneal*, the performance is improved more than 1.7× than

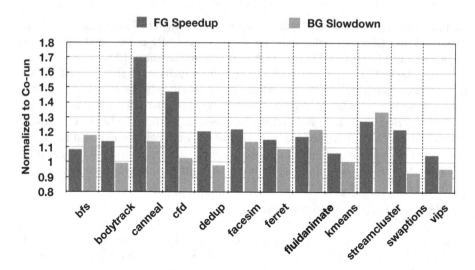

Fig. 6. Performance improvement of the batch foreground workload with *HIS* compared to the *co-run*. Each workload is initially allocated eight dedicated cores (background workload: SP).

co-run with simple core isolation that the workloads run on their dedicated cores, and the scheduler improves the performance of benchmarks on average 1.22× than *co-run*. On the other hand, the performance of the background workload is degraded, because our scheduler restricts the resource usage of the background workload to improve the performance and the responsiveness of foreground.

6.2.2 Latency-Sensitive Workloads

Figure 7 presents the performance of latency-sensitive workload running as the foreground. In order to evaluate the performance of latency-sensitive workload, we modified the ab which uses the *Pareto* distribution to reproduce situations where a few users are connected during most of the time and the connections are bursty. We measured the percentile latencies of requests.

In the figure, *HIS* can reduce the tail-latencies of web server below the performance of *solo-run* (8 cores) until 99.9th percentile, because the scheduler considers changes in dynamic load of the web server as well as the dominant resource contentions, and enforces various isolation techniques according to them. We also plot the tail-latencies of *solo-run* (12 cores) to compare with the proactive approach that reserves CPU cores as much as the maximum CPU cores that *HIS* allocates under the experiment. The latencies of *HIS* are higher than *solo-run* (12-cores), because *HIS* begins by allocating fewer cores to workload and increase the number of cores assigned to the workloads.

Compared with the *co-run*, *HIS* achieves the performance up to 2.14× speedup (for 99.9th percentile latency), while the performance of background

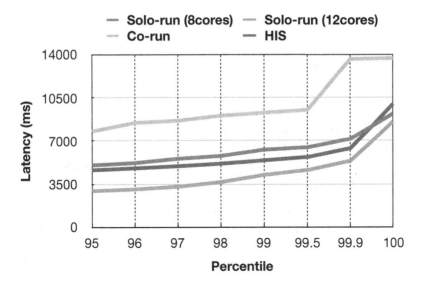

Fig. 7. Performance improvement of the latency-sensitive foreground workload (Apache web server) with *HIS* compared to the *co-run*. Each workload is initially allocated eight dedicated cores (background workload: SP).

workloads is slow down by 1.47×. We observed that the main reason for the performance improvement of foreground is due to fast and strict hardware isolation, core isolation which allocates more cores depending on the CPU demands, and adaptive isolations.

7 Related Work

There have been many studies on isolation approaches used in multicore systems. Software isolation is widely used in most multicore systems. CPI^2 [21] detects the performance anomaly and identifies the suffered a *victim* workload using statistics of CPI(Cycles Per Instruction), and throttles the CPU usage of the *antagonist* for performance isolation. Their work is inline with ours in terms of throttling background workloads with software isolations. However it only uses software techniques which provide less strict isolation, thereby needs harsh CPU hard-capping for antagoist for strictness (i.e., 0.01 CPU-sec/sec).

Memguard [20] isolates the memory bandwidth contention based on its memory budget. It utilizes a software isolation that throttles memory access of each workload by restricting CPU cycles, thus each workload's memory bandwidth can not exceed the assigned memory bandwidth. Similar to our work, it isolates memory resources by reserving memory bandwidth, but it does not utilize hardware isolation technique, so there is no guarantee for strict isolation. However, our work uses hardware isolation techniques to supplement strictness. Both CPI2 [21] and Memguard [20] isolate workloads by throttling CPU using a software technique, and they can mitigate memory contention easily. However software techniques may result in unintended interferences under the co-location of workloads showing bursty behaviors.

Dirigent [23] is a fine-grained isolation runtime system which partition an LLC and throttle CPUs. Similar to ours, it exploits hardware isolation techniques such as hardware cache partitioning and per-core DVFS to meet the SLOs of a latency-sensitive workload while backfilling batch workloads to improve resource efficiency. Our work is in line with their work [23] in terms of providing fine-grained isolations for considering the characteristics of workloads. However, we focus on the adaptive enforcement of multiple isolation techniques according to the characteristics of workloads, thus we can take more options for better performance isolation.

Quasar [6] utilizes a machine learning algorithm to infer which colocation mostly mitigates the shared resource contention, and uses scheduling and thread migration, which is the software approach, for isolation of consolidated workloads. Their work is inline with ours in terms of multiple isolation techniques In contrast, they only uses software isolation techniques for higher flexibility which can not provide strict and fast isolation.

Heracles [15] and PARTIES [4] isolate workloads by partitioning and throttling resources using both hardware and software isolation schemes to meet SLOs of production workloads while increasing resource efficiency. Similar to ours, their works are inline with ours in terms of using multiple isolation techniques for multicore systems. However, their works do not consider the tradeoffs between isolation techniques which can be harmful for the strictness and flexibility.

8   Conclusion

We developed a hybrid isolation system that utilizes hardware and software isolation techniques in a hybrid manner by the characteristics of the workloads. We have explored the tradeoffs between hardware and software isolation techniques, and illustrated how these properties affect performance of consolidated workloads. We have proposed an algorithm for isolation to use isolation techniques mutually complementary through characteristics analysis of workloads and comparison of each isolation technique. Our experimental results show that our approach can improve the performance of foreground workloads in terms of execution time than the static software isolation by from $1.7\times$–$2.14\times$ while improving resource efficiency for the selected benchmarks. For future work, we will evaluate our prototype with more diverse workload combinations. Also, we will investigate isolation techniques for the different micro-architectures such as AMD and ARM to generalize our ideas.

Acknowledgments. This research was supported by the National Research Foundation of Korea (NRF) grant funded by the Korea government (MSIT) (No. 2017R1A2B4004513, 2016M3C4A7952587, 2018R1C1B5085640), the Institute for the Information & communications Technology Promotion (IITP) grant funded by the

Korea government (MSIP) (No. R0190-16-2012), and BK21 Plus for Pioneers in Innovative Computing (Dept. of Computer Science and Engineering, SNU) funded by National Research Foundation of Korea(NRF) (21A20151113068).

References

1. Bailey, D.H., et al.: The NAS parallel benchmarks. Int. J. Supercomput. Appl. **5**(3), 63–73 (1991)
2. Bienia, C., Kumar, S., Singh, J.P., Li, K.: The parsec benchmark suite: characterization and architectural implications. In: Proceedings of the 17th International Conference on Parallel Architectures and Compilation Techniques, pp. 72–81. ACM (2008)
3. Che, S., Boyer, M., Meng, J., Tarjan, D., Sheaffer, J.W., Lee, S.H., Skadron, K.: Rodinia: a benchmark suite for heterogeneous computing. In: 2009 IEEE International Symposium on Workload Characterization, IISWC 2009, pp. 44–54. IEEE (2009)
4. Chen, S., Delimitrou, C., Martínez, J.F.: Parties: Qos-aware resource partitioning for multiple interactive services. In: Proceedings of the Twenty-Fourth International Conference on Architectural Support for Programming Languages and Operating Systems, pp. 107–120 (2019)
5. David, H., Gorbatov, E., Hanebutte, U.R., Khanna, R., Le, C.: RAPL: memory power estimation and capping. In: Proceedings of the 16th ACM/IEEE International Symposium on Low Power Electronics and Design, pp. 189–194. ACM (2010)
6. Delimitrou, C., Kozyrakis, C.: Quasar: resource-efficient and QoS-aware cluster management. ACM SIGPLAN Not. **49**(4), 127–144 (2014)
7. Derr, S.: Control Group Cpusets. BULL SA (2004). https://www.kernel.org/doc/Documentation/cgroup-v1/cpusets.txt
8. Elnikety, S., et al.Perfiso: Performance isolation for commercial latency-sensitive services
9. Hsu, C.H., et al.: Adrenaline: pinpointing and reining in tail queries with quick voltage boosting. In: 2015 IEEE 21st International Symposium on High Performance Computer Architecture (HPCA), pp. 271–282. IEEE (2015)
10. Intel, C.: Improving real-time performance by utilizing cache allocation technology. Intel Corporation, April 2015
11. Kim, S., Eom, H., Yeom, H.Y.: Virtual machine consolidation based on interference modeling. J. Supercomput. **66**(3), 1489–1506 (2013). https://doi.org/10.1007/s11227-013-0939-2
12. Lepers, B., Quéma, V., Fedorova, A.: Thread and memory placement on numa systems: asymmetry matters. In: USENIX Annual Technical Conference, pp. 277–289 (2015)
13. Leverich, J., Kozyrakis, C.: Reconciling high server utilization and sub-millisecond quality-of-service. In: Proceedings of the Ninth European Conference on Computer Systems, p. 4. ACM (2014)
14. Linden, G.: Make data useful (2006)
15. Lo, D., Cheng, L., Govindaraju, R., Ranganathan, P., Kozyrakis, C.: Heracles: improving resource efficiency at scale. ACM SIGARCH Comput. Architect. News **43**, 450–462 (2015)
16. Seo, D., Eom, H., Yeom, H.Y.: MLB: a memory-aware load balancing method for mitigating memory contention. In: Conference on Timely Results in Operating Systems (TRIOS 2014) (2014)

17. Teabe, B., Tchana, A., Hagimont, D.: Application-specific quantum for multi-core platform scheduler. In: Proceedings of the Eleventh European Conference on Computer Systems, p. 3. ACM (2016)
18. Turner, P., Rao, B.B., Rao, N.: CPU bandwidth control for CFS. In: Linux Symposium, vol. 10, pp. 245–254. Citeseer (2010)
19. Wysocki, R.J.: CPU Performance Scaling. Intel Corporation (2017). https://www.kernel.org/doc/html/v4.12/_sources/admin-guide/pm/cpufreq.rst.txt
20. Yun, H., Yao, G., Pellizzoni, R., Caccamo, M., Sha, L.: MemGuard: memory bandwidth reservation system for efficient performance isolation in multi-core platforms. In: 2013 IEEE 19th Real-Time and Embedded Technology and Applications Symposium (RTAS), pp. 55–64. IEEE (2013)
21. Zhang, X., Tune, E., Hagmann, R., Jnagal, R., Gokhale, V., Wilkes, J.: CPI 2: CPU performance isolation for shared compute clusters. In: Proceedings of the 8th ACM European Conference on Computer Systems, pp. 379–391. ACM (2013)
22. Zhao, Y., Rao, J., Yi, Q.: Characterizing and optimizing the performance of multithreaded programs under interference. In: 2016 International Conference on Parallel Architecture and Compilation Techniques (PACT), pp. 287–297. IEEE (2016)
23. Zhu, H., Erez, M.: DIRIGENT: enforcing QoS for latency-critical tasks on shared multicore systems. ACM SIGARCH Comput. Architect. News 44(2), 33–47 (2016)
24. Zhuravlev, S., Blagodurov, S., Fedorova, A.: Addressing shared resource contention in multicore processors via scheduling. ACM Sigplan Not. 45, 129–142 (2010)

Improving Resource Isolation of Critical Tasks in a Workload

Meghana Thiyyakat$^{(\boxtimes)}$, Subramaniam Kalambur, and Dinkar Sitaram

PES University, Bengaluru, India
meghanathiyyakat@pesu.pes.edu, {subramaniamkv,dinkars}@pes.edu

Abstract. Typical cluster schedulers co-locate critical tasks and background batch tasks to improve the utilization of resources in the cluster. However, this leads to resource contention and interference between the diverse co-located tasks. To ensure guaranteed resource allocation and predictability, critical tasks are executed within containers as they provide resource isolation using container resource allocation mechanisms. Linux-based containers achieve resource allocation and isolation using a kernel feature known as Control Groups (cgroups). Cgroups allow the division of CPU time into shares which can be allocated to different groups of tasks. In our study, we run workloads on servers with different hardware configurations and measure the CPU time per second, or the *CPU bandwidth*, that the critical tasks in the workloads can consume. Our workloads have been generated using a cluster trace published by Google, and contain a mixture of critical and background tasks. The results of the experiments show that under high CPU load conditions, the CPU bandwidth consumed by the critical tasks is inadequate and unstable because of the poor resource isolation offered by cgroups. However, when these tasks are scheduled with the careful use of SCHED_DEADLINE policy, which is based on the Global Earliest Deadline First and Constant Bandwidth Server algorithms, they steadily consume their required CPU bandwidth irrespective of the load on the CPU. As a result, when critical tasks are scheduled using SCHED_DEADLINE, they experience $3\times$–$40\times$ smaller delays than under cgroups.

Keywords: Resource isolation · Cgroups · Containers · CPU bandwidth

1 Introduction

As a result of the cost benefits of deploying multiple applications on shared infrastructure, companies are moving more and more of their computations to private and public clouds. The workloads running on these clouds comprise critical tasks and background tasks. Critical tasks need guaranteed resource allocations and/or have strict latency requirements. These are generally tasks of user-facing services such as web search that are deployed on stream processing frameworks like Storm [29] and Flink [7]. Background tasks comprise batch jobs from

© Springer Nature Switzerland AG 2020
D. Klusáček et al. (Eds.): JSSPP 2020, LNCS 12326, pp. 45–67, 2020.
https://doi.org/10.1007/978-3-030-63171-0_3

frameworks, such as Hadoop [30] which do not have stringent resource requirements and may be latency-tolerant. To improve the utilization of servers, tasks
with diverse characteristics and resource requirements are co-located. There have
been numerous works that use heuristics to find optimal combinations of tasks
to schedule on to systems such that the utilization of the infrastructure is maxi-
mized without violating service-level objectives [10,11,15,21,22,32]. Despite the
recognized benefits of shared infrastructure, it gives rise to two concerns: resource
isolation [4] and security. Today, containers have emerged as a popular lightweight virtualization solution to address both these issues [23]. In Linux-based
containers, two kernel features - control groups (cgroups) [8] and namespaces,
are used to implement resource-isolation and security, respectively. The cgroups
feature was introduced in Linux kernel version 2.6.24. It allows users to impose
constraints on the resource utilization of groups of tasks. While cgroups allow
users to manage multiple resources such as memory and network bandwidth,
in this paper, we focus on the resource isolation offered by cgroups for CPU
bandwidth.

SCHED_DEADLINE, originally designed for embedded systems [5,12,18],
is a real-time CPU scheduling policy available in Linux kernel version 3.14
onward. The policy is based on 2 algorithms - Earliest Deadline First (EDF)
and Constant Bandwidth Server (CBS). It schedules tasks based on their deadlines and performs admission control of tasks to prevent over-provisioning of
the CPU bandwidth, thereby ensuring that all the deadlines can be met. While
SCHED_DEADLINE has traditionally been used to guarantee temporal isolation of real-time tasks, that is, ensuring that deadlines of tasks are met, we show
that it can also be used to secure the required CPU bandwidth for critical tasks,
undeterred by the load on the CPU.

We use samples from the Google Cluster Trace [27] to emulate cluster workloads consisting of critical and background tasks. The results of our experiments
show that when critical tasks are allocated CPU bandwidth using cgroups, they
are unable to steadily consume their required bandwidth because of interference from the background tasks. When the same tasks are scheduled using
SCHED_DEADLINE, they are able to consistently consume their required CPU
bandwidth which results in smaller delays in their response times.

The contributions of the paper are a description of how we have used the
Google Cluster Trace to emulate cluster workloads, a method to estimate the
parameters required for scheduling with SCHED_DEADLINE, and a comparison
of the resource isolation offered by cgroups and SCHED_DEADLINE.

The rest of the paper is organized as follows. Section 2 summarizes scheduling
in the Linux operating system. Section 3 describes in detail the workloads used
and the experimental setup. Section 4 presents the results of the study. Section 5
discusses related works and finally, Sect. 6 concludes the paper.

2   Background

Linux is a multitasking general-purpose operating system and must concurrently
execute interactive as well as CPU bound jobs. Therefore, the scheduler needs

to give preference to interactive tasks to ensure quick responses, while ensuring that CPU-bound jobs do not starve. Linux also supports real-time scheduling policies to handle tasks with real-time constraints. SCHED_DEADLINE, SCHED_FIFO, and SCHED_RR are the real-time policies available in the Linux scheduler. The SCHED_DEADLINE policy, based on Global Earliest Deadline First [19] and Constant Bandwidth Server [2] algorithms, is used to grant temporal isolation to tasks and predictability in their execution. In our work, we show that SCHED_DEADLINE offers better resource isolation than cgroups.

2.1 Completely Fair Scheduler

The Completely Fair Scheduler [25] is Linux's default scheduling policy. Tasks scheduled under SCHED_OTHER, SCHED_IDLE and SCHED_BATCH policies are all handled by CFS. In our work, we only consider one of CFS's policies: SCHED_OTHER. Since CFS does not provide implicit resource isolation, we have used the results of critical tasks scheduled under CFS (SCHED_OTHER) as a baseline to compare the CPU bandwidth allocation with and without resource isolation. In all the scheduling scenarios in our study, the background tasks are scheduled using SCHED_OTHER only.

2.2 SCHED_DEADLINE

The SCHED_DEADLINE policy was added to the Linux kernel in 2014, to version 3.14 and is based on the Global Earliest Deadline First and Constant Bandwidth Server algorithms. Tasks scheduled under this policy are given the highest priority in the system and can preempt tasks of all other policies. Since the scheduling policy is based on CBS it ensures non-interference between tasks by throttling threads that try to consume more than their allotted share of the CPU. While CFS ensures maximum utilization of the CPU and that no process starves, SCHED_DEADLINE provides predictability to tasks that have strict deadlines and latency constraints. To schedule a task using SCHED_DEADLINE, 3 parameters are passed to the scheduler—sched_runtime (budget), sched_period (period) and sched_deadline (deadline). The budget denotes the amount of CPU time the task needs every period. Hence, the share of CPU time allotted to the task is sched_runtime ÷ sched_period. The sched_deadline parameter conveys to the scheduler that it must allocate sched_runtime seconds of CPU time to the task within sched_deadline seconds of each period. If a task tries to consume more CPU time than its budget, it is throttled until its next period. This property, combined with the fact that the tasks of this policy are assigned the highest priority, enforces resource isolation between the tasks. To ensure that deadlines can be met and that the required budget can be sanctioned to each task every period, the scheduler performs a schedulability test. The schedulability test only allows a new thread to enter the runnable thread pool if the sum of the CPU usage rates of the new thread and the existing threads in the pool continues to be less than the number of processors. That is,

$$\sum_{i=1}^{n} \frac{sched\_runtime}{sched\_period} <= N \qquad (1)$$

where N is the number of processors, and n is the runnable threads in the system, including the new task. However, to ensure that non-real-time tasks do not starve, an upper limit is enforced on the total CPU usage rate of real-time tasks. To reflect this the above equation is modified:

$$\sum_{i=1}^{n} \frac{sched\_runtime}{sched\_period} <= N \times rt\_quota\% \qquad (2)$$

where rt_quota% is the cap on the aggregate CPU usage rate of real-time tasks. rt_quota is equal to 95% by default in Linux.

In our work, we make use of the resource isolation offered by SCHED_DEADLINE while scheduling critical tasks. However, since the tasks may be long-running, aperiodic, and have dynamic resource requirements, we use the SCHED_DEADLINE policy differently from its conventional usage for real-time tasks. In our work, we show that the policy can also be used to secure the CPU bandwidth necessary for the critical tasks to run without delays. Since the bandwidth requirements may vary with time, for every window of time during which the CPU bandwidth is constant, SCHED_DEADLINE is used to secure the needed CPU bandwidth. A description of this modified usage of SCHED_DEADLINE is given in Sect. 3.3. When scheduling critical tasks using SCHED_DEADLINE, if a task fails the schedulability test, we put the task to sleep for 0.1 s, and then try to reschedule the task. We repeat this step until the task is successfully scheduled. The sleep duration was determined empirically based on the trade-off between the polling overhead and delay in scheduling the thread.

2.3   Control Groups

Control groups, or cgroups, were introduced as a part of the Linux kernel in version 2.6.24. They allow system administrators to make resource reservations and partitions for groups of tasks. The cgroups interfaces to resources such as CPU or memory are known as subsystems. In our work, we focus on the CPU only and have thus made use of the CPU subsystem. Linux-based containers use the CPU subsystem to enforce CPU bandwidth isolation with the help of shares. Shares are integers used to describe the relative share of total CPU bandwidth that a cgroup is assigned. That is, a cgroup's portion of the total CPU bandwidth is the number of shares assigned to the cgroup divided by the total number of shares available. If a task is not assigned explicitly to a cgroup, it comes under the root cgroup. In our study, we assign the critical tasks to a cgroup, group_p. We have allocated group_p with 95% in the initial runs, and then with 99% of the CPU shares. The number of shares assigned to group_p is calculated using the following formulae:

$$\frac{group\_p\_shares}{group\_p\_shares + root\_shares} = share\% \qquad (3)$$

The root cgroup has 1024 shares by default. If the subsystem has only one explicitly defined group—group_p, it has to be assigned 19456 shares to give the tasks in group_p access to a minimum of 95% of the total CPU bandwidth (using Eq. 3).

Cgroups also allow users to enforce hard upper limits on the amount of CPU Time that can be consumed in a specified period. This is done by defining quotas. In our work, we have not used quotas for the background tasks to ensure optimum CPU utilization. When the critical tasks do not require the remaining CPU bandwidth, the background tasks scheduled using quotas cannot make use of this bandwidth, thereby reducing the overall utilization of the CPU and introducing unnecessary delays in the background tasks.

Scheduling of tasks under cgroups is undertaken by CFS by default. In our work, the critical tasks assigned to cgroups are scheduled using CFS (SCHED_OTHER).

3   Methodology

The objective of our study was to compare the resource isolation offered by cgroups and SCHED_DEADLINE policy. To do so, we measured the CPU bandwidth consumed by the critical tasks in the workloads under different scheduling scenarios. When resource isolation is not robust, interference from the co-located tasks does not allow critical tasks to consume the required CPU time at the rate needed by the tasks. This leads to delays in their response times. While robust resource isolation could be guaranteed to critical tasks by scheduling them on dedicated CPU cores, such course-grained allocation leads to severe underutilization of the CPU resources. Hence, we have used cgroups and SCHED_DEADLINE to allocate resources at a finer granularity.

In this paper, the terms *CPU usage rate, bandwidth, share* and *utilization*, all represent the amount of CPU Time that is consumed or required every second. While the terms all measure the same quantity, they have been used depending on the context of the measurement and cannot be used interchangeably. The quantity, *CPU usage rate*, used by Google in their cluster trace, is measured in core-second/second. We have used the term *CPU bandwidth* to refer to the ratio of the CPU Time consumed or required per second, to the total CPU Time available per second. We use the term "Total CPU bandwidth" to denote 100% CPU bandwidth. Therefore, if a task running on a 4-core machine has a CPU bandwidth requirement of 20%, it consumes 20% of the total CPU time available every second, that is, 20% of 4 core-seconds. Therefore, its CPU usage rate is 0.8 core-second/second. We have used the term *share*, as per the cgroups definition, for the relative amount of CPU Time allotted to a cgroup per second. The term

CPU utilization has been used to denote the utilization of the entire CPU of the server when executing a workload or a part of it.

3.1 Workloads

The two workloads used in our experiments were created from the Google Cluster Trace [27]. The trace, published by Google in 2011, contains data about the different tasks that run on a 12k node cluster for 29 days. It includes measurements such as CPU and memory usage, task characteristics such as priorities and scheduling classes, and the attributes of the machines on which the tasks are deployed. All the dimensions in the trace have been normalized relative to the largest capacity of a resource.

3.2 Workload Generation

To generate the High CPU Utilization (HCU) workload, we first chose a machine from the trace that had experienced a high CPU load. To do so, we selected all machines from the machine_events table with CPU capacity 1 (maximum capacity, since all the resource dimensions are normalized). The utilization of the cluster is maximum during days 22 and 23 of the trace [28]. We found the average utilization of the selected machines on these days by joining tables task_usage and task_events. The tasks_events table contains information about the priority and scheduling class of each task and the task_usage table holds a log of the resource consumption of each task for every measurement window. The measurement window is typically 300s unless it is the beginning or end of a task's execution lifetime. From the top 10 machines with the highest average utilization, we chose a machine that had tasks with a diverse mixture of priorities and scheduling classes. For our second workload, the Low CPU Utilization (LCU) workload, we sampled the resource usage data for the same machine but for day 10—during which the CPU utilization was relatively lower. The LCU workload, therefore, has a lower overall CPU utilization.

Since our study only concerns CPU time, each row of the resulting trace sample consisted of the following values:

1. Start time of the measurement period
2. End time of the measurement period
3. Mean CPU usage rate
4. Priority
5. Scheduling class

As all measurements in the trace are normalized, the "Mean CPU usage rate" in the sample, measured in core-second/second, ranged from 0–1. Google has chosen not to disclose their machine specifications to the extent we require, hence, to be able to denormalize the resource measurements, we made assumptions about the values of the CPU clock speed of the machine chosen. We used the parameters of a typical machine of that period to assume that the chosen machine, machine A, was a 4-core machine with a processing speed of 2.1 GHz. While generating the workload, we have made a simplifying assumption that the CPU clock speed is constant for the values reported in the trace. However, we have executed the workload on real systems with varying CPU speeds. The assumption holds since we use the results to perform comparisons between different runs on a given system only, and not across systems. We calculated the following values for each measurement period in the trace as per the assumptions made:

$$ExecutionTime = Endtime - Starttime \tag{4}$$

$$CPU\,RuntimeA = Normalized\_CPU\_Usage\_Rate \times 4 \times ExecutionTime \tag{5}$$

Here, *Starttime* and *Endtime* are the beginning and end of the measurement window in the trace. $CPU\,RuntimeA$ is the runtime of the task on machine A and $Normalized\_CPU\_Usage\_Rate$ is the normalized mean CPU usage rate given in the trace for each measurement window. We multiply by 4 to undo the normalization based on the assumed number of cores. To run the workloads on the target machine, machine B, we scaled them appropriately by performing the following calculations:

$$ClockCycles = CPU\,RuntimeA \times ClockSpeedA \tag{6}$$

$$= CPU\,RuntimeB \times ClockSpeedB \tag{7}$$

$$\therefore CPU\,RuntimeB = \frac{CPU\,RuntimeA \times ClockSpeedA}{ClockSpeedB} \tag{8}$$

$CPU\,RuntimeB$ is the denormalized CPU time the task is to consume on machine B, $ClockSpeedA$ and $ClockSpeedB$ are the CPU speeds of the chosen machine, machine A, and the target machine, machine B, respectively.

Each task in the workloads was executed as a separate multi-threaded process. When the CPU usage rate of a task was greater than 1 core-second/second, the rate was split equally among multiple threads and scheduled to run on multiple cores. To consume $CPU\,RuntimeB$ seconds of the CPU, the task thread executed a few mathematical statements for $CPU\,Slice$ seconds and was then put to sleep for $SleepSlice$ seconds. The task thread repeated these steps until the total CPU Time consumed by it equaled $CPU\,RuntimeB$. The parameters were calculated as follows:

$$SleepTimeB = ExecutionTime - CPU\,RuntimeB \tag{9}$$

$$NumSlices = \frac{ExecutionTime}{Slice} \tag{10}$$

$$CPU\,Slice = \frac{CPU\,RuntimeB}{NumSlices} \tag{11}$$

$$SleepSlice = \frac{SleepTimeB}{NumSlices} \tag{12}$$

The value of *Slice* was set to 0.05. Algorithm 1 summarizes how the tasks were modeled and emulated based on the calculated values.

Algorithm 1: Pseudo-code for running a task in the workloads.

Input: trace sample *trace*
begin
  | Function RUN_ON_CPU(*row*)
  | *slice* = 0.05 *num_slices* = *row.window/slice*
  | *cpu_slice* = *cpu_time/num_slices sleep_slice* = *sleep_time/num_slices*
  | *current_cpu_time* = 0
  | **while** *current_cpu_time* < *cpu_time* **do**
  | | Run math operations on CPU till CPU time equal to *cpu_slice* is
  | | consumed;
  | | Sleep for *sleep_slice* seconds;
  | | *current_cpu_time* = *current_cpu_time* + *cpu_slice*;
  | **end**
  | Function Main(*trace*)
  | **foreach** *row* ∈ *trace* **do**
  | | **if** *row.cpu_time* > *row.window* **then**
  | | | *num_threads* = *ceil(row.cpu_time/row.window)*
  | | | *row.cpu_time* = *row.cpu_time/num_threads*
  | | | **for** *i* ← 0*tonum_threads*1 **do**
  | | | | execute *RUN_ON_CPU(row)* on a new thread
  | | | **end**
  | | **else**
  | | | *RUN_ON_CPU(row)*
  | | **end**
  | **end**
  | **return** Task Completed
end

For each task, a logger thread maintained a log of the CPU usage rate of the task. The aggregate CPU usage rate of each task class was later found and plotted. The average delay in the tasks, as well as the delay observed in each measurement window, were plotted for each scheduling scenario. We also recorded the overall CPU utilization % of the workloads every second.

Only tasks with priority 9 or higher and scheduling class greater than 0 were considered as "critical". Other tasks were labeled as "background". We did so based on the analysis of the trace by Reiss et al. [28] and the description of the trace parameters published by Google [27]. Since there are no descriptions of the jobs and tasks in the trace, we assume that critical tasks are those tasks that have stringent-latency constraints and/or need strict resource allocation guarantees.

We created two different workloads to study resource isolation under different CPU load conditions. The HCU workload consisted of 7 critical tasks and 7 background tasks. A summary of the tasks in the workload scaled for the 4-core machine according to the methodology described in Sect. 3.2, can be found in Table 1. The LCU workload contained 9 critical tasks and 33 background tasks. Both workloads had a runtime of around 2 h. The CPU bandwidth requirements of the two categories of tasks in the HCU and LCU workloads are shown in Fig. 1.

Table 1. Description of the HCU workload tasks on the 4-core machine.

Task No	Type	Mean CPU Usage Rate [Std Dev] (in core-second/second)	Duration (in s)
1	Critical	0.186 [0.024]	5700
2	Critical	0.179 [0.018]	5700
3	Critical	0.162 [0.019]	6300
4	Critical	0.039 [0.042]	6600
5	Critical	0.030 [0.025]	6600
6	Critical	0.042 [0.040]	6600
7	Critical	0.705 [0.154]	6600
8	Background	1.398 [0.266]	6600
9	Background	0.247 [0.085]	6600
10	Background	0.239 [0.090]	6600
11	Background	0.231 [0.120]	6600
12	Background	0.261 [0.124]	5438
13	Background	0.247 [0.094]	6600
14	Background	0.001 [0.0]	246

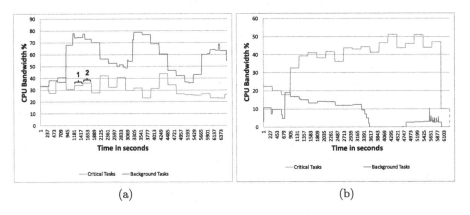

Fig. 1. CPU bandwidth requirement of each task category in the a) HCU workload, and b) LCU workload.

The delay in the response time was calculated as follows:

$$ResponseTime = Task\_ETime - Task\_STime \tag{13}$$

$$Delay = ResponseTime - TaskExecutionTime \tag{14}$$

Where $TaskExecutionTime$ is defined as the duration between the start and end of the task as per the trace. $Task\_STime$ and $Task\_ETime$ are the actual wall clock times recorded at the start and end of the task thread's execution, respectively.

3.3   Experimental Setup

To compare the resource isolation offered by the two resource allocation mechanisms, the upper limit on the CPU bandwidth allocated to critical tasks had to be set equally for both. In our experiments, we set the upper limit as 95% of the total CPU bandwidth. This is because, in Linux, the CPU bandwidth that real-time tasks are allowed to consume is capped, by default, at 95% of the total CPU bandwidth. The 2 system-wide settings: `sched_rt_period_us` and `sched_rt_runtime_us`, found in `/proc/sys/kernel/`, determine the CPU bandwidth that real-time tasks are allowed to consume [26] and have default values of 1s and 0.95s, respectively, restricting the CPU usage of real-time tasks to 95% of the total CPU bandwidth. Therefore, for a fair comparison of the two scheduling scenarios, we assigned 95% of the CPU shares to the cgroup with the critical tasks. While the critical tasks scheduled using SCHED_DEADLINE were allotted a *maximum* of 95% of total the CPU bandwidth, the tasks scheduled using cgroups were allotted a *minimum* of 95% of the total CPU bandwidth. However, since SCHED_DEADLINE tasks are always assigned the highest priority in the system, the tasks can consume up to 95% of the total CPU bandwidth without being throttled or having to wait for lower priority tasks to yield the CPU. Therefore, in both scenarios, 95% of the total CPU bandwidth was allocated to the running of the critical tasks. We ran the workloads under 3 scenarios: i) using neither cgroups or SCHED_DEADLINE (only SCHED_OTHER), ii) selectively assigning the critical tasks to a cgroup with 95% share of the total CPU bandwidth, and iii) selectively scheduling critical tasks using SCHED_DEADLINE. The results of scenario (i) were used as a baseline to compare the performance of tasks with and without resource isolation.

We ran the workloads on two Intel Xeon machines. Since some cloud-workloads comprise tasks deployed on containers which, in turn, run on Virtual Machines (VMs), we also conducted our experiments on two EC2 instances. The details of the servers are summarized in Table 2. In the table, HT stands for Hyperthreading.

Cgroups: For the cgroups scenario, the critical tasks were scheduled to a cgroup `group_p`. Since the CPU bandwidth of real-time tasks is capped, by default, at

Table 2. Server configurations

Type	CPU speed GHz	Logical cores or vCPUs	Linux kernel version
EC2 instance- c5n.xlarge	3.0	4	4.15
EC2 instance- c4.2xlarge	2.6	8	4.15
Intel Xeon E3-1220	3.1	4	5.5
Intel Xeon E5-2683 v4 (with HT)	2.1	32	5.5

95% of the total CPU bandwidth, we assigned 95% of the total CPU shares to group_p to allow us to compare the two scheduling scenarios. The experiment was also repeated with 99% of the total CPU shares being allotted to group_p.

Dynamic Parameter Estimation For SCHED_DEADLINE: To schedule tasks using SCHED_DEADLINE, 3 parameters need to be set: sched_runtime, sched_deadline and sched_period. A task thus scheduled is given sched_runtime seconds of CPU Time every sched_period seconds with a relative deadline of sched_deadline seconds from when the task begins execution.

Since the value of sched_runtime required by a task is generally unknown before-hand, we use a dynamic profiling method to estimate the value of sched_runtime. We split the execution of every task in each measurement window of the trace into 2 stages: a short profiling stage at the beginning of the window, and an execution stage spanning the rest of the window. We utilised the resource isolation offered by SCHED_DEADLINE even during the profiling stage to get an accurate estimate of the CPU usage rate required by the task. During its short profiling stage, each thread in every runnable task was allotted an entire CPU core for the duration of the profiling stage. That is, if the duration of the stage is t seconds, sched_runtime, sched_deadline and sched_period are all set to t. This allowed the task to run unhampered at the CPU usage rate it required without being throttled or having to deal with interference from other tasks. After the short profiling stage, we measured the required CPU usage rate of the task as:

$$CPU\_usage\_rate = \frac{CPUTime}{ProfilingWindow}$$

Where $ProfilingWindow$ is the duration of the profiling stage, and $CPUTime$ is the amount of CPU time (on a single core) consumed by the task during the profiling stage. A representation of the stages can be found in Fig. 2. SCHED_DEADLINE performs a schedulability test (Eq. 2) before admitting tasks into its runnable pool. Hence, if the server has N cores, and t_n is the number of concurrent tasks that are executing in their profiling stage at an instant, $t_n <= N$. When the number of tasks that wish to enter their profiling stages, t_p, is greater than N, then at least t_p - N tasks fail the schedulability test and need to wait for at least one task to exit its profiling stage before they can enter their own. We empirically determined the size of the Profiling Window such that the wait time of the tasks did not cause significant delays in their response times. Once the CPU_usage_rate was found, the sched_runtime parameter was set to CPU_usage_rate seconds and the sched_period and sched_deadline parameters were set to 1 s. By doing so, we guaranteed that the task got its required CPU bandwidth every second. Therefore, instead of using SCHED_DEADLINE to guarantee a deadline was met, we used it to secure the CPU bandwidth required by the task.

Since the Google Cluster trace only reports the mean CPU usage rate for every measurement window (usually 300 s long), we modeled the tasks such that they had a constant CPU usage rate during a measurement window—equal to the value given in the trace. After every window, we ran the profiling stage again to find the current required rate and rescheduled the tasks with the updated parameter values. In the future, we wish to extend our work to tasks with continuously varying CPU usage rates.

By default, Linux restricts the total usage rate of real-time tasks to 95% of the total CPU bandwidth to ensure that non-real-time tasks are not starved. We retained the default value while running our workloads under SCHED_DEADLINE.

4   Results

In this section, we discuss the results of running the LCU and HCU workloads on the 4 servers under the different scheduling scenarios described in Sect. 3.

4.1   CPU Bandwidth Consumption

Figure 3 shows the CPU bandwidth consumed by the critical and background tasks of the HCU workload on the 32-core physical machine. In Fig. 4 and Fig. 5, the CPU bandwidth consumed by the critical tasks in the HCU workload, scheduled using CFS, cgroups, and SCHED_DEADLINE, is plotted.

The standard deviation of the CPU bandwidth consumed during the intervals of time indicated by the numbers 1 and 2 in Fig. 1a is tabulated in Table 3 and Table 4, respectively. From the table it is observed that the standard deviation of the bandwidth consumption is consistently smaller in the SCHED_DEADLINE scenario, proving that the CPU bandwidth consumption under SCHED_DEADLINE is steadier. We have chosen the two intervals towards the beginning of the runs because, towards the latter part of the runs, the CPU bandwidth curve for the cgroups scenario lags behind due to delays arising from

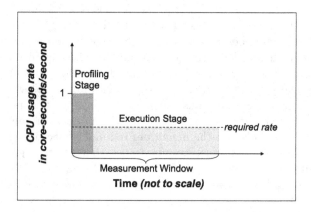

Fig. 2. Dynamic sched_runtime estimation

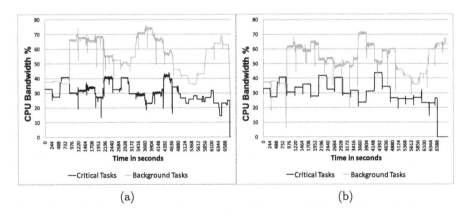

Fig. 3. CPU bandwidth consumed by each task category in the HCU workload when scheduled on the 32-core physical machine, using a) cgroups, and b) SCHED_DEADLINE.

insufficient bandwidth allocation. During intervals 1 and 2, the transitions in the CPU bandwidth consumption in the two time-series are still aligned with respect to time, therefore, allowing us to compare them.

Table 3. Standard deviation of the CPU bandwidth % consumed in Interval 1 by critical tasks scheduled using SCHED_DEADLINE and cgroups

Server	SCHED_DEADLINE	Cgroups
4-core physical machine	0.032	0.422
32-core physical machine	0.031	1.235
EC2 instance- c4.2xlarge	0.026	1.409
EC2 instance- c5n.xlarge	0.049	1.518

The results show that on all the servers, the bandwidth consumed by the critical tasks under CFS and cgroups was unsteady and lesser than the required CPU bandwidth for most of the run. However, the CPU bandwidth consumed by the critical tasks scheduled with SCHED_DEADLINE did not fluctuate as much and was equal to the required bandwidth for most of the run. This observation also validates our methodology used for the dynamic estimation of the sched_runtime parameter for the critical tasks (Sect. 3.3). The mean absolute percentage error (MAPE) and the standard error (SE) in the estimation of sched_runtime for the critical tasks in the HCU workload are recorded for each server in Table 5.

A similar trend was found when the critical tasks were scheduled under a cgroup allotted with 99% of the CPU shares (Fig. 6). The standard deviation of the CPU bandwidth consumed in intervals 1 and 2 is given in Table 6.

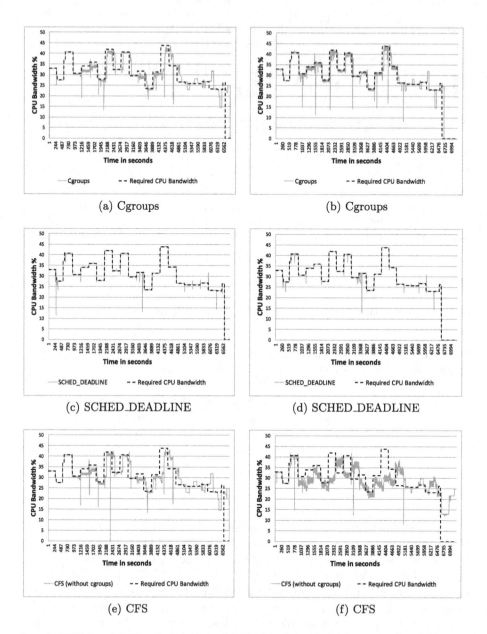

Fig. 4. CPU bandwidth consumption of critical tasks under cgroups on the a) 32-core physical machine and b) 4-core physical machine, under SCHED_DEADLINE on the c) 32-core physical machine and d)4-core physical machine, and under CFS on the e) 32-core physical machine and f) 4-core physical machine

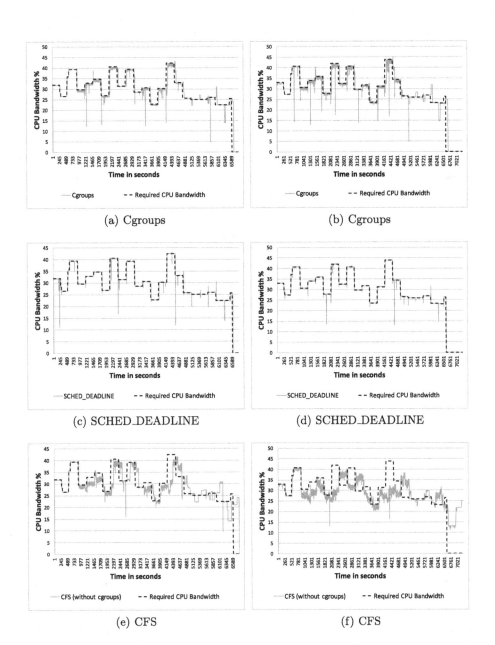

Fig. 5. CPU bandwidth consumption of critical tasks under cgroups on the a) c4.2xlarge instance, and b) c5n.xlarge instance, under SCHED_DEADLINE on the c) c4.2xlarge instance and d) c5n.xlarge instance, and under CFS on the e) c4.2xlarge instance and f) c5n.xlarge instance

Table 4. Standard deviation of the CPU bandwidth % consumed in Interval 2 by critical tasks scheduled using SCHED_DEADLINE and cgroups

Server	SCHED_DEADLINE	Cgroups
4-core Physical Machine	0.044	1.745
32-core Physical Machine	0.054	0.578
EC2 Instance- c4.2xlarge	0.027	0.805
EC2 Instance- c5n.xlarge	0.028	1.120

Table 5. Mean Absolute Percentage Error and Standard Error of the estimated sched_runtime parameter in the HCU workload

Server	Mean absolute percentage error	Standard error (in core-second/second)
EC2 Instance- c5n.xlarge	4.694%	0.043
EC2 Instance- c4.2xlarge	3.726	0.052
Intel Xeon E3-1220	5.349%	0.052
Intel Xeon E5-2683 v4	1.249%	0.030

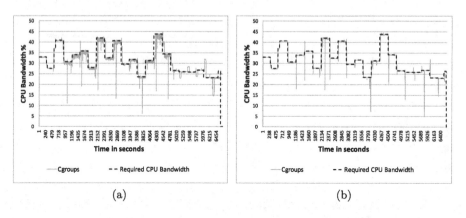

(a)   (b)

Fig. 6. CPU bandwidth consumption of critical tasks under cgroups (99% share allotted) on the a) 4-core physical machine, and b) 32-core physical machine.

Table 6. Standard deviation of the CPU bandwidth % consumed in intervals 1 and 2, by critical tasks scheduled under the cgroup with 99% of the CPU shares

	32-core physical machine	4-core physical machine
Interval 1	0.087	0.783
Interval 2	1.139	1.296

The CPU bandwidth consumed by the critical tasks in the LCU workload, under the different scheduling scenarios, on the 32-core physical machine is reported in Fig. 7.

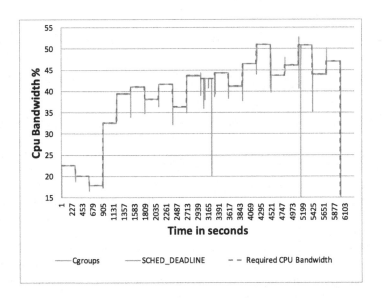

Fig. 7. CPU bandwidth consumption of the critical tasks in the LCU workload, under cgroups and SCHED_DEADLINE, on the 32-core physical machine.

Since the background tasks in the LCU workload have a lower CPU utilization than those in the HCU workload, the interference posed by the tasks is bound to be lesser. Hence, it can be seen that the CPU bandwidth consumed under both scheduling scenarios was nearly equal to the bandwidth required. However, the CPU bandwidth consumed by critical tasks under SCHED_DEADLINE was still found to be marginally greater than that consumed under cgroups. Since the difference is not apparent from the plot, we have briefly summarized the distribution of the CPU bandwidth consumed by the critical tasks in Table 7.

Table 7. Distribution of the CPU bandwidth % consumed by the critical tasks in the LCU workload on the 32-core physical machine.

	SCHED_DEADLINE	Cgroups
1st Quartile	36.32%	36.28%
Median	41.66%	41.61%
3rd Quartile	44.28%	44.25%

4.2   Delay in Tasks

The maximum CPU utilization of the critical tasks in the workloads was found to be far less than 95% (e.g., only 43.8% on the 32-core physical machine). Therefore, it is expected that if the critical tasks are assigned to a cgroup with 95% of the CPU shares, the tasks must execute without considerable delay in their response times. The average delay in the response times of tasks in the HCU workload, for the 3 scenarios: CFS, selective scheduling of critical tasks using a cgroup with 95% of the CPU shares, and selective scheduling of critical tasks using SCHED_DEADLINE (with the default 95% cap on CPU usage rate), is reported for the 4 servers in Fig. 8. The average delay for each task category has been calculated as the sum of the delays in each of its task, divided by the number of tasks in the category. The delay in each task was found using Eq. 14.

From the plots, it is evident that despite the cgroup having been allotted with more than the required number of CPU shares, the response times of the critical tasks assigned to it were very poor. The average delay of critical tasks when they were assigned to cgroups was 3 to 40 times larger than the average delay of the tasks under SCHED_DEADLINE. These results were found to be consistent across all 4 servers.

The average delay in the response times of the tasks in the LCU workload under the different scheduling scenarios is shown in Fig. 9. While the delays were smaller than those in the HCU workload, it can be seen that, here too, the delay in the critical tasks scheduled with SCHED_DEADLINE was smaller than the delay under cgroups. However, unlike the HCU workload, the average delay in the background tasks in the LCU workload is smaller than the average delay in the critical tasks. We suspect this is due to two reasons. First, the CPU bandwidth requirement of the critical tasks in the LCU workload is much higher than that of the background tasks. Second, the background tasks in the LCU workload are short-lived while the critical tasks are long-running tasks. Both these factors cause the critical tasks to be more adversely affected by resource contention leading to larger delays. In the case of the HCU workload, the background tasks had a higher CPU bandwidth requirement when compared to the critical task. Since the background tasks are scheduled using CFS which penalizes CPU-bound jobs, larger delays were found in the background tasks of the HCU workload. We also suspect that the reason behind the slightly higher average delay in the critical tasks of the LCU workload under cgroups, when compared to CFS, is due to contention within the cgroup itself.

To further study the resource isolation, the delays observed in the critical tasks at the end of each measurement period and the CPU utilization of the HCU workload were recorded throughout the run (Fig. 10). It was found that under cgroups, the delays of the critical tasks in each measurement period increased considerably when the CPU utilization of the workload was high. Hence, it is evident that the performance of the critical tasks under cgroups was not immune to the load on the CPU. However, under SCHED_DEADLINE, the magnitude of the delay in the critical tasks was not only considerably smaller but also remained nearly constant throughout the run, unaffected by the changes in the CPU load.

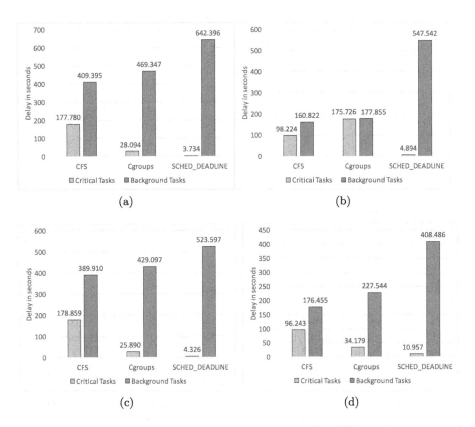

Fig. 8. Average delay in the response time of tasks of the HCU workload on the a) 4-core physical machine, b) 32-core physical machine, c) c5n.xlarge instance, and d) c4.2xlarge instance.

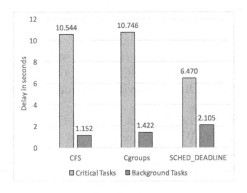

Fig. 9. Average delay in LCU workload tasks on the 32-core physical machine.

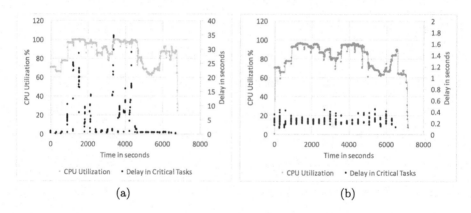

Fig. 10. Total CPU utilization of the 32-core physical machine while running the HCU workload and the corresponding delay in the critical tasks scheduled using a) cgroups and b) SCHED_DEADLINE.

5   Related Work

In this section, we survey work that is related to resource isolation, cgroups, and the performance of scheduling policies such as SCHED_DEADLINE that enforce temporal isolation in the CPU.

Several enhancements have been proposed to the cgroups feature to improve its I/O resource management capabilities on NUMA machines with SSDs [3,24]. Gao et al. [13], studied the different ways in which it is possible to circumvent the resource isolation enforced by cgroups and how an adversarial container can take advantage of the weaknesses inherent in cgroups to consume more resources than it is allowed to. From our work, too, it is evident that cgroups are unable to provide robust resource isolation for CPU time and background hogs can interfere with the tasks running in cgroups, thereby reducing their chances of getting the required share of CPU time.

PINE [20] is a performance isolation optimization strategy that dynamically adjusts disk space and I/O concurrency levels based on the performance requirements of tasks— either throughput or latency.

Vitucci et al. [31] compared the performance of SCHED_DEADLINE with non-resource isolating algorithms like SCHED_FIFO and SCHED_OTHER concluding that SCHED_DEADLINE provides an almost stable throughput compared to the other scheduling policies.

AIRS [16] is based on two algorithms—Flexible CBS and EDF with Window-constraint Migration (EDF-WM). The results show that AIRS is able to achieve higher frame rates than SCHED_DEADLINE when running multiple movies due to the use of the EDF-WM algorithm. The work, however, does not touch on resource isolation or stability of CPU bandwidth allocation. It instead focuses on improving overall system utilization by allowing tasks to divide runtime among multiple cores and to share excess CPU bandwidth allocation.

In [9], the authors make use of the IRMOS real-time scheduler with KVM to provide stable performance to real-time applications running on VMs. The IRMOS scheduler allocates CPU time to a group of threads, such that the threads share the specified CPU time within a given period. Since our paper focuses specifically on the isolation of individual critical tasks, rather than VMs, we make use of the SCHED_DEADLINE policy without having to modify underlying system software. Our `sched_runtime` parameter estimation methodology is dynamic, and unlike the benchmarking in the aforementioned work, it does not require dedicated resources. This is because we use the SCHED_DEADLINE policy to provide the resource isolation necessary to estimate the CPU bandwidth requirement of critical tasks.

In [1], the authors present a hierarchical scheduler to execute the tasks in real-time control groups. The runqueues associated with the CPUs of a real-time cgroup are scheduled using the SCHED_DEADLINE policy. While the paper is related to cgroups and SCHED_DEADLINE, the objective of the work greatly differs from ours. Firstly, our work focuses on non-real-time workloads with unknown resource requirements and non-real-time cgroups which are scheduled using CFS. Secondly, the objective of our paper is to show that non-real-time cgroups, which are used as the default resource allocation mechanism in containers, provide poor resource isolation when compared to SCHED_DEADLINE.

PerfIso [14] is a performance isolation framework that uses a method known as CPU Blind Isolation that restricts the cores on which background tasks run to ensure that critical tasks always have some headroom. In our work, we use SCHED_DEADLINE to provide robust resource isolation to critical tasks such that the background tasks can utilize the remaining CPU bandwidth, without affecting the performance of the critical tasks. By allowing background tasks unrestricted access to the CPU bandwidth that has not been allocated to critical tasks, we improve the overall CPU utilization.

SCHED_DEADLINE is most effective when the CPU usage rate required by a task can be known or predicted accurately. Hence, our study complements other works [6,11,17], whose objective is to profile workloads and predict the dynamic resource requirements of tasks.

6   Conclusion

Cgroups are a kernel feature which enforce resource isolation between tasks in Linux-based containers. In this paper, we compare the resource isolation offered by cgroups and the SCHED_DEADLINE scheduling policy in the context of CPU bandwidth. While SCHED_DEADLINE has traditionally been used to guarantee temporal isolation of real-time tasks, we demonstrate that it can also be used to secure guaranteed CPU bandwidth allocation for critical tasks, undeterred by the load on the CPU. Our experiments reveal that under cgroups, the critical tasks are unable to secure the required CPU bandwidth because of interference from co-located tasks. Since the tasks scheduled using cgroups do not get adequate CPU bandwidth in a timely manner, delays are introduced in the tasks' execution. However, when the critical tasks in the workloads are scheduled using SCHED_DEADLINE, the CPU bandwidth consumption of the tasks is nearly equal to the required CPU bandwidth, irrespective of the load on the CPU. As a result, the average delay of critical tasks scheduled using SCHED_DEADLINE was found to be 3x-40x smaller than cgroups. From this, we conclude that under high CPU load conditions, if critical tasks are scheduled using SCHED_DEADLINE rather than cgroups, they are assured better resource isolation, which results in stable resource allocations, smaller delays and predictable response times. We, therefore, recommend that existing execution environments for critical tasks be modified to exploit the resource isolation and the consequent benefits (such as dynamic estimation of CPU bandwidth requirement and reduction in task delays) offered by SCHED_DEADLINE.

Acknowledgments. We thank Akarsh Dsouza for his assistance with the implementation of the emulation and modelling of tasks in the cluster trace.

References

1. Abeni, L., Balsini, A., Cucinotta, T.: Container-based real-time scheduling in the Linux kernel. ACM SIGBED Rev. **16**(3), 33–38 (2019)
2. Abeni, L., Buttazzo, G.: Integrating multimedia applications in hard real-time systems. In: Proceedings 19th IEEE Real-Time Systems Symposium (Cat. No. 98CB36279), pp. 4–13. IEEE (1998)
3. Ahn, S., La, K., Kim, J.: Improving i/o resource sharing of linux cgroup for NVME SSDS on multi-core systems. In: 8th USENIX Workshop on Hot Topics in Storage and File Systems (HotStorage 2016) (2016)
4. Barker, S.K., Shenoy, P.: Empirical evaluation of latency-sensitive application performance in the cloud. In: Proceedings of the First Annual ACM SIGMM Conference on Multimedia Systems, pp. 35–46. ACM (2010)
5. Bini, E., et al.: Resource management on multicore systems: the actors approach. IEEE Micro **31**(3), 72–81 (2011)
6. Calheiros, R.N., et al.: Workload prediction using ARIMA model and its impact on cloud applications Qos. IEEE Trans. Cloud Comput. **3**(4), 449–458 (2014)
7. Carbone, P., et al.: Apache flink: stream and batch processing in a single engine. Bull. IEEE Comput. Soc. Tech. Commit. Data Eng. 36(4) (2015)
8. Cgroups. https://www.kernel.org/doc/Documentation/cgroup-v1/cgroups.txt
9. Cucinotta, T., Giani, D., Faggioli, D., Checconi, F.: Providing performance guarantees to virtual machines using real-time scheduling. In: Guarracino, M.R., et al. (eds.) Euro-Par 2010. LNCS, vol. 6586, pp. 657–664. Springer, Heidelberg (2011). https://doi.org/10.1007/978-3-642-21878-1_81
10. Delimitrou, C., Kozyrakis, C.: Paragon: Qos-aware scheduling for heterogeneous datacenters. ACM SIGPLAN Not. **48**, 77–88 (2013)
11. Delimitrou, C., Kozyrakis, C.: Quasar: resource-efficient and QoS-aware cluster management. ACM SIGARCH Comput. Architect. News **42**, 127–144 (2014)
12. Faggioli, D., et al.: An EDF scheduling class for the linux kernel. In: Proceedings of the 11th Real-Time Linux Workshop, pp. 1–8. Citeseer (2009)
13. Gao, X., et al.: Houdini's escape: Breaking the resource rein of linux control groups (2019)

14. Iorgulescu, C., et al.: Perflso: performance isolation for commercial latency-sensitive services. In: 2018 USENIX Annual Technical Conference, pp. 519–532 (2018)
15. Julian, S., Shuey, M., Cook, S.: Containers in research: initial experiences with lightweight infrastructure. In: Proceedings of the XSEDE16 Conference on Diversity, Big Data, and Science at Scale, XSEDE16, New York, NY, USA, pp. 25:1–25:6. ACM (2016). ISBN 978-1-4503-4755-6. https://doi.org/10.1145/2949550.2949562. http://doi.acm.org/10.1145/2949550.2949562
16. Kato, S., Rajkumar, R., Ishikawa, Y.: AIRS: supporting interactive real-time applications on multicore platforms. In: 2010 22nd Euromicro Conference on Real-Time Systems, pp. 47–56. IEEE (2010)
17. Kishore, Y., et al.: Qos aware resource management for apache Cassandra. In: 2016 IEEE 23rd International Conference on High Performance Computing Workshops (HiPCW), pp. 3–10. IEEE (2016)
18. Lelli, J., et al.: Deadline scheduling in the Llinux kernel. Softw. Pract. Exp. **46**(6), 821–839 (2016)
19. Li, J., et al.: Global EDF scheduling for parallel real-time tasks. Real Time Syst. **51**(4), 395–439 (2014). https://doi.org/10.1007/s11241-014-9213-9
20. Li, Y., et al.: Pine: optimizing performance isolation in container environments. IEEE Access **7**, 30410–30422 (2019)
21. Lo, D., et al.: Heracles: improving resource efficiency at scale. ACM SIGARCH Comput. Architect. News **43**, 450–462 (2015)
22. Mars, J., et al.: Bubble-up: increasing utilization in modern warehouse scale computers via sensible co-locations. In: Proceedings of the 44th Annual IEEE/ACM International Symposium on Microarchitecture, pp. 248–259. ACM (2011)
23. Merkel, D.: Docker: lightweight linux containers for consistent development and deployment. Linux J. **2014**(239), 2 (2014)
24. Min, J., et al.Cgroup++: enhancing I/O resource management of linux cgroup on Numa systems with NVMe SSDs. In Proceedings of the Posters and Demos Session of the 16th International Middleware Conference, p 7. ACM (2015)
25. Pabla, C.S., et al.: Completely fair scheduler. Linux J. **2009**(184), 4 (2009)
26. Real-time group scheduling. https://www.kernel.org/doc/Documentation/scheduler/sched-rt-group.txt
27. Reiss, C., Wilkes, J., Hellerstein, J.L.: Google cluster-usage traces: format+schema, pp. 1–14. Google Inc., White Paper (2011)
28. Reiss, C., et al.: Heterogeneity and dynamicity of clouds at scale: google trace analysis. In: Proceedings of the Third ACM Symposium on Cloud Computing, p 7. ACM (2012)
29. Toshniwal, A., et al.: Storm@ twitter. In: Proceedings of the 2014 ACM SIGMOD International Conference on Management of Data, pp. 147–156. ACM (2014)
30. Vavilapalli, V.K., et al.: Apache Hadoop YARN: yet another resource negotiator. In: Proceedings of the 4th Annual Symposium on Cloud Computing, p. 5. ACM (2013)
31. Vitucci, C., et al.: A Linux-based virtualized solution providing computing quality of service to SDN-NFV telecommunication applications. In: Proceedings of the 16th Real Time Linux Workshop (RTLWS 2014), pp. 12–13 (2014)
32. Xu, R., et al.: Pythia: improving datacenter utilization via precise contention prediction for multiple co-located workloads. In: Proceedings of the 19th International Middleware Conference, pp. 146–160. ACM (2018)

Optimizing Biomedical Ultrasound Workflow Scheduling Using Cluster Simulations

Marta Jaros[1]($^{\boxtimes}$) , Dalibor Klusáček[2], and Jiri Jaros[1]

[1] Faculty of Information Technology, Centre of Excellence IT4Innovations,
Brno University of Technology, Brno, Czech Republic
{martajaros,jarosjir}@fit.vutbr.cz
[2] CESNET a.l.e., Brno, Czech Republic
klusacek@cesnet.cz

Abstract. Therapeutic ultrasound plays an increasing role in dealing with oncological diseases, drug delivery and neurostimulation. To maximize the treatment outcome, thorough pre-operative planning using complex numerical models considering patient anatomy is crucial. From the computational point of view, the treatment planning can be seen as the execution of a complex workflow consisting of many different tasks with various computational requirements on a remote cluster or in cloud. Since these resources are precious, workflow scheduling plays an important part in the whole process.

This paper describes an extended version of the k-Dispatch workflow management system that uses historical performance data collected on similar workflows to choose suitable amount of computational resources and estimates execution time and cost of particular tasks. This paper also introduces necessary extensions to the Alea cluster simulator that enable the estimation of the queuing and total execution time of the whole workflow. The conjunction of both systems then allows for fine-grain optimization of the workflow execution parameters with respect to the current cluster utilization. The experimental results show that this approach is able to reduce the computational time by 26%.

Keywords: Scheduling · Workflow · k-Dispatch · Simulation · Alea

1 Introduction

The use of ultrasound as a diagnostic imaging tool is well-known, particularly during pregnancy where ultrasound is used to create pictures of developing babies. In recent years, a growing number of therapeutic applications of ultrasound have also been demonstrated [17]. The goal of therapeutic ultrasound is to modify the function or structure of biological tissue in some way rather than produce an anatomical image. This is possible because the mechanical vibrations caused by ultrasound waves can affect tissue in different ways, for example, by

© Springer Nature Switzerland AG 2020
D. Klusáček et al. (Eds.): JSSPP 2020, LNCS 12326, pp. 68–84, 2020.
https://doi.org/10.1007/978-3-030-63171-0_4

causing the tissue to heat up or by generating internal forces that can agitate the cells or tissue scaffolding. These ultrasound bioeffects offer enormous potential to develop new ways to treat major diseases. In the last few years, clinical trials of different ultrasound therapies have demonstrated the ability of ultrasound to destroy cells through rapid heating for the treatment of cancer and neurological disorders, target the delivery of anticancer drugs, stimulate or modulate the excitability of neurons, and temporarily open the blood-brain barrier to allow drugs to be delivered more effectively [12]. These treatments are all completely noninvasive and have the potential to significantly improve patient outcomes.

The fundamental challenge shared by all applications of therapeutic ultrasound is that the ultrasound energy must be delivered accurately, safely, and noninvasively to the target region within the body identified by the doctor. This is difficult because bones and other tissue interfaces can severely distort the shape of the ultrasound beam. In principle, it is possible to predict and correct for these distortions using models of how ultrasound waves travel through the body. However, the underlying physics is complex and typically must consider nonlinear wave propagation through absorbing media with spatially varying material properties. Simple formulas do not exist for this scenario, so models used for studying therapeutic ultrasound are instead based on the numerical solution of the wave equation (or the corresponding constitutive equations) [19].

The k-Wave toolbox designed for the time-domain simulation of acoustic waves in biomedical materials has become very popular in the international ultrasonic community [18]. Nevertheless, modelling ultrasound treatments using this toolbox requires very complex and intensive computations that generally cannot be satisfied by desktop computers or small servers [6]. It is thus essential to offload the computational work to cloud or HPC clusters. Unfortunately, using these facilities and composing the processing workflow representing the treatment is complex even for experienced developers. Therefore, it is crucial to offer clinical end-users a middleware layer that features a simple interface (e.g., web page, medical GUI, etc.) to upload treatment setups with related data and automate the execution. This middleware layer is implemented by our software package called k-Dispatch [9].

k-Dispatch, however, offers much more than simple job submission with semi-automated execution and monitoring such as HTCondor [8] or Pegasus [3]. k-Dispatch additionally provides a low level automatization by selecting suitable execution parameters specifying the amount of compute resources and estimates required execution time for particular tasks. This is enabled by a fixed set of medically certified binaries serving as building blocks for user's workflows, and collected performance data updated after every successful run. Based on the task input data, k-Dispatch searches the performance database to estimate scaling of particular binaries on the fly, and tune the execution parameters to minimize execution time and/or computational cost. Nevertheless, since the computational resources are shared by multiple users and workflows, the queuing times and user interference may depreciate the execution plan.

Therefore, this paper deals with the extension of the Alea cluster simulator [10] to estimate the workflow makespan, i.e., the overall execution time including the queuing times as well as the computational cost for complex biomedical ultrasound workflows. For every workflow, k-Dispatch prepares a candidate set of execution parameters and passes them to Alea which simulates the workflow execution with respect to the cluster parameters, job scheduling system setup, and background workload.

This paper is organized as follows. In Sect. 2, the considered workflow scheduling problem is discussed thoroughly. Section 3 describes the Alea simulator and its new workflow-related functionality. Next, Sect. 4 demonstrates the newly developed simulation capabilities which are crucial for the k-Dispatch's scheduling module when analyzing the quality of considered workflow execution plan(s). The paper is concluded and the future work is discussed in Sect. 5.

2   Problem Description

The k-Dispatch's mission is to enable fully automated offloading of biomedical ultrasound workflows built on the top of the acoustic k-Wave toolbox to the HPC and cloud environment. These workflows are used for pre-operative treatment planning based on the patient specific images to maximize the treatment outcome. Every treatment plan consists of many tasks carrying out data processing, ultrasound sonications, and thermal and tissue model evaluations. Their orchestration is encoded in the form of a directed acyclic graph (DAG) describing the data dependency and precedence relations [14]. Every task is evaluated by an appropriate piece of software included in the k-Wave toolbox. The most time consuming ultrasound tasks can be executed by a variety of simulation codes optimized for particular hardware platform including shared memory systems, single Nvidia GPU, and distributed memory CPU and GPU clusters. Each binary is suitable for a different simulation size and complexity and has associated a different simulation cost. The shared memory/GPU versions can be used for treatment planning in small volumes such as prostate, while the distributed versions are suitable for large treatments in the brain, liver or kidney.

Working within the medical environment implies all software must undergo a strict regulatory and certification process. It is thus not possible for users to use their own binaries. Instead, only authorized personnel are allowed to deploy the simulation binaries within a strictly controlled environment, e.g., inside Singularity [7] or Docker [13] containers. The clinical users are, of course, allowed to compose different workflows from predefined modules, change the number of sonications, their parameters or upload different patient images.

These restrictions, on the other hand, open great opportunity for automated performance tuning and resource allocation. Since the binaries are fixed, their execution can be monitored, and the performance data collected and analysed for future use. k-Dispatch maintains a complex performance database including information about every successful task containing binary name, cluster name, queue name, amount of resources, simulation medium size and properties, wall clock time and computational cost. Once a new ultrasound workflow is received, k-Dispatch decodes individual tasks and assigns them suitable binaries, appropriate resources, and estimates the wall clock time. Then, the tasks are handed over to the cluster job scheduler that is responsible for their execution.

The optimizations of execution parameters help minimizing the computational cost and/or the execution time of individual tasks. However, since every workflow contains many tasks and there are usually multiple workflows being simultaneously executed, the isolated optimization of individual tasks may lead to poor cluster utilization or long queuing times. It is necessary to focus on bigger picture and take into account the dependencies between tasks of (multiple) DAGs. However, the optimization complexity can become exponential [15]. Therefore, there is a need for heuristics that include fast cluster simulations to evaluate the overall execution time of all workflows currently in the system. This information provides the feedback to the planning logic to adjust the amount of resources for particular tasks.

2.1   Workflows and Infrastructure

There are many workflow templates supported by k-Dispatch [9]. Figure 1 shows an intracranial neuromodulation workflow used for treatment planning of essential tremor and Parkinson's disease procedures. The purpose of this workflow is to verify the ultrasound hits the desired target but does not rise the tissue temperature above safety levels.

The workflow starts with the aberration correction pre-processor converting the treatment parameters and patient data into input files for the following ultrasound simulations. This task is usually simple and only employs a single compute node for a couple of minutes per sonication. The total execution time thus increases with the number of sonications (N) being executed (see the first line in Table 1). Next, a number of independent aberration correction simulations is executed. For this particular example, an ultrasound transducer with a driving frequency of 550 kHz, and a medium of 25 cm × 29 cm × 19 cm is used.

Table 1. Execution time and amount of resources for particular tasks within the neurostimulation workflow measured on the Anselm Supercomputer. The number of sonications (denoted by N) influences the total execution time.

Code type	Number of nodes	Execution time
Aberration correction pre-processor	1	$400 + 250 \cdot N$ [s]
Aberration correction simulation	1–16	$< 34.31, 4.96 >$ [h]
Aberration correction post-processor	1	$115 + 95 \cdot N$ [s]
Forward planning pre-processor	1	$650 + 310 \cdot N$ [s]
Forward planning simulation	1–16	$< 30.90, 4.72 >$ [h]
Forward planning post-processor	1	$105 + 60 \cdot N$ [s]
Thermal simulation	1	$30 + 720 \cdot N$ [s]

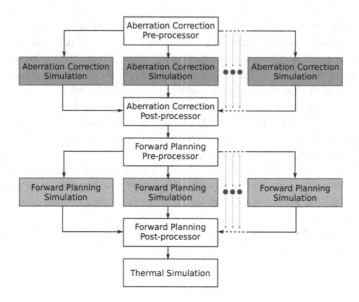

Fig. 1. Typical neurostimulation simulation workflow using the reverse focusing for aberration corrections. After pre-processing, reverse ultrasound propagation simulation from particular targets are executed. After aberration correction, forward ultrasound simulations are executed to calculate energy deposition. Finally, a thermal simulation is executed to estimate overall heat deposition and temperature rise in the tissue.

A simulation of such a size can be executed by the distributed CPU code running on 1 to 16 nodes. The number of sonications is usually between 1 and 32. After all aberration correction simulations have completed, the aberration correction post-processor joins the results from the previous step and derives corrected transducer signals. The forward planning pre-processor consequently generates new ultrasound simulation files. Both these tasks require a single node only. The forward planning simulations use the same code as the aberration correction simulations but with different driving signal. The execution times are therefore very similar. This stage is closed by the forward planning post-processors, which collects the heat deposition from particular sonications. Again, a single node is sufficient for this task. Finally, the thermal simulation is executed to calculate the temperature rise in the brain and evaluate the treatment outcome. This code uses a single simulation node only.

The target infrastructure used for the evaluation of the planning capabilities is based on a 16 node partition of the Anselm supercomputer run by the IT4Innovations National Supercomputing Centre[1]. Each node is equipped with two 8-core Sandy Bridge processors, 64 GB RAM and 40 GB InfiniBand connection. The supercomputer is managed by the PBS Pro scheduler with a backfilling job scheduling.

---

[1] https://docs.it4i.cz/anselm/compute-nodes/.

2.2 Optimization Criteria

In general, k-Dispatch aims to find the best execution parameters for particular tasks to minimize the *overall execution time, computational cost* and *queuing times*. This is achieved by using the database maintaining information about previously completed tasks that allows us to approximate execution time and amount of resources for new workflows, and cluster simulations that evaluate queuing times for given execution parameters.

The optimization criteria can be minimized independently using a multi-objective approaches to create a Pareto front, or aggregated into a single criterion by associated weights. To limit the time complexity of the optimization process, the following aggregated criteria f is used:

$$f = w_t * (t + q) + w_c * c \tag{1}$$

where w_t and w_c are the weights promoting the execution time and computation cost, respectively, t is the wall clock execution time of all tasks, q is the aggregated queuing time, and c is the overall computation cost. Five different combinations of the weights are evaluated in this paper:

- $w_t = 1 \wedge w_c = 0$ minimizing execution time but ignoring cost,
- $w_t = 0 \wedge w_c = 1$ minimizing execution cost but ignoring time
- $w_t = 0.5 \wedge w_c = 0.5$ looking for a trade-off between execution time and cost,
- $w_t = 0.7 \wedge w_c = 0.3$ preferring execution time to cost,
- $w_t = 0.3 \wedge w_c = 0.7$ preferring execution cost to time.

2.3 Execution Parameters Selection

Before the workflow is submitted to the cluster, the execution parameters for particular tasks have to be set. For this purpose, k-Dispatch employs four modules: (1) *Optimizer* that employs a simple hill climbing algorithm traversing the search space of promising execution parameters, (2) *Interpolator* that provides estimations of execution time and cost for given tasks and their execution parameters, (3) *Simulator* that evaluates the queuing times and calculates the overall execution time of the complete workflow, see Eq. (1), and (4) *Collector* that updates the performance database after the workflow execution.

Let us start with Interpolator which is supposed to estimate the execution time and cost for a given task and execution parameters provided by Optimizer. This module searches the performance database for similar tasks. If there is a direct match, i.e., a task of the same type and size has already been executed, the records are filtered by the age and sorted according to the execution parameters used. If there are multiple records for the same execution parameters, the median value is taken. Consequently, a strong scaling plot is constructed, see Fig. 2. From this plot, it is straightforward to estimate the execution time and cost for given execution parameters (number of nodes in this case). If some values are missing, e.g., Optimizer asks about an odd number of compute nodes, the execution time and cost are interpolated. If there is not a direct match, which indicates

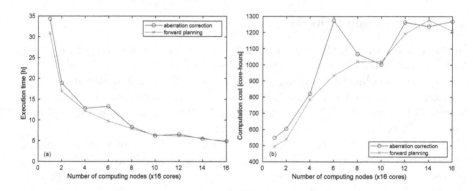

Fig. 2. Strong scaling of the (a) execution time and (b) execution cost for aberration correction and forward planning simulations. The anomalies in the plots are caused by unbalanced work distribution over compute nodes.

such a task has not been executed before, a dual interpolation is performed. Interpolator searches all tasks of similar size, constructs multiple scaling plots, and interpolates between them. If the interpolation fails due to oscillations of the interpolation polynomial or a low number of records found, a default wall clock time with the associated cost are returned. This is, however, a very rare situation, since the more tasks get executed, the more records are in the database, and the more precise interpolations are.

Once the execution parameters have been set for all tasks, the workflow schedule is handed over to Simulator. Although many job schedulers offer some kind of queuing time estimation, the number of such requests is very limited, e.g., one per 5 min. Therefore, the actual state of the cluster is downloaded and fed into the Alea simulator. After the evaluation, the overall execution time (makespan) is calculated as the sum of the estimated execution and queuing times over all tasks. Since the queuing times are not included in the execution cost, the simulator only returns the overall time. Let us note that on a real system, the execution times of particular tasks may slightly vary due to cluster workload (network and I/O congestion, varying temperature and clock frequency between nodes, etc.). These oscillations are, however, neglected since being usually below 5%, and if there is a significant transient performance drop, the k-Dispatch monitoring module detects such an anomaly and terminates affected tasks.

Optimizer tries to select appropriate execution parameters to minimize the aggregated criteria for the whole workflow, see Fig. 3. The parameters of the tasks may be initialized randomly, using the recently best known values, or by individual optimization of each task. In order to search the space, the execution parameters are slightly perturbed in every iteration, the compute time and cost estimated by Interpolator, and the makespan evaluated by Simulator. After a predefined number of iterations, the best workflow parameters are used to submit the workflow to the cluster. In order to broaden the performance database, there is a small probability that Optimizer selects such execution parameters that have not been tried before. This helps adapt the workflow schedules to changes in the cluster software configuration, hardware upgrades, long-term performance anomalies, etc. After the workflow has been executed by the cluster, the amount of resources used is stored in the performance database along with the actual execution time and cost.

Figure 3 shows two examples of the execution plans designed by k-Dispatch. In the first example, all aberration correction simulations use the same amount of resources, which may yield the best value of the optimization criteria for individual tasks. This may however lead to a suboptimal execution schedule when the cluster size is limited. A better solution may be to use 2 nodes for first 16 tasks and 4 nodes for the last four. Should the number of nodes assigned per task happen not to be a divider of the cluster size, there would be wasted computing slots. The main objective of k-Dispatch is to prevent such inefficiencies.

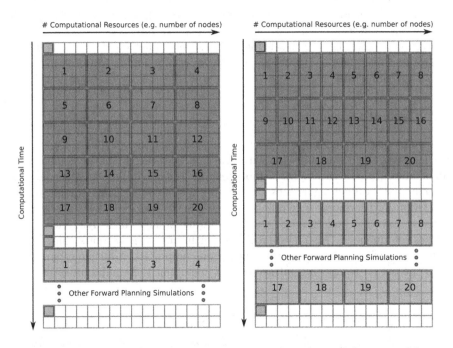

Fig. 3. Example of two different execution plans of the neurostimulation workflow on a 16-node cluster. On the left, every job was optimized independently neglecting the queuing times. On the right, the complete workflow was optimized leading to different resources allocations for particular simulations to minimize the overall execution time.

3   Simulator

As the basis for our workflow scheduling simulator, we have adopted the *Alea* job scheduling simulator [10]. Alea is a platform-independent event-driven discrete time simulator written in Java built on the top of the GridSim simulation toolkit [16]. GridSim provides the basic functionality to model various entities in a simulated computing system, as well as methods to handle the simulation events. The behavior of the simulator is driven by an event-passing protocol. For each simulated event, such as job arrival or completion, one message defining this event is created. It contains the identifier of the message recipient, the type of the event, the time when the event will occur and the message data. Alea extends this basic GridSim's functionality and provides a model allowing for detailed simulation of the whole scheduling process in a typical HPC/HTC system. To do that, Alea either extends existing GridSim classes or it provides new classes on its own, especially the core `Scheduler` class and classes responsible for data parsing and collection/visualization of simulation results.

Figure 4 shows the overall scheme of the Alea simulator, where boxes denote major functional parts and arrows express communication and/or data exchange within the simulator.

3.1   General Description

The main part of the simulator is the centralized job scheduler. The scheduler manages the communication with other parts of the simulator. It maintains important data structures such as job queue(s). Job scheduling decisions are performed by scheduling algorithms that can be easily added using existing simple interfaces. Furthermore, scheduling process can be further influenced by using additional system policies, e.g., the fair-sharing policy which dynamically prioritizes job queue(s). Also, system queues including various limits that further refine how various job classes are handled are supported. Additional parts simulate the actual computing infrastructure, including the emulation of machine

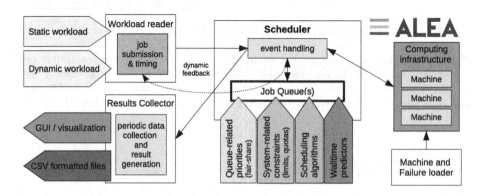

Fig. 4. Main components of the Alea jobs scheduling simulator.

failures/restarts. Workload readers are used to feed the simulator with input data about jobs being executed and the simulator also provides means for visualization and generation of simulation outputs. Alea is freely available at GitHub [1].

The primary benefit of Alea is that it allows for realistic testing of workload execution subject to (different) scheduling policies or setups of computing systems. It models all important features that have significant impact on the performance of the system. These features enable us to mimic real-life systems properly with a reasonably high realism [11].

3.2 Workflow Support

One of the main contributions of this work is the development of workflow (DAG) execution support in Alea. This has been mostly achieved by modifying two components in the simulator: the workload reader and the scheduler. Workload reader has been modified to properly parse new DAG-compatible workload format (see Sect. 3.3). In the scheduler, new logic has been added to properly handle inter job dependencies. The most important modification was the addition of a new *hold queue* for all jobs with unfinished predecessors. Using this queue, these jobs are excluded from the normal scheduling loop until all their dependencies are resolved, i.e., all their predecessors are completed.

The list of all *unfinished predecessors* is kept up-to-date throughout the execution of DAGs. Once a job completes its execution, it is removed from the list of *unfinished predecessors* and the *hold queue* is scanned to check if any job now has all of its precedence constraints satisfied. If so, this job is immediately moved to the normal *scheduling queue* where it waits until it is actually started. Figure 5 demonstrates how the inter-DAG dependencies are handled, using the *hold queue* together with the list of all *unfinished predecessors*.

Otherwise, only minor changes were necessary in Alea, e.g., job definition as well as simulation outputs have been extended to reflect that each job (task) may have predecessors.

3.3 DAG Workload Format

For convenience, we use slightly extended Standard Workload Format (SWF) which is used in the Parallel Workloads Archive [4]. SWF is a simple format where each workload is stored in a single ASCII file [5]. Each job (or task) is represented by a single line in the file. Lines contain a predefined number of fields, which are mostly integers, separated by whitespace. Fields that are irrelevant for a specific log or model appear with a value of −1. To represent DAGs, we have extended the standard 18 entries with two new entries that allow us to distinct which line corresponds to which DAG (DAG_id) and which task within a given DAG this job represents (task_id). Also, we have modified the existing Preceding Job Number such that it can point to more than one job (task). If a given job has more than one predecessor in the DAG, then & character is used

Job Submission Logic (with DAG support)

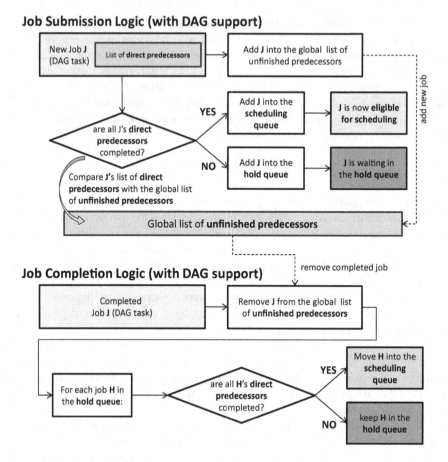

Fig. 5. Added logic handling correct execution order of DAG-like workflows within Alea simulator. Job dependencies are checked during new job arrival (top) and updated once a job completes its execution (bottom). At this point, waiting jobs from the *hold queue* are moved to the *scheduling queue* if their dependencies are satisfied.

to concatenate the list of these predecessor IDs. For example, 1&2&3 means that the given job can only start once jobs 1, 2 and 3 are all completed[2].

4   Alea Simulation Capabilities

Alea job scheduling simulator is well known for its capability to simulate and also optimize various setups of HPC/HTC systems [2,10]. In this section we will demonstrate the novel DAG-oriented simulation capability. We illustrate how the newly extended Alea simulator can be used to evaluate various setups of ultrasound simulations in order to choose the best available setup.

---

[2] This string corresponds to the list of *direct predecessors* used in Fig. 5.

As discussed in Sect. 2, k-Dispatch keeps its internal performance database to predict rather accurately what the execution time needed to complete such a task will be. The problem is, that task-level optimization does not guarantee that good results will be achieved. Instead, we need to optimize the execution parameters of the whole workflow(s) to achieve good performance. An example of such situation has been shown in Fig. 3. Also, as the available computing infrastructure may change over the time, k-Dispatch must be able to adapt existing scheduling plans once, e.g., the amount of available resources has changed.

In the first example, we use Alea to model and execute (simulate) the problem depicted previously in Fig. 3. In this case, the same workflow uses two different sets of task execution parameters which influence the total execution time. The Gantt chart presented in Fig. 6 shows the execution of all tasks (Y-axis) over the time (X-axis). Clearly, these results correspond to the illustration used in Fig. 3.

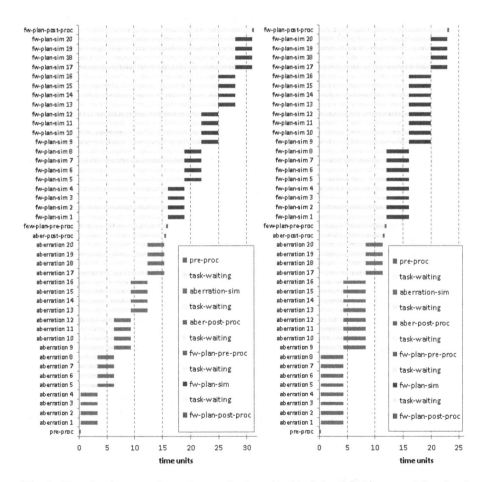

Fig. 6. Alea simulator used to measure the impact of task-level (left) vs. workflow-level (right) optimization on the total workflow execution time (makespan).

We can observe, that task-level execution time optimization (see the Gantt chart on the left in Fig. 6) is suboptimal compared to the workflow-level optimization (right). In this particular case, the second (right) scenario decreased the total execution time from 31 time units to just 23, representing 26% improvement by means of cost/time.

Of course, there are more scenarios that can be modelled and analysed in Alea. For example, we may analyse how several workflows will perform when executed simultaneously. Such an experiment may be very useful when finding the trade-off between total execution time and cost. In other words, we can use such experiment to see how many resources are needed to compute N workflows in a given time T. We illustrate this situation in Fig. 7. Here we show the impact of concurrently executed workflows on the queuing time and the total execution time (makespan). Also, the impact of varying number of available number of CPU cores (i.e., the cost) is shown.

For this demonstration, we use identical workflows, each consisting of 3 tasks that are directly dependent upon each other[3]. We start with a scenario where we execute 3 such workflows together (see the top chart in Fig. 7). As we can see, the system (16 nodes) is capable of executing all 3 workflows concurrently. The situation changes once we add the fourth workflow (see the middle chart in Fig. 7). In this case, the system is not large enough to execute all four tasks no. 2 simultaneously, i.e., the task no. 2 from the fourth workflow (denoted as DAG-4 [2]) has to wait until at least one task no. 2 of the remaining workflows is completed. As a result, the makespan gets higher. As illustrated in the bottom chart in Fig. 7, the makespan gets even worse once we shrink the available resources to a half (8 nodes).

Clearly, the Alea simulator allows us to compare various alternatives and decide which combination of parameters and/or what cost leads to acceptable makespan. Simulations like these can be then used by the k-Dispatch's scheduling module when deciding which parameter settings to choose for the tasks that must be scheduled.

Finally, we would like to briefly mention the simulation overhead of Alea when dealing with DAG-like workflows. Naturally, we need the simulator to be fast when emulating the execution of realistically complex workflows. Therefore, we have performed a set of experiments, where we measured the time needed to perform a simulation. We investigated the influence of both DAG complexity (number of tasks within a workflow) and the number of DAGs being simulated simultaneously[4]. The results are shown in Fig. 8. Simulations use various number of DAGs (up to 64 DAGs) while each such DAG has different number of tasks (2, 4, 8, 16, 32 or 64 tasks per DAG). The figure shows that the simulator is capable to simulate DAG executions in a reasonable amount of time. Even with the most demanding setup (64 DAGs, each having 64 tasks per DAG) the total simulation time is below 2.5 s.

---

[3] The corresponding DAG looks like this: task 1→ task 2→ task 3.

[4] The experiments were performed on a machine running Windows 10 with Intel Core i7-7500U CPU running at 2.7 Ghz and having 8 GB of RAM.

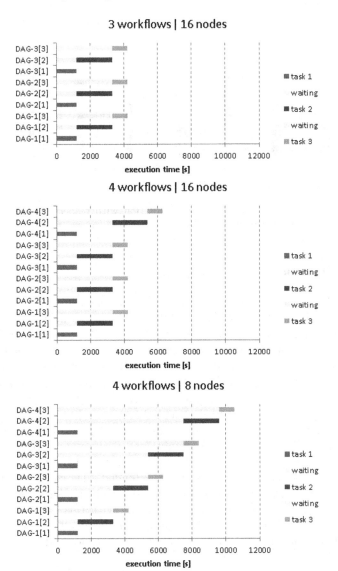

Fig. 7. Makespan and wait time (queuing time) as impacted by the number of concurrently executed workflows and the size of the infrastructure.

This means that Alea is capable of evaluating many different workflow parameter setups within just few seconds. Such a small overhead is clearly no issue for the k-Dispatch workflow management system.

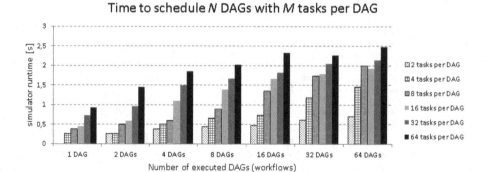

Fig. 8. The time needed to execute one simulation with respect to the number and complexity of simulated workflows (DAGs).

5   Conclusions

In this paper, we have described the scheduling problem related to proper setup of complex biomedical ultrasound workflows. Moreover, we have provided an example of real life-based problem instances (workload describing DAG-like workflows) and developed an extension for the open source job scheduling simulator Alea. Using this extension, basic DAG-like workflows can be simulated and the impact of varying workflow execution parameters (number of tasks and their requirements) can be quickly analysed. Also, thanks to the main focus of the Alea simulator, detailed system-oriented setups and resource policies (e.g., scheduling algorithms, queue setup or fair-share priorities) can be easily emulated, thus providing more realistic outputs and performance predictions.

In the future, we would like to integrate this functionality with the k-Dispatch workflow management system. The newly extended Alea simulator with DAG scheduling support can be freely obtained on GitHub [1]. Also, we invite other researchers to look into the data provided along with this paper that describe real-life based workflows used within the international ultrasonic community. These workloads include the examples used in this paper and will be available at the website of the workshop[5].

This work has a significant impact on the biomedical ultrasound community. Not only the clinicians do not have to bother with selecting suitable computing facilities, deploying simulation codes, moving data forth and back, job submission, execution and monitoring, but their workflows are executed efficiently minimizing the execution time and cost. This all is done without any user intervention, actually, the users do not even know such a process exists.

Acknowledgments. We kindly acknowledge the support provided by the project Reg. No. CZ.02.1.01/0.0/0.0/16_013/0001797 co-funded by the Ministry of Education, Youth and Sports of the Czech Republic. Computational resources were supplied by

---

[5] http://jsspp.org/workload/.

the project "e-Infrastruktura CZ" (e-INFRA LM2018140) provided within the program Projects of Large Research, Development and Innovations Infrastructures.

This work was also supported by The Ministry of Education, Youth and Sports from the National Programme of Sustainability (NPU II) project IT4Innovations excellence in science - LQ1602 and by the IT4Innovations infrastructure which is supported from the Large Infrastructures for Research, Experimental Development and Innovations project IT4Innovations National Supercomputing Center - LM2015070. This project has received funding from the European Union's Horizon 2020 research and innovation programme H2020 ICT 2016–2017 under grant agreement No 732411 and is an initiative of the Photonics Public Private Partnership.

References

1. Alea job scheduling simulator, May 2020. https://github.com/aleasimulator/alea/tree/FIT
2. Azevedo, F., Klusáček, D., Suter, F.: Improving fairness in a large scale HTC system through workload analysis and simulation. In: Yahyapour, R. (ed.) Euro-Par 2019. LNCS, vol. 11725, pp. 129–141. Springer, Cham (2019). https://doi.org/10.1007/978-3-030-29400-7_10
3. Deelman, E., et al.: Pegasus: a workflow management system for science automation. Future Gener. Comput. Syst. **46**, 17–35 (2014)
4. Feitelson, D.G.: Parallel workloads archive, May 2020. http://www.cs.huji.ac.il/labs/parallel/workload/
5. Feitelson, D.G.: The standard workload format, May 2020. https://www.cse.huji.ac.il/labs/parallel/workload/swf.html
6. Georgiou, P.S., et al.: Beam distortion due to gold fiducial markers during salvage high-intensity focused ultrasound in the prostate. Med. Phys. **44**(2), 679–693 (2017)
7. Godlove, D.: Singularity. In Proceedings of the Practice and Experience. In: Advanced Research Computing on Rise of the Machines (learning), pp. 1–4, New York, NY, USA. ACM, July 2019
8. HTCondor. HTCondor - high throughput computing (2019)
9. Jaros, M., Treeby, B.E., Georgiou, P., Jaros, J.: k-Dispatch: a workflow management system for the automated execution of biomedical ultrasound simulations on remote computing resources. In: Proceedings of the Platform for Advanced Scientific Computing Conference, PASC 2020, New York, NY, USA. Association for Computing Machinery (2020)
10. Klusáček, D., Soysal, M., Suter, F.: Alea – complex job scheduling simulator. In: Wyrzykowski, R., Deelman, E., Dongarra, J., Karczewski, K. (eds.) PPAM 2019. LNCS, vol. 12044, pp. 217–229. Springer, Cham (2020). https://doi.org/10.1007/978-3-030-43222-5_19
11. Klusáček, D., Tóth, Š.: On interactions among scheduling policies: finding efficient queue setup using high-resolution simulations. In: Silva, F., Dutra, I., Santos Costa, V. (eds.) Euro-Par 2014. LNCS, vol. 8632, pp. 138–149. Springer, Cham (2014). https://doi.org/10.1007/978-3-319-09873-9_12
12. Konofagou, E.E.: Trespassing the barrier of the brain with ultrasound. Acoust. Today **13**(4), 21–26 (2017)
13. Merkel, D.: Docker: lightweight Linux containers for consistent development and deployment. Linux J. **2014**(239), 2 (2014)

14. Robert, Y.: Task graph scheduling. In: Padua, D. (ed.) Encyclopedia of Parallel Computing, pp. 2013–2025. Springer, Boston (2011). https://doi.org/10.1007/978-0-387-09766-4_42

15. Sarkar, V.: Partitioning and scheduling parallel programs for multiprocessors. In: Research Monographs in Parallel and Distributed Computing, pp. 1–183. MIT Press, Cambridge (1989)

16. Sulistio, A., Cibej, U., Venugopal, S., Robic, B., Buyya, R.: A toolkit for modelling and simulating data Grids: an extension to GridSim. Concurr. Comput. Pract. Exp. **20**(13), 1591–1609 (2008)

17. Szabo, T.L.: Diagnostic Ultrasound Imaging: Inside Out (2014)

18. Treeby, B.E., Cox, B.T.: k-Wave: MATLAB toolbox for the simulation and reconstruction of photoacoustic wave fields. J. Biomed. Optics **15**(2), 021–314 (2010)

19. Treeby, B.E., Jaros, J., Martin, E., Cox, B.T.: From biology to bytes: predicting the path of ultrasound waves through the human body. Acoust. Today **15**(2), 36–44 (2019)

Evaluating Controlled Memory Request Injection to Counter PREM Memory Underutilization

Roberto Cavicchioli$^{(\boxtimes)}$ (ID), Nicola Capodieci(ID), Marco Solieri(ID),
Marko Bertogna(ID), Paolo Valente(ID), and Andrea Marongiu(ID)

Department of Physics, Informatics and Mathematics, University of Modena
and Reggio Emilia, Modena, Italy
{roberto.cavicchioli,nicola.capodieci,marco.solieri,marko.bertogna,
paolo.valente,andrea.marongiu}@unimore.it

Abstract. Modern heterogeneous systems-on-chip (HeSoC) feature high-performance multi-core CPUs tightly integrated with data-parallel accelerators. Such HeSoCS heavily rely on shared resources, which hinder their adoption in the context of Real-Time systems. The predictable execution model (PREM) has proven effective at preventing uncontrolled execution time lengthening due to memory interference in HeSoC sharing main memory (DRAM). However, PREM only allows one task at a time to access memory, which inherently under-utilizes the available memory bandwidth in modern HeSoCs. In this paper, we conduct a thorough experimental study aimed at assessing the potential benefits of extending PREM so as to inject controlled amounts of memory requests coming from other tasks than the one currently granted exclusive DRAM access. Focusing on a state-of-the-art HeSoC, the NVIDIA TX2, we extensively characterize the relation between the injected bandwidth and the latency experienced by the task under test. The results confirm that for various types of workload it is possible to exploit the available bandwidth much more efficiently than standard PREM arbitration, often close to its maximum, while keeping latency inflation below 10%. We discuss possible practical implementation directions, highlighting the expected benefits and technical challenges.

Keywords: Heterogeneous systems-on-chip · Memory interference · Predictable execution

1 Introduction

In recent years, embedded systems designs have been increasingly embracing the heterogeneous system-on-chip paradigm (HeSoC), where several and possibly non-identical general-purpose CPUs are coupled to various accelerators (e.g., GPUs for general purpose computing, Digital Signal Processors, etc.), achieving high processing capacity at a comparatively low cost. While these systems are capable of achieving very high GOps/W targets, they are designed for optimal best-effort performance, not at all for timing predictability. Designing a predictable system requires characterizing its schedulability, i.e., formally assessing

© Springer Nature Switzerland AG 2020
D. Klusáček et al. (Eds.): JSSPP 2020, LNCS 12326, pp. 85–105, 2020.
https://doi.org/10.1007/978-3-030-63171-0_5

whether the timing constraints of each work unit (task) can be satisfied with the available computing resources (CPU cores, accelerator cores, memory). In the real-time literature [2], applications are generally composed of tasks characterized by a *period* (minimum time span between two instances of the same task), a Worst-Case Execution Time (*WCET*) and a *deadline*. A taskset is *schedulable* if there exists a mapping of its tasks to the available compute/memory resource that does not cause a deadline miss at runtime.

In HeSoCs, CPU cores or other computing units can concurrently access shared memory resources such as caches and system DRAM. The best-effort, throughput-oriented arbitration mechanisms of such on-chip shared resources – which increasingly becomes a point of contention, severely impacting the execution time of concurrent tasks – coupled to the often undisclosed nature of their internal working poses severe challenges to the adoption of HeSoCs in the context of real-time applications. Real-time scheduling has traditionally focused on scheduling CPU computation, assuming that the Worst-Case Execution Time can be computed for each task running in the system. However, when considering different applications running concurrently on a modern HeSoC, with several actors featuring different bandwidth usage, the measured WCET can vary significantly, depending on the global system schedule.

The Predictable Execution Model (PREM) was originally proposed in the context of single-core CPUs [11] to provide robustness to memory-access interference from I/O devices, and was later extended to avoid inter-core interference in multi-core CPUs [1] and in HeSoCs [6]. PREM assumes that tasks are split into *memory* and *compute phases*, with all shared-memory accesses in the memory phases. By scheduling memory phases separately, the system designer has full control on shared-memory interference. In particular, interference can be canceled completely by executing one memory phase at a time.

While this greatly reduces WCET pessimism, the very method for canceling interference entails one of the main drawbacks of PREM: executing only one memory phase at a time implies severe under-utilization of the shared-memory bandwidth in most cases.

In this paper, we conduct a thorough experimental study aimed at assessing the potential benefits of extending PREM with a technique capable of *injecting controlled amounts of memory accesses* coming from other tasks than the one currently granted exclusive access to the memory. Focusing on a state-of-the-art HeSoC, the NVIDIA Tegra X2, we extensively characterize the relation between the injected bandwidth and the memory-access latency experienced by the task(s) under test. The NVIDIA TX2 features a *host* CPU design architected as two *clusters*, one made of four ARM Cortex-A57 and the other made of two DENVER cores, each featuring local, shared L2 cache. On both the Cortex-A57 and the DENVER clusters, if the workload is memory-intensive, *controlled injection* allows reaching over 80% of the maximum cluster bandwidth with virtually no impact on the execution time of the PREM task. If the workload has more sporadic/random accesses to main memory, we can improve over PREM by at least 600%, in some cases reaching maximum exploitation of the available bandwidth.

Based on these observations, we discuss possible practical implementation directions, highlighting the expected benefits and technical challenges.

This paper is organized as follows: Sect. 2 discusses background notions related to the PREM execution model and the target hardware platform, as well as our benchmarking methodology and the experimental setup. Section 3 presents and discusses the results of the various experiments we conduct to assess the benefits of *controlled injection*. Section 4 discusses possible practical ways to implement and deploy the presented approach in real-life application scenarios. Section 5 presents related works, before concluding the paper in Sect. 6, highlighting future research directions.

2   Controlled Injection: Background, Experimental Methodology and Setup

The Predictable Execution Model (PREM) is designed to isolate accesses to shared main memory from different actors. The original proposal in [11] was meant to provide robustness to CPU memory-access interference from peripheral devices, and was later extended to avoid inter-core interference in multi-core CPUs [1]. This is achieved by partitioning programs into contention-sensitive memory and contention-free computation phases, and scheduling these such that two memory phases are never executed in parallel. By scheduling only a single memory phase at a time, contention at the main memory level is effectively avoided. This allows a system designer to tightly bound memory access latencies, leading to shorter worst-case execution times (WCET) and, ultimately, less pessimism in traditional timing and schedulability analysis.

Most modern multi-core SoC designs leverage heterogeneity at different levels. Typically, a powerful multi-core, general-purpose CPU (the *host* processor) is coupled to some type of acceleration fabric, like a data-parallel co-processor (e.g., a GPGPU, DSPs) or programmable logic (FPGA). For energy efficiency, the design of the *host* CPU itself is typically heterogeneous, with a number of *compute clusters* locally grouping a small number of homogeneous CPUs sharing interconnection and memory resources. Globally, these heterogeneous *clusters* share the last-level cache or the main system memory. The latter is also shared with other acceleration devices. These systems must sustain tremendous bandwidth to the main memory, to satisfy requests coming from many actors. Table 1 shows the effect of inter-core bandwidth sharing on a variety of commercial heterogeneous SoCs, highlighting the portion of the total SoC bandwidth that is used by the *host* CPU cores (the focus of this paper). The rightmost column indicates the nominal main memory bandwidth as reported in the official datasheets (where available). We use the *bw_mem* benchmark from the *LMBench* suite [10] to measure the maximum bandwidth request generated by a single CPU (*host*) core and the maximum aggregated bandwidth requested by all the cores inside the CPU complex[1] For each of the tested SoCs where a total nominal bandwidth value is available (i.e., those featuring a GPU), the comparison with the aggregated CPU bandwidth shows that a significant share of this bandwidth is reserved to other devices than the CPU

---

[1] *bw_mem* performs a pointer walk over a >100 MiB buffer, using a stride such that consecutive memory accesses request a different L2 cache line. The test is executed for a predefined time window (3 s) to measure the average bandwidth.

Table 1. Baseline and composite bandwidth on recent SoCs.

SoC/Board	CPU core count	Arch	BW from single core [GiB/s]	aggreg CPU BW [GiB/s]	Total BW (nominal) [GiB/s]
NVIDIA Jetson Xavier	8	Carmel (ARM v8.2-A)	18	74	137
NVIDIA Jetson TX2	6	Denver2 + Cortex-A57	12(4)	22	59.7
Intel i7-9700K	8	x86_64	22	27	39.4
Xilinx UltraScale Zynq ZCU 102	4	Cortex-A53 (ARM v8-A)	2.3	6.7	-
Xilinx Zedboard Zynq-7000	2	Cortex-A9 (ARM v7)	0.404	0.505	-

(the acceleration logic). Focusing on the CPU complex, we observe a significant difference between the maximum bandwidth used by a single core and the aggregated memory bandwidth used by the whole CPU *compute cluster*. Even though the bandwidth request in general does not grow up linearly with the number of cores, it is evident that a single CPU core only consumes a fraction of the bandwidth budget allotted to the CPU complex.

In this scenario, the *one-core-at-a-time* memory arbitration model implied by PREM is bound to poorly fit this increasing gap in bandwidth reservation. PREM could be enhanced with techniques to admit more than one task at a time to access memory. We will explain that for such techniques to be successful, the rate at which the new task injects its own transactions should be controlled in a fine-grained manner. We call this technique *Controlled memory-transaction Injection*, proposing a synthetic benchmark that allows evaluating this concept by a thorough characterization of the system.

2.1 Target Architecture

For our benchmarking, and to assess the potential benefits of a *Controlled Injection* scheme, we have selected the NVIDIA Jetson TX2 as our reference HeSoC hardware. The NVIDIA Jetson TX2 is a widely available commercial HeSoC featuring a GPU accelerator governed by a heterogeneous *host* processor.

The *host* is organized in two different *compute clusters*: a quad-core ARMv8 Cortex-A57, and a dual-core ARMv8-compliant *DENVER* processor (NVIDIA proprietary design). Each of the six cores integrates a 32 KiB L1 data cache and a 48 KiB L1 instruction cache. Furthermore, each *cluster* features a 2 MiB L2 cache shared among its local cores.

The main system memory is an 8 GiB LPDDR4 128 bit DRAM with a total bandwidth of 59.7 GiB/s, needed to sustain requests coming from the two CPU *clusters* and the GPU accelerator.

In this paper, we focus on the characterization of the *host* memory behavior.

2.2 Benchmarking Methodology

There are many ways to implement *Controlled Injection* (see Sect. 4 for a discussion on practical solutions). In this paper, our focus is on exhaustively studying

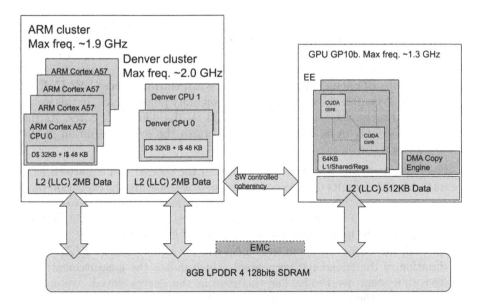

Fig. 1. Block diagram of the Tegra X2 architecture.

the potential benefits of this technique, stressing corner cases via a custom-designed synthetic benchmark, called *mem_bench*[2].

Controlling the Access Pattern. The first thing we need to be able to control is the type of access pattern our benchmark generates. Traditionally, *sequential* and *random* patterns are adopted for this type of bandwidth/latency measurements, with the former reading memory addresses one word aside (i.e., consecutive words, with unit *stride*) and the latter reading with random *stride*. The NVDIA TX2, like most modern HeSoCs, features a number of hardware blocks aimed at improving the average-case performance (cache prefetchers, DRAM row buffers, etc.). As all these features are platform-specific, for our benchmarking methodology to be general, we need a convenient knob to control the extent to which our workload bypasses such mechanisms, spanning a range of access patterns that goes from purely sequential to fully random (where each memory access really pays the worst-case cost). To achieve this goal, we implement a simple pointer walk over a portion of a statically pre-allocated large array (64 MiB) of data structures, each containing: (i) a pointer to the next address to read/write; (ii) padding, to fill the remainder of a whole L2 cache line.

To model a *sequential* access pattern, we only need to define a $SIZE_{MEM}$ and a *stride* parameter. The pointer walk can then be initialized to read $SIZE_{MEM}/$ *stride* cache lines at that fixed *stride*. In this case, the $SIZE_{MEM}$ is the size of the L2 cache divided by the number of cores, and the *stride* is the size of a cache line (64B). For the *random* access pattern, *mem_bench* accepts two parameters:

---

[2] Available for download: https://git.hipert.unimore.it/msolieri/membench.

1. **the size of the memory portion within the static array from which the addresses to initialize the pointer walk are taken** ($SIZE_{MEM}$): this is key to control the actual distance of the loads/stores (i.e., their cost) when modeling a *random* traffic pattern[3];
2. **the number of cache lines the pointer walk should access** ($NLINES$): this is key to control the size of the PREM memory phase, which, in this work, is assumed to be the L2 cache size divided by the number of cores. As the data is read only once, this parameter dictates the overall duration of the benchmark.

The first parameter is in fact used to model the desired traffic pattern mix. Figure 2 shows the results of an experiment where we measure the execution time to read a memory portion of increasing size (on the X axis) on both the Cortex-A57 and the DENVER CPU cores. More specifically, here $SIZE_{MEM} = NLINES * SIZE_{cache\_line}$. The bandwidth is computed as $SIZE_{MEM}/exec\_time$.

For both the Cortex-A57 and the DENVER, for small values of $SIZE_{MEM}$, the duration of the transfer is very small, which makes the measurement very sensitive to system overheads. For this reason, the curves initially ramp up, getting closer to their peak value at around 16 and 32 KB, respectively. This is the operating point where the use of prefetching mechanisms is still predominant. The more we move to the right, the higher the probability that the strides are wider than the prefetch buffers size and that the requests are difficult to reorder at the DRAM side for better row usage. We can see that for $SIZE_{MEM} \geq 4096B$ the traffic pattern generated by our benchmark is truly *random*[4].

Controlling the Injection Rate. To evaluate the benefits of *Controlled Injection* as well as to assess the capability of controlling it at a fine granularity, we extend *mem_bench* with an option that allows interleaving a sequence of memory accesses (representative of one PREM task memory phase) with a parametric number of stall cycles, so as to finely tune the injected memory bandwidth request.

To this aim, we add two more parameters:

1. the number of cache lines (L) that the task can read before being throttled;
2. the number of cycles (C) the task will be throttled for before reading again.

L and C define the *duty cycle* of the memory requests issued by the task performing *controlled injection*. In our experimental evaluation, we call *LOAD intensity* the ratio between number of cache lines and the number of throttling cycles. The *LOAD intensity* affects in different ways the *injection rate* that a given task can sustain, based on the type of access pattern the task performs[5]. Intuitively, there

---

[3] Randomly computing the next address inside a memory portion that fits the size of the prefetch buffer generates the same behavior of a *sequential* traffic pattern, as most of the loads/stores will hit in the L2 cache.

[4] In the remainder of the paper, we use the value $SIZE_{MEM} = 12$ MiB to generate random interference traffic.

[5] As we will explain later on, the *injection rate* is defined as the ratio between the bandwidth request generated by a task at a given *LOAD intensity* value and the bandwidth request generated by the same task at 100% *LOAD intensity*.

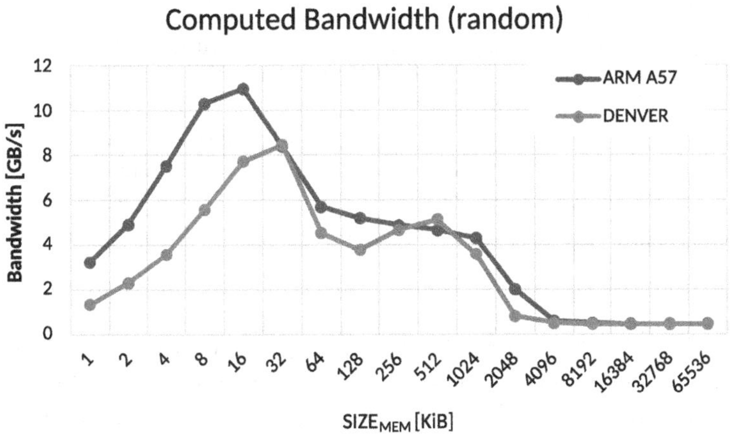

Computed Bandwidth (random)

Fig. 2. Bandwidth request for increasingly larger memory portions. Random traffic.

are several ways of organizing the memory access pattern so as to obtain a given injection rate. Depending on the granularity at which the injection is done, the generated interference will be different. Our synthetic benchmarking methodology is aimed at capturing the effects of the most fine-grained injection scheme one could conceive, i.e., a single memory access, followed by a controllable number of stall cycles. Evaluating this particular injection scheme (as compared, for example, to coarser grained ones like [21]) in combination with an experimental setup that stresses the most pessimistic operating conditions (see Sect. 2.3) is in our opinion the fairest way to assess the benefits of *controlled injection*.

mem_bench can be configured to operate in two modes:

1. ***mem_bench_LAT***: in this mode, the benchmark only **reads once** the $SIZE_{MEM}$ bytes specified as the memory phase. This is the most accurate mode for latency measurements;
2. ***mem_bench_BW***: in this mode, the benchmark **reads multiple times** the $SIZE_{MEM}$ bytes to ensure the duration (in seconds) of the benchmark exceeds the value specified via an additional $DURATION$ parameter. This is the most accurate mode for bandwidth measurements.

2.3   Experimental Setup

Our experiments are aimed at assessing the benefits of *Controlled Injection* as a complementary technique to a standard PREM scheme. In such a system, all the tasks are transformed according to the PREM rules (memory + compute phase), and their memory phases are augmented with the fine-grained *controlled injection* mechanism described in the previous section.

Our target is to exhaustively assess the benefits of this fine-grained *controlled injection* system under the most pessimistic conditions. To model such conditions, we model the PREM taskset as follows: The task under test (UT) is

Table 2. Maximum bandwidth request (in MiB) generated by a single Cortex-A57 or DENVER core when executing in isolation (Alone) or with the other CPU complex and GPU generating maximum bandwidth request (All together).

	Alone		All together	
	Sequential	Random	Sequential	Random
Cortex-A57	4204	425	3650	400
DENVER	9078	409	8760	395

representative of the PREM task currently allowed to access the main memory (in a traditional mutually-exclusive PREM scheduling scheme). The task reads once the amount of data decided by the code generation policy in the compiler: typically the whole cache [5]). The rest of the tasks, which in a standard PREM system would be idle while this UT task is executing, are in our experiments allowed to inject their own memory transactions at varying rates, acting as interfering tasks (IF). In the real PREM+*Controlled Injection* system that we envision, these IF tasks would also be transformed according to the PREM rules: their memory phases would have defined duration and they would be scheduled to maximize their memory bandwidth usage. To model the worst-case interference that the IF tasks could generate, we execute them for the whole time that the UT task is running. Specifically, IF tasks start execution before we launch the UT task, and complete execution after the UT task has terminated.

This is representative of an ideal PREM+*Controlled Injection* system, where the interference is constant, because we always have sustained injection traffic and we can schedule it so as to never leave gaps. In a real system, such gaps would be present, so the interference suffered by the UT task would in general be smaller. In this sense, the results we show here are pessimistic with respect to the benefits of *controlled injection*.

Considering the cluster-based nature of the target hardware, we conduct our experiments in three settings:

1. inside the Cortex-A57 CPU cluster;
2. inside the DENVER CPU cluster;
3. across the two compute clusters.

For experiments 1 and 2, we consider a single UT task, which represents the task that a regular PREM scheme would grant exclusive access to memory. On top of that, we explore the effect of allowing *controlled injection* by IF tasks, mapped on the remaining cores from the same compute cluster (each task is pinned to a different core). For these, we vary (with exponential spacing) the LOAD intensity (and thus the injection rate) from near-zero to 100%.

The Cortex-A57 and the DENVER cores read memory chunks of 512 KiB and 1024 KiB respectively (the size of their whole L2 cache divided by the number of cores in each cluster). Table 2 shows the measured bandwidth in MiB for a single Cortex-A57 or DENVER core considering both *sequential* and *random* access patterns. The two groups of columns refer to the case when the observed core is the only one that generates memory requests (*Alone*) and to the case when the cores from the other CPU complex and from the GPU are all generating memory requests at full speed (*All together*). We have observed that the interconnects and the memory controller implement static partitioning of the bandwidth between the Cortex-A57 complex, the DENVER complex and the GPU complex. Cores from a given complex are allowed to use some of the bandwidth allocated to a different complex if this is not used, as the difference between the *Alone* and *All together* numbers show. For this reason, while we run our experiments on a target complex, we keep the rest of the complexes active and reclaiming as much as possible of their own bandwidth (e.g., to conduct experiment 1, we keep all the cores from the DENVER and GPU complexes active executing *sequential* access patterns).

The third set of experiments studies the effect of interference among the two compute clusters. One ARM core and one DENVER core run one of two UT tasks. we run four IF tasks on the remaining cores (three Cortex-A57, one DENVER) from both clusters. The GPU is active and generates as many *sequential* memory requests as possible.

To stress all the possible corner cases, we consider various combinations of access patterns. Indeed, even if PREM compilers try hard to generate sequential patterns for their memory phases, random patterns are unavoidable in certain applications [6]. Using the benchmarks described in the previous sections, we generate four different combinations for UT and IF tasks, considering both *sequential* (SEQ) and *random* (RAN) access patterns:

1. UT=SEQ, IF=SEQ;
2. UT=SEQ, IF=RAN;
3. UT=RAN, IF=SEQ;
4. UT=RAN, IF=RAN.

For increasing *LOAD intensity/injection rates*, each of our plots shows a breakdown of the bandwidth usage among different cores (stacked areas) and the latency increase experienced by the UT task. In this way, it is easy to appreciate how much *controlled injection* can be tolerated in the various configurations before the UT task significantly suffers from the interference. Note that bandwidth and latency for the UT tasks are measured in different runs of the benchmark: as already mentioned, *mem_bench_LAT* provides the most accurate way of measuring the effect of interference on PREM tasks (which are characterized by relatively small burst transfers), while *mem_bench_BW* provides the most accurate way of measuring how much bandwidth the UT tasks can utilize under interference.

To limit the noise from operating system services (power management, graphics server, etc.), we do the following for all the experiments: (i) we set the maximum operating frequencies on both the CPU clusters, the GPU and the memory controller via the `jetson_clock` command with root privileges; (ii) the operating system (Linux for Tegra (L4T) Ubuntu 18.04) is set to run level 2 via the `telinit` command; and (iii) all the tasks are pinned to a core using the `taskset` command, and their priority is set to -15 using the `nice` command.

For the latencies, we run each experiment 100 times, and we take the worst-case value, filtering out outliers due to OS activities. In all our experiments, outliers can be easily spotted, as their values are one to two orders of magnitude higher than the vast majority of the samples. Quantitatively, in all our experiments less than 5% of the samples were discarded.

3   Evaluation

3.1   Effects of Controlled Injection Within the Cortex A57 Cluster

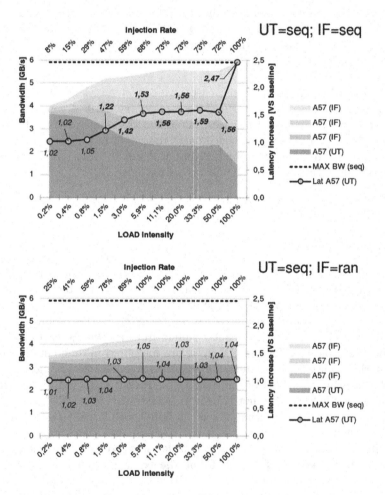

Fig. 3. Effects of controlled injection within the ARM cluster. Task under test has sequential traffic, cache transfer is 512 KiB.

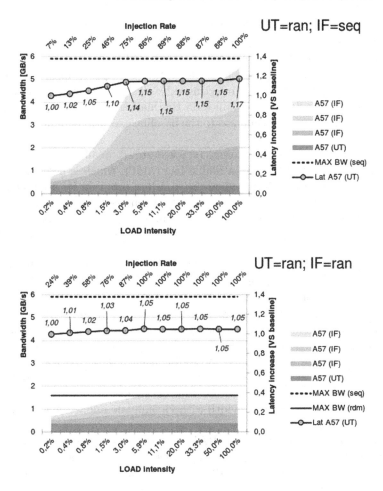

Fig. 4. Effects of controlled injection within the ARM cluster. Task under test has random traffic, cache transfer is 512 KiB.

Figures 3 and 4 show the results for our experiments within the Cortex-A57 compute cluster. The plots show *LOAD intensity* on the bottom X-axis, and the *injection rate* of a single IF task on the top X-axis. This metric is computed as the bandwidth requested by an IF task for a particular *LOAD intensity*, normalized to the maximum bandwidth that the same IF task can request for the same experiment (i.e., when the *LOAD injection* reaches 100%). It represents probably the most significant way of visualizing the degree of *controlled injection* the system is sustaining, which allows for a more direct comparison between bandwidth usage and latency increase. The plots show measured bandwidth on the left Y-axis, and latency on the right Y-axis. The stacked area plots show the breakdown of the total utilized memory bandwidth (to be read on the left Y-axis) by the UT task (the darker area) and the IF tasks. The plots also highlight the measured MAX bandwidth that the four ARM cores can cumulatively request when generating memory transactions at full throttle (for both SEQ and RAN access patterns). The black line with yellow markers shows the increase in execution time (latency, to be read on the right Y-axis) experienced by the UT task while IF tasks are injecting extra memory transactions at increasing rates. More specifically, the values on the markers represent the latency of the test with interference normalized to the baseline execution latency in absence of interference.

If we focus on the bandwidth usage (stacked areas), in all these plots it seems that a significant portion of the available bandwidth, which is not exploited by the PREM task alone (as shown when the *injection rate* is at its minimum), can be utilized by *controlled injection* (as shown when we move to the right). By combining the information from the latency curve and the bandwidth areas it is possible to identify the sweet spot where, for each traffic pattern combination, we can gain the most.

Focusing on the first subplot, (UT=SEQ; IF=SEQ), where both the task under test and the interference traffic feature sequential access pattern (i.e., the most sensitive case to interference), we see that the cumulative bandwidth request from all the Cortex-A57 cores is limited to only around 6 GB. As already mentioned, the breakdown shows that this is due to system-level bandwidth partitioning, as a single core utilizes 66% of that maximum bandwidth.

If we focus on the latency curve, we notice that a 0.8% *LOAD intensity* by any IF task implies 30% *injection rate*, perturbing the execution time of the UT task by a tiny 5%. Overall, in this case *controlled injection* allows to reach 81% of the maximum sequential bandwidth with virtually no impact on the execution time of the UT task.

When the IF workload is of type RAN, the SEQ UT task is never perturbed, even when 100% *controlled injection* is allowed. This brings a 37% increase in bandwidth usage, overall reaching 72% of the maximum sequential bandwidth. Focusing on a RAN UT task (Fig. 4), when the IF task is of type SEQ we see that *controlled injection* has a tremendous effect on increasing memory bandwidth usage. Clearly, the tolerated increase in execution time for the UT task varies from one system (or one application domain) to another, but we can see that even with 100% injection rate the latency never exceeds 17%. In this case we observe a staggering 1365% increase in bandwidth usage, reaching 93% of the maximum sequential bandwidth. If a more conservative 10% is chosen as a maximum tolerated increase in latency, we can see that this is achieved for a *LOAD intensity* of around 1.5% (46% *injection rate*). Even in this case, *controlled injection* allows for a 626% increase in bandwidth usage.

Finally, when both the UT and the IF tasks are of type RAN, we see that the bandwidth requests can be fully summed up, increasing bandwidth usage by 300% without impacting the execution time of the UT task.

3.2   Effects of Controlled Injection Within the DENVER Cluster

Figures 5 and 6 show the results for our experiments within the DENVER compute cluster. The setup is identical to the Cortex-A57 compute cluster, as is the information in the plots and the general observations that can be drawn. The benefits of *controlled injection* in the DENVER cluster are even more pronounced, as one single DENVER core roughly uses half the available bandwidth for the cluster, as can be seen in the UT=SEQ, IF=SEQ plot (whereas in the Cortex-A57 case a single core used 66% of the total). Although the numbers are slightly less stable in this experiment, it can be seen that even when the *injection rate* reaches 100% the increase in the latency of the UT task stays around 10%. The bandwidth usage reaches full efficiency, as it gets doubled.

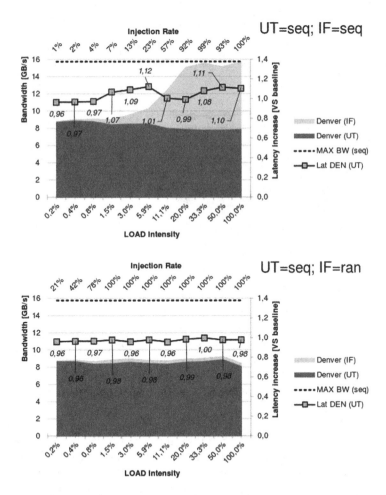

Fig. 5. Effects of controlled injection within the DENVER cluster. Task under test has sequential traffic, cache transfer is 1024 KiB.

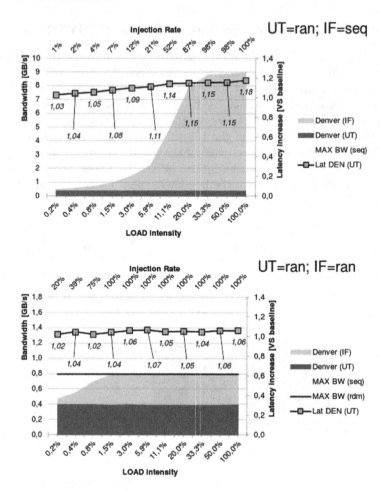

Fig. 6. Effects of controlled injection within the DENVER cluster. Task under test has random traffic, cache transfer is 1024 KiB.

Similar to the Cortex-A57, there is not a lot to be gained when the IF task is of type RAN and the UT task is of type seq, as the bandwidth generated by the random access pattern is an order of magnitude smaller than the sequential for the DENVER core. Still, *controlled injection* can be applied at full throttle without disturbing the UT task.

When the UT task is of type RAN, there is always to gain from *controlled injection*. If the IF task is of type SEQ, we increase bandwidth usage by 465% while keeping latency increase below 10% (and we could increase it by 2300% if a latency increase of up to 18% could be tolerated). When the IF task is of type RAN, we can double the bandwidth usage without impacting the UT task at all.

3.3   Inter-Cluster Effects of Controlled Injection

After studying the benefits of *controlled injection* within each compute cluster in isolation, we experiment with inter-cluster interference. We first elect a single ARM or DENVER core, in turn, to host the UT task, and we place the IF tasks on the sole cores belonging to the other cluster. Thus, when one DENVER hosts the UT task, the IF tasks run on the ARM cluster (the second DENVER core is inactive), and vice-versa. We don't show whole plots for this experiment (which we consider preliminary to what follows), but we report here the most important findings.

When a DENVER core hosts the UT task, its latency is virtually unmodified (<5%) independent of the *injection rate* of the IF tasks running on the ARM

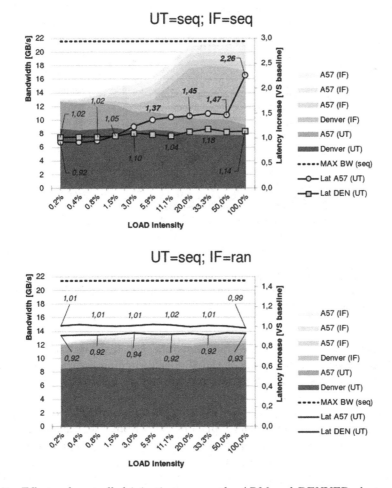

Fig. 7. Effects of controlled injection among the ARM and DENVER clusters (SoC level). Task under test has sequential traffic, cache transfer is 512 KiB for the ARM and 1024 KiB for the DENVER.

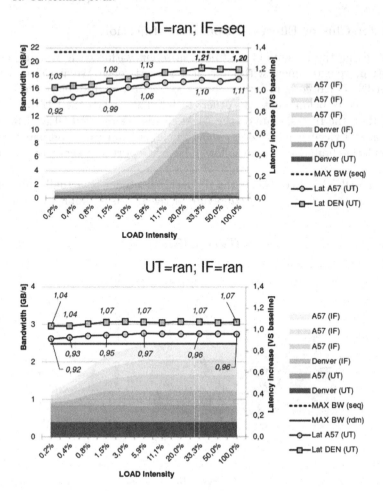

Fig. 8. Effects of controlled injection among the ARM and DENVER clusters (SoC level). Task under test has random traffic, cache transfer is 512 KiB for the ARM and 1024 KiB for the DENVER.

cores. When it is an ARM core that hosts the UT task, its latency is more susceptible to the *injection rate* of the IF tasks running on the other cluster (the DENVER cores), but the variation always stays below 10% if the *LOAD intensity* stays within 33%.

These findings suggest that the best way to support PREM on a platform of this type is that of always allowing one core from each cluster to access memory. This still leaves plenty of room for better bandwidth exploitation, which *controlled injection* can effectively achieve.

Figures 7 and 8 show the results for our last experiment, where an ARM core and a DENVER core both run an UT task, while the remaining cores from both clusters run IF tasks. At the system level, the benefits of *controlled injection* already seen within each cluster are consolidated. When both the UT and IF tasks generate SEQ requests we can tune IF tasks to inject up to a *LOAD intensity* of 3%, with an increase in the UT tasks latency within 10%. This brings a 35% increase in bandwidth usage compared to only allowing a single Cortex-A57 and a single DENVER core to access memory (a basic PREM scheme). If the IF tasks are of type RAN, no significant interference is generated on the UT tasks on both clusters. The benefits are more modest (as already observed within the individual clusters), with an increase in bandwidth usage of around 13%. Note that the values in the latency curves (in particular for the DENVER) might sometimes drop below one. This is due to the fact that as a baseline value for normalization we consider the latency measured when a single core from a given cluster executes (SEQ or RAN) while all cores from the other cluster (and from the GPU) execute SEQ IF tasks. In this particular experiment, we have less interference coming from the other cluster, as one of the cores hosts the UT task. As a consequence, particularly when the UT task is of type RAN, the amount of interference generated for the other cluster is smaller.

When the UT tasks are of type RAN, we see the highest potential for making a better use of the available bandwidth. If the IF tasks are of type SEQ, they can inject at a *LOAD intensity* of up to 3% to keep the latency increase below 10%, improving bandwidth usage by 628% compared to PREM (a single Cortex-A57 and a single DENVER). Note that it is only the Cortex-A57 that poses this limitation. The maximum interference observed on the UT task running on the DENVER core is 11%, when the *LOAD intensity* reaches 100%. At this point, the overall increase in bandwidth usage is 1822%. If the IF tasks are of type RAN, they can inject at full throttle, stacking up additively all the bandwidth requests and improving bandwidth usage by 202%.

4   Practical Realization of the Injection Scheme

Implementing *controlled injection* requires design choices that are inherently tight not only to the specific real-time requirements, but also to the particular software stack of interest. Hence, since it would be impossible to provide a definitive reference implementation, we guide the reader along the most important points.

Injection Rate Limit. Although effective in increasing the system utilization, bandwidth injection on a PREM-like setup needs to be bounded to preserve the memory access determinism.

Safe Approach. Given a platform of interest, and an expendable relative latency for memory phases l and characterization of the platform's memory subsystem like the one we presented, it is easy to to find the greatest injection load intensity i such that, for any intensity $i' \leq i$, we measure a relative intensity $l' \leq l$. On a TX2 platform, for instance, if we assume $l = 5\%$, and look at the less favourable worst case for injection SEQ-SEQ, we find $i = 0.8\%$. This practically means that we are gaining: 2.1 GiB/s from 3 cores injecting on A57; 0.3 GiB/s from 1 core injecting on Denver; and 2.7 GiB/s for 3+1 cores injecting on the whole SoC. Although it produces experimental guarantees, this approach may be considered expensive or rigid. Also, it is prone to a tradeoff between bandwidth underutilization and latency degradation, similarly to the m-PREM technique discussed in Sect. 5.

Dynamic Approach. Alternatively, if a hot measurement of the latency impact can be performed, then such information can be fed to a suitable adaptive algorithm which dynamically increases the injection rate, until reaching an oscillation around the optimal value. In this case, the optimization function has to be constructed or parameterized in order to provide a bounded latency impact that meets the safety requirements.

Injection Control. Regardless of the injection rate limitation approach, such limit has to be enforced, when injecting tasks are allowed to execute alongside a PREM task. We discuss two mutually non-exclusive techniques.

Fine-Grained Control. When tasks' code is automatically transformed to adhere to the PREM scheme, a compiler is also part of the PREM runtime [6]. This enables the memory interval compiled code to be regularly interleaved by an idle instruction sequence, whose length can be dynamically determined, or statically hard-coded. In this case, the control on the injection rate is the finest possible, exactly as the idle cycle C used in the empirical section, but we need all tasks to be rebuilt on the custom-compiler.

Transparent Control. A centralized and secure injection control mechanism can be integrated in the underlying system-layer software, where the PREM admission control also usually resides. For example, an injection server can conveniently be implemented in a hypervisor, to periodically throttle an injecting task, and possibly measure the impacted latencies. Feasibility has been already been proven by the implementation of a memory guarding server [21] for the memory paritioning version [7] of Jailhouse [3], Experiments on Nvidia TX2 showed [13] that such server may run with a period of $16\,\mu s$ without costing more than 2% time utilization on the injecting task, or even every $1\,\mu s$, costing the 30%. Although courser-grained than the previous one, this technique is compatible with PREM-foreign code, thus enabling injection on third-party proprietary portion of the software stack (e.g., OS and libraries).

5   Related Work

The effects of memory contention in modern system-on-chips have been abundantly discussed in previous literature. Efforts to study the deterioration in the WCET of memory-contending applications have been performed on multi-core embedded systems [12], HPC-oriented systems [8,15] and even the magnitude on memory interference of co-running integrated and discrete GPUs [4,18,19] has been measured in previous work.

PREM was originally proposed for single-core CPUs [11] to provide robustness to memory-access interference from peripheral devices, and was later extended to avoid inter-core interference in multi-core CPUs [1,14]. After that, there has been extensive work on controlling CPU-GPU interference with PREM on HeSoCs [5,6,9]. PREM splits tasks into memory and compute phases, and schedules memory phases one at a time to prevent interference. While this simple approach allows to greatly reduce the pessimism in WCET estimates, it also heavily under-utilizes the memory bandwidth available in modern HeSoCs.

This fact was highlighted by the original authors of PREM [20], which experimentally proved that the latency of main-memory accesses does grow less than linearly with the number of cores accessing memory at the same time. In particular, if each core accesses a different bank, then the latency stays unchanged, independent of the number of competing cores. Based on this observation, the authors define a parameterized algorithm that schedules up to m phases at the same time. The main drawback of this approach is that the user must guess the right value for m for avoiding interference or for keeping it sufficiently low.

This may be particularly tricky if the accesses generated by a task set are not even: for the memory phases of some tasks, a given value of m may be fine, but for other tasks it may be either too low or too high. Even worse, $m = 2$ may be too high for some tasks (or even all tasks), thereby making any utilization boost impossible. Controlled injection, as our evaluation demonstrates, seems able to improve bandwidth utilization also in these unfriendly scenarios, due to its finer granularity.

Memguard [21] provides a different approach to protecting a task's WCET from the adverse effects of memory interference, based on throttling the bandwidth at which every core can access the shared memory, in an attempt to guarantee that each core gets its assigned bandwidth. Although simple and effective, such a mechanism may provide less control on interference compared to PREM, because memory accesses cannot be controlled explicitly. In addition, PREM is a much more general solution, because it is a building block for arbitrary schedules, while throttling is a well-defined control policy. Consider for example a constrained-deadline task[6]. To meet the task's deadlines with Memguard, the task must be assigned a (much) higher bandwidth than that sufficient to complete each instance before the arrival of a new one. This results in (high) bandwidth waste. With PREM, such a task can be scheduled with efficient scheduling algorithms for constrained-deadline tasks, resulting in minimum or even zero bandwidth waste. Previous work has characterized the effects of memory interference on modern HeSoCs [4,16], but the focus has always been on latency only, with no study of the bandwidth utilization, or the correlation between the two. More in general, none of the aforementioned contributions assess whether it is convenient on a performance and predictability perspective to arbitrate

---

[6] i.e., a task with a relative deadline (much) shorter than the minimum inter-arrival time of the task instances.

simultaneous memory accesses in modern HeSoCs through controlled injection of memory clients' requests.

6   Conclusion and Future Work

In this paper we presented how, with various types of workload, it is possible to exploit the available bandwidth of HeSoCs in a more efficient way than the canonical PREM arbitration, which conservatively considers main memory as a *one-user-at-a-time* resource. The proposed *controlled injection* technique allows in most practical cases to get close to the maximum available bandwidth, without significantly impacting the latency of the original PREM task. With regards to practical scenarios, authors in [17], for instance, present CAVBench, a collection of applications for autonomous driving vehicles. Profiling these applications leads to the conclusion that such workloads are extremely memory bound, hence the importance of accurately controlling memory bandwidth becomes paramount in latency sensitive scenarios.

As part of our future work, we envision the development of a practical *controlled injection* scheme, built on top of existing PREM implementations that consider both the CPU and the GPU of a HeSoC [5,6,9]. *Controlled Injection* also paves the way to new, more effective PREM-based scheduling algorithms. We are currently evaluating scheduling policies where both the UT and the IF tasks are slowed down by the same factor, rather than leaving full bandwidth to a core and allowing the others to inject small amounts of requests.

Acknowledgment. This article is part of a joint collaboration between researchers that work on two projects that have received funding from the European Union's Horizon 2020 research and innovation programme under the ECSEL-JU programme No 826653 (New control), the ECSEL project No. 826610 (COMP4DRONES) and the POR-FSE 2014–2020 (thematic objective 10) funding assigned by the Regional Authority to the project CUP E96C18001200009.

References

1. Alhammad, A., Pellizzoni, R.: Time-predictable execution of multithreaded applications on multicore systems. In: DATE 2014. IEEE (2014)
2. Baruah, S., Bertogna, M., Buttazzo, G.: Multiprocessor scheduling for real-time systems. Springer, Berlin (2015)
3. Baryshnikov, M.: Jailhouse hypervisor. B.S. thesis, České vysoké učení technické v Praze. Vypočetní a informační centrum (2016)
4. Cavicchioli, R., Capodieci, N., Bertogna, M.: Memory interference characterization between cpu cores and integrated gpus in mixed-criticality platforms. In: 2017 22nd IEEE International Conference on Emerging Technologies and Factory Automation (ETFA). pp. 1–10 (2017). https://doi.org/10.1109/ETFA.2017.8247615
5. Forsberg, B., Marongiu, A., Benini, L.: GPUguard: Towards supporting a predictable execution model for heterogeneous SoC. In: DATE 2017 (2017)
6. Forsberg, B., Benini, L., Marongiu, A.: Heprem: A predictable execution model for gpu-based heterogeneous socs. IEEE Trans. Comput. (2020, to appear)

7. Kloda, T., Solieri, M., Mancuso, R., Capodieci, N., Valente, P., Bertogna, M.: Deterministic memory hierarchy and virtualization for modern multi-core embedded systems. In: 2019 IEEE Real-Time and Embedded Technology and Applications Symposium (RTAS). pp. 1–14 (2019). https://doi.org/10.1109/RTAS.2019.00009

8. Majo, Z., Gross, T.R.: Memory management in numa multicore systems: trapped between cache contention and interconnect overhead. In: ACM Sigplan Notices. vol. 46, pp. 11–20. ACM (2011)

9. Matějka, J., et al.: Combining prem compilation and static scheduling for high-performance and predictable mpsoc execution. Parallel Comput. **85**, 27–44 (2019). https://doi.org/10.1016/j.parco.2018.11.002

10. McVoy, L.W., Staelin, C., et al.: lmbench: Portable tools for performance analysis. In: USENIX Annual Technical Conference. pp. 279–294. San Diego, CA, USA (1996)

11. Pellizzoni, R., et al.: A predictable execution model for COTS-based embedded systems. In: RTAS 2011. IEEE (2011)

12. Pellizzoni, R., Schranzhofer, A., Chen, J.J., Caccamo, M., Thiele, L.: Worst case delay analysis for memory interference in multicore systems. In: 2010 Design, Automation & Test in Europe Conference & Exhibition (2010). pp. 741–746. IEEE (2010)

13. Solieri, M., Kloda, T., Bertogna, M., Sojka, M., Baryshnikov, M.: D5.3: Integrated schedulability analysis. Deliverable of the HERCULES project (12 2018)

14. Soliman, M.R., Pellizzoni, R.: Prem-based optimal task segmentation under fixed priority scheduling. In: 31st Euromicro Conference on Real-Time Systems (ECRTS 2019). Leibniz International Proceedings in Informatics (LIPIcs), vol. 133, pp. 4:1–4:23 (2019). https://doi.org/10.4230/LIPIcs.ECRTS.2019.4

15. Tudor, B.M., Teo, Y.M., See, S.: Understanding off-chip memory contention of parallel programs in multicore systems. In: 2011 International Conference on Parallel Processing. pp. 602–611. IEEE (2011)

16. Vogel, P., Marongiu, A., Benini, L.: An evaluation of memory sharing performance for heterogeneous embedded socs with many-core accelerators. In: Proceedings of the 2015 International Workshop on Code Optimisation for Multi and Many Cores, COSMIC@CGO. pp. 1–9 (2015). https://doi.org/10.1145/2723772.2723775

17. Wang, Y., Liu, S., Wu, X., Shi, W.: Cavbench: A benchmark suite for connected and autonomous vehicles. CoRR abs/1810.06659 (2018), http://arxiv.org/abs/1810.06659

18. Wen, H., Wei, Z.: Interference evaluation in cpu-gpu heterogeneous computing. In: IEEE High Performance Extreme Computing Conference (HPEC) (2017)

19. Yamagiwa, S., Wada, K.: Performance study of interference on gpu and cpu resources with multiple applications. In: 2009 IEEE International Symposium on Parallel & Distributed Processing. pp. 1–8. IEEE (2009)

20. Yao, G., Pellizzoni, R., Bak, S., Yun, H., Caccamo, M.: Global real-time memory-centric scheduling for multicore systems. IEEE Trans. Comput. **65**(9), 2739–2751 (2016). https://doi.org/10.1109/TC.2015.2500572

21. Yun, H., Yao, G., Pellizzoni, R., Caccamo, M., Sha, L.: Memguard: Memory bandwidth reservation system for efficient performance isolation in multi-core platforms. In: Real-Time and Embedded Technical and Application Symposium (RTAS). IEEE (2013)

Accelerating 3-Way Epistasis Detection with CPU+GPU Processing

Ricardo Nobre$^{(\boxtimes)}$, Sergio Santander-Jiménez, Leonel Sousa, and Aleksandar Ilic

INESC-ID, Instituto Superior Técnico, Universidade de Lisboa, Lisboa, Portugal
{ricardo.nobre,sergio.jimenez,leonel.sousa,aleksandar.ilic}@inesc-id.pt

Abstract. A Single Nucleotide Polymorphism (SNP) is a DNA variation occurring when a single nucleotide differs between individuals of a species. Some conditions can be explained with a single SNP. However, the combined effect of multiple SNPs, known as epistasis, allows to better correlate genotype with a number of complex traits. We propose a highly optimized GPU+CPU based approach for epistasis detection. The GPU portion of the approach relies only on CUDA cores to score sets of SNPs, based on the copresence of genetic variants and a specific outcome (case or control), making it suitable for a large number of computing devices. Considering datasets with different shapes (more SNPs than patients, or vice versa) and sizes, combining an analytical analysis and an experimental evaluation with five CPU+GPU configurations covering different GPU architectures from the last five years, we show that the performance achieved by our proposal is close to what is theoretically possible on the targeted GPUs. Comparing, in 3-way epistasis detection, with a state-of-the-art GPU-based approach which also does not rely on specialized hardware cores, MPI3SNP, the proposal is on average $3.83\times, 2.72\times, 2.44\times$ and $2.71\times$ faster on systems with a Titan X (Maxwell 2.0), a Titan XP (Pascal), a Titan V (Volta) and a GeForce 2070 SUPER (Turing) GPU, respectively.

Keywords: Epistasis detection · Parallel processing · GPU · Heterogeneous system.

1 Introduction

Throughout the years, Genome-Wide Association Studies (GWAS) have been promoting significant advances in genetics research by shedding light into the relationship between genetic variants and phenotypic traits. The analysis of Single Nucleotide Polymorphisms (SNPs) plays a prevailing role in this context, since they represent the most frequent type of variation in the human genome.

This work was supported by the FCT (Fundação para a Ciência e a Tecnologia, Portugal) and the ERDF (European Regional Development Fund, EU) through the projects UIDB/50021/2020 and LISBOA-01–0145-FEDER-031901 (PTDC/CCI-COM/31901/2017, HiPErBio). Sergio Santander-Jiménez is supported by the Post-Doctoral Fellowship from FCT under Grant SFRH/BPD/119220/2016.

© Springer Nature Switzerland AG 2020
D. Klusáček et al. (Eds.): JSSPP 2020, LNCS 12326, pp. 106–126, 2020.
https://doi.org/10.1007/978-3-030-63171-0_6

In the pursuit of a better understanding of genotype-phenotype relationships, increasing research efforts have been focused on identifying the impact of multiple, interactive SNPs, a phenomenon known as epistasis [10]. In fact, the accurate identification of epistatic interactions represents a hot research topic, since a number of complex traits (such as Alzheimer's disease [20], breast cancer [14] and Crohn's disease [8]) are consequence of the joint effect of several SNPs at different interaction orders.

The epistasis detection not only introduces additional layers of biological complexity but it also represents a computationally intensive optimization problem. This challenging nature becomes even more noticeable when an exhaustive (as precise as possible) evaluation of interactive SNP combinations (i.e., triplets in 3-way detection) is needed to explain very complex traits. In order to address this issue, given the data-parallel nature of epistasis detection searches (same operations performed to evaluate each set of SNPs), there are a number of exhaustive strategies implementing GPU-based approaches [3,5,12,17,19]. However, for a number of reasons (e.g., differences in the architectures), some of those approaches might not be able to efficiently use recent hardware.

This work proposes a novel GPU+CPU approach for epistasis detection based on exhaustive examination of SNP combinations, which aims at fully exploiting the computational capabilities offered by the joint, collaborative action of CPU and GPU devices. With this purpose in mind, the proposed method relies on the architectural differences between CPU and GPU to undertake the efficient evaluation of epistatic interactions, accurately scheduling and distributing these tasks according to their properties and suitability to the underlying hardware. The main contributions of this paper are the following:

– High-Performance GPU+CPU based high-order epistasis detection approach based on optimized parallel algorithms;
– Analytical and experimental analysis of the proposal when performing 3-way detection on five CPU+GPU systems (comprising Maxwell 2.0, Pascal, Volta and Turing GPU architectures and Xeon, i7, and i9 CPU architectures);
– In-depth discussion of theoretical and achieved parallel performance on different dataset shapes and problem sizes, with validation of results through comparisons with other state-of-the-art strategies.

Experimental results show that the proposed approach is capable of outperforming MPI3SNP [12], a state-of-the-art approach, for about $2.9\times$ (on average) across four different NVIDIA architectures. In addition, the proposal achieves near-theoretical maximum performance according to the characteristics of the algorithm.

This paper is structured as follows. Section 2 formulates the epistasis detection problem. Section 3 provides insight into the proposed method and the design strategies adopted to enhance epistasis searches on CPU+GPU systems. Section 4 presents the experimental campaign herein undertaken and contrasts the results achieved with the state-of-the-art. Section 5 situates the proposal in the related work on optimized algorithms for epistasis detection. Section 6 concludes the paper.

2   Problem Formulation

Certain phenotypic traits, e.g. diseases, are strongly correlated to the joint inter-action of different SNPs in the genome of a particular individual (patient). The accurate identification of such interactions represents the main goal in epistasis detection. Epistasis analyses therefore deal with the processing of information on SNPs from different individuals, which are classified according to a binary outcome (e.g., having –case– or not having –control– the phenotypic trait under study). Such information is contained in a dataset D of size $N \times (M+1)$, where N is the number of individual samples and M the number of SNPs subject to analysis. Each entry $D[i,j], i \in \{1, ..., N\}, j \in \{1, ..., M\}$ provides the genotypic value observed at the j-th SNP for the i-th individual, encoded as 0 (homozygous major allele, AA), 1 (heterozygous allele, aA or Aa), or 2 (homozygous minor allele, aa). The entry $D[i, M+1]$ in a sample represents the phenotypic state observed for the i-th individual (0 in control samples and 1 in case samples).

Epistasis detection is usually formulated as an optimization problem that is aimed at identifying the combination of k-interactive SNPs $x = [x_1, x_2, ..., x_k]$ ($x_i \in \{1, ..., M\}$) that most likely governs the occurrence of the examined trait, where k is the epistasis interaction order assumed for that trait. The identifica-tion of the optimal solution to the problem requires exploring an epistasis search space of $^M C_k = \frac{M!}{k!(M-k)!}$ sorted and non-repeated combinations of SNPs [13]. The suitability of each possible combination x is measured by means of objective functions, which measure the degree of impact of the evaluated interaction in the studied trait. In this work, the proposed approach adopts the widely-used Bayesian K2 score [2,15] as the scoring objective function:

$$K2 = \sum_{i=1}^{I} \left(\sum_{b=1}^{r_i+1} \log(b) - \sum_{j=1}^{J} \sum_{d=1}^{r_{ij}} \log(d) \right), \tag{1}$$

where I is the number of possible genotypic combinations among k SNPs ($I = 3^k$, since each SNP can take one out of three possible genotypic values), J the number of phenotypic states ($J = 2$ in case-control scenarios), r_i the frequency of a certain genotypic combination i at the evaluated SNPs $x = [x_1, x_2, ..., x_k]$, and r_{ij} the number of samples that satisfy the occurrence of the phenotypic state j with the genotypic combination i at x. That is, given a k-order SNP interaction, the occurrences of each possible genotype combination for the examined k SNPs are counted through all the samples recorded in the dataset, taking into account each record type (case or control). This results in a total of 2×3^k frequency values. These values, forming what is known as a *contingency* or *frequency* table, are used to compute a score that aims to discriminate predictive strength, between the different sets of SNPs, in relation to the binary outcome under study. Lower K2 scores denote better solution quality, in such a way that the interaction that minimizes Eq. 1 represents the best potential solution.

In terms of computational effort, the exhaustive identification of optimal solutions depends on the interaction order and the dimensions of the input data.

Specifically, the number of possible candidate solutions to the problem exponentially grows in harder epistasis scenarios (increasing k and M), while the amount of calculations in the objective function depends on N. These issues demand efficient parallel strategies and orchestration of computing devices to tackle the problem, accurately exploiting the combined capabilities of CPU+GPU systems.

3 GPU+CPU Hybrid Epistasis Detection

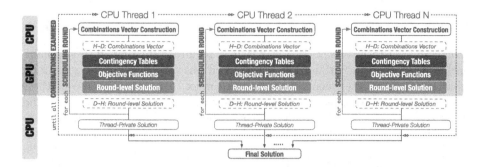

Fig. 1. Overview of scheduling between CPU and GPU.

The approach proposed in this paper is aimed at exploiting the collaborative execution among CPU and GPU devices to conduct computationally demanding epistasis detection tasks, particularly the exhaustive search for optimal 3-way SNP interactions according to the K2 score. Figure 1 provides the general overview of the proposed CPU+GPU approach, which is designed in such a way that both device types cooperate in the process of determining the optimal solution by executing different sets of tasks. This task distribution is conducted due to the architectural differences between CPU and GPU, thus each device type is assigned with the tasks whose characteristics allow better exploitation of the computational and memory resources on a per device architecture basis.

In a nutshell, the host CPU cores are responsible for generating the sets of combinations of SNP indexes (*Combinations Vector*) to be processed in the GPU. The evaluation of SNP combinations is a task rich in data-parallelism, thus highly suitable for GPU execution, while the generation of combinations vectors requires a large amount of complex control and synchronization primitives, thus better fitting the CPU architecture. The combinations vectors (chunks) are simultaneously constructed within several CPU threads and offloaded to the GPU in a streaming fashion. This process is repeated in several scheduling rounds until all possible SNP combinations have been examined.

Upon reception of a combinations vector, the GPU performs the following set of tasks: 1) *Contingency table construction*, i.e., counting the frequencies of combined genotypes for each of the unique sets of SNPs (resulting from combining SNPs all-to-all) generated by a particular CPU thread in a given round,

2) *Objective function (K2 score) calculation*, i.e., scoring each set of SNPs based on the constructed contingency table; and 3) determination of the local optimal solution (the one with the minimum K2 score) from the set of tuples of SNP indexes in the combinations vector, i.e., *Round-level Solution*.

For each scheduling round, the host CPU threads maintain the information regarding the best solution obtained across all executed rounds on the GPU (and initiated by that thread). Upon all possible SNP combinations are processed, the final/global optimum solution is determined by the CPU master thread by gathering the partial solutions from each host CPU thread.

3.1   CPU as Orchestration Engine and Generator of Unique Sets

Exhaustive epistasis searches in 3-way fashion require evaluating all-to-all combinations three SNPs at a time. There are algorithms specialized in the generation of a combination of elements from a given index (e.g., [1]). The use of these algorithms allows arriving at a given combination faster than exhaustively and iteratively enumerating all combinations up to that combination. This is especially the case when those combination indexes are large.

Direct calculation of the combination (i.e., the triplet of indexes of SNPs) to process inside each GPU thread, from the GPU global thread identifiers, introduces a considerable overhead as it does not suit the parallel architecture of GPUs. Generation of the triplets of indexes of SNPs inside the GPU threads can result in an overhead that can only be offset when processing datasets with a large number of patient records. Notice that, given the nature of epistasis detection, we only want to process unique sets of SNPs. If what was required was to process all permutations, it would not be challenging to achieve direct mapping of thread identifiers into the triplets to process inside the GPU threads.

In the proposal presented in this paper, it is the host (i.e., the CPU) that generates combinations of indexes of SNPs, to be sent to the GPU for evaluation. Generation of combination vectors and communication of these vectors to the GPU for evaluation are performed in multiple rounds. The number of rounds is given by $\left\lceil \frac{{}^{M}C_3}{s} \right\rceil$, where ${}^{M}C_3$ is the total number of combinations to evaluate in a particular epistasis detection 3-way search (SNPs combined all-to-all in sets of three) and s is the number of combinations processed per round. Herein we refer to the later as *chunk size*.

Multiple rounds are processed concurrently by multiple CPU threads (a parameter). This results in more efficient use of the CPU resources to generate sets while also improving bandwidth utilization between CPU and GPU devices. While some CPU threads are generating combination vectors or waiting for GPU kernel executions to complete, other threads are sending new combination vectors to the GPU. Each CPU thread, when starting a new round, generates the first combination of three SNPs (i.e., three indexes) from a given starting combination index (assigned to that round). The calculation of the first combination for a given round is accomplished through an adaptation of the algorithm presented in [1].

Algorithm 1 depicts the operations the proposal performs for determining the configuration of the l_{th} combination (starting from 1), represented in output vector c, considering combinations of three SNPs chosen from m SNPs numbered from 0 to $m - 1$.

Data: m, l
Result: c
$r = l$;
$c[0] = -1$;
for $i = 0$; $i < 2$; $i = i + 1$ **do**
    while $r > 0$ **do**
        $c[i] = c[i] + 1$;
        $d = comb(m - (c[i] + 1), 2 - i)$;
        $r = r - d$;
    end
    $r = r + d$;
    $c[i + 1] = c[i]$;
end
$c[2] = c[2] + r$;

Algorithm 1: Generation of the l_{th} combination of three elements chosen from m elements.

The *for* loop executes for two iterations ($i = 0$ and $i = 1$), determining the value for the first and the second positions—$c[0]$ and $c[1]$—in the combination configuration vector c. The value for the third (and last) position—$c[2]$—is equal to the value found for the previous position (the second)—$c[1]$—plus a remainder (rest) stored in the r variable. In each of the two *for* loop iterations, the nested *while* loop executes until $r \leq 0$, which signals that the SNP index value for $c[i]$ ($i = 0$ or $i = 1$) has been found. Variable r, decremented by $comb(m - (c[i] + 1), 2 - i)$—number of combinations that exist between $\{c[0], c[0] + 1, c[0] + 2\}$ and $\{c[0] + 1, c[0] + 2, c[0] + 3\}$ ($i = 0$) or between $\{c[0], c[1], c[1] + 1\}$ and $\{c[0], c[1] + 1, c[1] + 2\}$ ($i = 1$)—for any increment to $c[i]$, holds the distance to the l_{th} combination. When the *while* loop condition is evaluated to *false*, the previous value of r (the remainder) is restored—$r = r + d$—and the starting value of $c[i + 1]$, the next combination configuration index, is set $c[i]$, the value found in the current *for* loop iteration. In order to avoid having to calculate (and recalculate) $^j C_2$ during execution of a given epistasis detection search, the proposal relies on a lookup table that is only required to store values for j up to the number of SNPs. Thus, in the first *for* loop iteration ($i = 0$), the term $comb(m - (c[i] + 1), 2 - i)$ maps to precomputed values that are loaded at the application start. In the second (and final) *for* loop iteration ($i = 1$), there is no need to resort to precomputed values, as the number of combinations of one element chosen from $m - (c[i] + 1)$ elements is equal to the latter.

After the configuration of the first combination to be processed in a given round is known, all other combinations to be processed in that round are sequentially enumerated (assuming lexicographical order) by the CPU thread operating the round. For example, the next combination after $\{32, 41, 1854\}$ is

$\{32, 41, 1855\}$ if the number of SNPs to select from is larger than 1855 (the indexes of the SNPs start at 0), and $\{32, 42, 43\}$ otherwise. This offsets the initial cost of determining the first combination to be part of the combinations vector to be generated on a given round, as generating the next combination from a given other combination is considerably less computationally expensive.

While combination vectors are being processed on GPU kernel executions launched by some CPU threads, additional combination vectors are concurrently being generated on the CPU by other threads, and combination vectors pertaining to other rounds are being transferred to the GPU (i.e., host to device memory transfer). This behavior is achieved using OpenMP, with a parallel *for* loop (`#pragma omp parallel for schedule(dynamic)`) iterating over the total number of sets to process (i.e., $^{M}C_3$) with a step equal to the number of combinations to be evaluated on a given round (i.e., the chunk size). These chunks must be large enough (a parameter of the proposal) to saturate the GPU compute units, while at the same time not large to the point of severely reducing the number of threads that can execute concurrently on the host. Each iteration of the parallel OpenMP loop, executed by a given CPU thread (each with its own private CUDA stream) is responsible for generating a chunk of triplets of indexes representing combinations of SNPs (i.e., the combinations vector), sending them to the GPU and launching the GPU kernel that evaluates the combinations. After that particular kernel execution completes, the CPU thread transfers back (i.e., device to host memory transfer) the index identifying the locally optimal combination found on the GPU kernel execution and corresponding score. Each CPU thread keeps track of the best solution found up to any given point, with the final reduction done on the master thread after the parallel *for* loop completes execution, i.e., once all combinations of SNPs are exhausted.

3.2   GPU as a Combinations Processor

Due to the challenging nature of the epistasis detection problem tackled herein, the way the input dataset is represented and processed represents a crucial aspect in ensuring its high performance execution, especially on GPU devices. In order to efficiently encode the input data set, we rely on binarization techniques, first used in the context of epistasis detection in [16]. In the proposed approach, the GPU receives as input two arrays, representing the controls and cases in the dataset (phenotype), respectively. As it is depicted in Fig. 2(a), all genotypic information pertaining a given SNP X in relation to the samples in the dataset is represented by $3 \times (N_0 + N_1)$ binary values, where N_0 and N_1 represent the number of controls and the number of cases, respectively. Each of these binary values is stored in the array representing controls (phenotype 0) or in the array representing cases (phenotype 1), respectively. For each pair composed of a sample and a SNP, one of three particular bits is set to 1 (in the cases or the controls array), identifying which genotype (0, 1 or 2) the sample has regarding that SNP. In total, these two arrays represent $M \times 3 \times N$ binary values, where M is the number of SNPs and N is the total number of samples ($N_0 + N_1$).

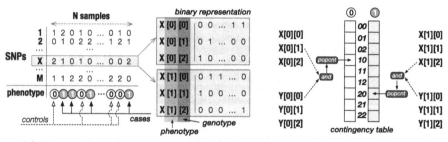

(a) Binary representation of input dataset

(b) Contingency table construction from binary encoding

Fig. 2. Representation of basic notions in epistasis detection.

As previously referred, the GPU receives an array holding triplets of indexes of the SNPs to process in a specific kernel execution (i.e., the combinations vector), one triplet to be processed per GPU thread. When processing a single SNP combination, the binary representation of input data allows calculating the frequency of any given combined genotype (out of the 27 possible genotypic combinations) using only bitwise AND and POPC (population count, which counts the number of bits set to 1) instructions, and accumulating until all bit-packs concerning cases or controls (for a given genotype) have been processed.

Cases and controls are represented in distinct bit arrays and thus processed from separate bit-packs of data. Both AND and POPC instructions process 32-bit of data in all GPUs that are part of the systems targeted in this paper. Thus, for interaction order k (i.e., k-way epistasis detection searches), the total number of POPC instructions is equal to $^{M}C_k \times 3^k \times (\lceil \frac{N_0}{32} \rceil + \lceil \frac{N_1}{32} \rceil)$, while the total number of AND instructions is $(k-1)$ times higher (M being the number of SNPs, N_0 the number of controls and N_1 the number of cases). In particular, for 2-way epistasis detection, depicted in Fig. 2(b), an equal amount of and POPC instructions is required. However, for 3-way detection (considered in the work proposed herein), the number of AND instructions to be performed is 2 times higher than the amount of POPC instructions. This is due to the fact that, in order to calculate a single entry in the contingency table, two AND operations are needed to be performed over three binary encoded SNP inputs, before a single POPC operation is applied.

To facilitate the calculation of the objective function, the main GPU kernel also receives as input an array with precalculated values, specific to the particular function used (logarithms of factorials for the K2 Bayesian score [2,15]), for up to the maximum that can possibly be needed to calculate scores given the number of cases and controls in the dataset, the number of SNPs, and the total number of sets resulting from the number of SNPs and the interaction order. Some of these values could be calculated inside each particular GPU thread, but it makes for a more efficient solution to pass values that are to be the same in all GPU threads as input to the kernel.

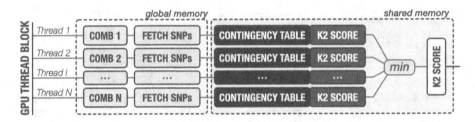

Fig. 3. Round of combinations being processed on a given GPU thread block.

The main GPU kernel is launched with a grid composed of as many thread blocks as the number of sets of SNPs to be processed by it (the chunk size) divided by the number of threads per thread block. The global identifier of each GPU thread pertaining to a given kernel execution (`blockDim.x * blockIdx.x + threadIdx.x`) identifies the combination of SNPs to be processed from the sets of SNPs represented in the combinations vector sent by the CPU in a given round. Thus, it is mapped to the positions in global memory holding the indexes representing the three SNPs to be evaluated by a given GPU thread.

Each GPU thread processes a set of SNPs, whose indexes are identified in the combinations vector previously transferred from the CPU for that particular round, at positions $s \times i + global\_id$, where s is the number of combinations of SNPs to be processed per round and i is the particular SNP index out of the three involved. Reading the triplet of indexes identifying the SNPs to evaluate from global memory in each GPU thread does not significantly increase the execution time of the GPU kernel. These indexes are read in a coalesced access pattern, at a small cost in relation to the overall execution of the GPU kernel.

Figure 3 illustrates how combinations are processed within a single GPU thread block, including which parts in the memory subsystems are used at each step. Each thread in a thread block iterates over all cases and then over all controls, reading packed binarized genotype patient data for a particular triplet of SNPs. The read operations to fetch patient data from global memory are in general efficiently performed. Within each array, SNP genotype values are binary encoded as follows. Each bit-pack n of w binary encoded patient data records (i.e., representing w patients) concerning one of the three possible genotype configurations $(0, 1$ or $2)$, represented as g, of an SNP of index m is stored in position $g \times M \times \lceil \frac{N}{w} \rceil + n \times M + m$ in global memory. Given that the number of SNPs in the dataset is expected to be significantly larger than the size of a warp, and that GPU threads with contiguous *thread id* access lexicographically contiguous combinations, GPU threads in a given warp are likely to access data concerning the third SNP in the combination being processed from contiguous positions in memory, i.e., in a coalesced access pattern. For instance, the combination after $\{23, 354, 661\}$ is likely $\{23, 354, 662\}$. In addition, the global memory reads to data concerning the first and the second SNPs from the combination being evaluated in each GPU thread will typically access the same memory positions as other threads from the same warp.

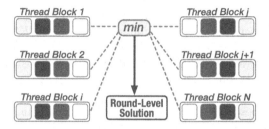

Fig. 4. Reduction of scores between different GPU thread blocks.

Iterating over individuals, cases or controls, the three vectors of data per SNP and per genotype (a total of nine vectors of binarized patient data) in a given GPU thread are combined to determine the number of occurrences of each genotype combination (27 possible genotype combinations) in the samples represented by the bit-packs of binarized data. This is accomplished with bitwise AND and POPC instructions. The proposal relies on __popcll(), which is the 64-bit equivalent of the __popc() 32-bit CUDA intrinsic. Both map to the POPC 32-bit instruction, but processing bit-packs of 64-bit of data at a time allowed to achieve a slightly higher overall performance. Iteratively processing 64-bit of binarized patient data instead of 32-bit allows a better use of the GPU memory subsystem, by reducing the amount of write accesses needed for incrementing the frequency counters during construction of the contingency table to half. Genotype frequencies are accumulated for cases and controls (processed separately) until all bit-packs of patient data concerning a given triplet of SNPs have been processed, at which point the construction of the contingency tables for all GPU threads in a warp is complete.

The GPU threads in a given thread block store the counts of observed combined genotype frequencies (for cases and controls) in an array of size $2 \times 27 \times T$ in shared memory, where T represents the number of GPU threads in a thread block. All write memory accesses during the generation of the contingency tables are coalesced. Each frequency counter for a given combined genotype g (from 0 to 26) and phenotype p (0 for controls and 1 for cases), pertaining to a GPU thread with a given *local id*, is mapped to position $2 \times g \times T + p \times T + local\_id$ of the array in shared memory. In any given thread block, the specific shared memory 32-bit slot used in a GPU thread is indexed by its local identifier (`threadIdx.x`) in the thread block. Thus, there is no possibility of collision with other threads in the same warp (i.e., multiple threads accessing the same memory slot). These optimizations maximize the utilization of shared memory, thus benefiting from its low latency and high bandwidth nature (when compared to the global memory).

After all data (for all cases and controls) regarding the set of SNPs assigned to a given GPU thread has been processed, a score is calculated based on the counts for the 27 combined genotype frequencies (for cases and controls) stored, per GPU thread, in shared memory. Afterwards, the score is reduced in shared memory across the GPU threads in the same thread block, and finally, in global memory across all thread blocks, as illustrated in Fig. 4, in order to determine the best overall objective score (minimum in the case of the K2 score) for a given round. The *global id* of the thread achieving local minimum and the corresponding score are transferred to the CPU thread responsible for that particular GPU kernel execution and stored, after mapping the *global id* to a combination index (adding the index of the first combination processed in the round), if the score is better than the best score found in the previous rounds in that CPU thread.

Particularities of the exhaustive epistasis detection algorithm used and knowledge about the type of data being processed are leveraged to attain high performance. For instance, the proposal improves performance of the objective function by using a lookup table for storing precomputed values that are to be used by the scoring function. Note that this makes the performance of the proposal, in regards to the evaluation of the sets of SNPs from the genotype frequency counts (i.e., the contingency table values for cases and controls), to a great extent independent of the particular scoring function used. The only requirement is that the range of precomputed values includes all the values that might be needed when computing the scores, which depends both on the scoring function and the number of cases and controls, and that access to those values is fast. The later aspect is assured by the use of the read-only GPU data cache load function (i.e., __ldg()). In the case of the K2 Bayesian score, the logarithms of factorials calculated by this scoring function are precomputed on the CPU and sent to the GPU (once for the whole execution). Thus, assuring that no actual expensive computation of logarithms of factorials needs to be performed on the GPU. Even compared with the use of the lgamma() CUDA math intrinsic, which allows to calculate the factorials efficiently through the use of the gamma function ($\Gamma(x) = (x-1)!$), using the lookup tables allows achieving highest performance.

3.3   CPU+GPU Execution Orchestration

In order to get the maximum performance out of a given CPU+GPU system, the proposal relies on several CPU threads executing concurrently. Thus, overlapping the generation of combination vectors on the CPU with computation on the GPU and with data transfers between CPU/GPU at any given time. This results in making efficient use of the available bandwidth between CPU/GPU, all available CPU cores and GPU compute resources. This kind of orchestration is suitable even in the presence of multi-GPU systems. In such systems, GPU devices on the same machine are assigned to CUDA streams private to different CPU threads. The way the proposal divides combinations of SNPs to be evaluated into smaller work units improves efficiency of work distribution between GPUs on the same system. Depending on the capability of a given GPU, compared with other GPUs in the system, more/less rounds are assigned during execution to the CPU threads responsible for orchestrating work for that GPU.

The overall wall-clock time required to execute the proposal is dominated by execution on the GPU. Generation of combinations on the CPU might only be a performance deterrent in unbalanced systems (i.e., high-end GPU or multi-GPU paired with weak CPU). The number of threads is by default set to be equal to the number of CPU cores identified at runtime to exist in the system. This assures that there are enough concurrently running CPU threads to send the GPU new combination vectors to process at a pace that allows CUDA cores to be utilized close to their potential.

A suitable chunk size, i.e., number of sets to process per kernel execution, is important to achieve high performance. Chunk size determines the time taken by CPU threads to generate combinations and the time required to evaluate them on the GPU. The range of values that best suit the execution of the proposal is expected to depend on the dataset (number of SNPs and patient records) and on the given target CPU+GPU configuration. A value that is too low implies that the GPU compute resources will be severely underutilized and/or result in more time spent on preparation and launching the kernel in relation to the kernel execution. A value that is too large can also result in performance degradation, impacting negatively the load balancing between the CPU threads. This is especially the case in scenarios where the input dataset has a small number of SNPs, and thus the resulting number of total sets to process is also small. The latter scenario can result, in the worst case, in the complete serialization of the work, being all SNP combinations processed in a single round.

Data transfer between CPU and GPU devices is mostly in the direction from the CPU to the GPU. Data transfer from the GPU to the CPU is only performed at the end of the execution of the main GPU kernel in a given CPU thread, i.e., an index identifying the SNP set evaluated as having the best score and the score itself. Compared with the wall-clock time required by the GPU to evaluate combinations of SNPs, the time required for sending the combination vectors is not expected to limit overall performance on well balanced systems. This is especially the case on systems with CPUs with a large number of cores.

4   Experimental Results

Our experimental campaign is aimed at thoroughly evaluating the impact of different numbers of SNPs and individual samples on the throughput of the proposal for systems with different CPU+GPU configurations. We performed experiments on datasets with different shapes (more SNPs than patient records, or vice versa) and sizes in order to cover different use cases. In addition, we evaluate the combined performance impact of the number of concurrently executing CPU threads and the number of combinations processed per scheduling round. Finally, the performance of the proposal is compared with MPI3SNP [12], a GPU-based state-of-the-art approach for 3-way epistasis detection.

4.1   Experimental Setup and Datasets

We rely on five different workstations/servers for our experiments. The systems are comprised of a Xeon E3-1245 V3 and a GeForce 2070 SUPER (designated as S1), a Core i9-7900X and a Titan V (S2), a i7-4770K and a Titan Xp (S3), a i7-5960X and a Titan X (S4) or a i7-6700K and two GeForce 980 GPUs (S5).

Table 1 shows the specifications of the systems, including GPU, CPU, DRAM, operating system, CUDA and GPU driver[1] versions. The systems are ordered based on GPU architecture, from the most recent (Turing) to the one released earliest (Maxwell 2.0).

Table 1. Overview of systems used in the experiments.

Systems	GPU (NVIDIA) arch. | cuda | driver	CPU (Intel) #cores | freq	DRAM #channels | freq	Operating System
S1	**GeForce 2070S** Turing | 10.1 | 430.40	**Xeon E3-1245 V3** 4 | 3.6GHz	16GB DDR3 dual | 2400MHz	Ubuntu 18.04
S2	**Titan V** Volta | 9.2 | 396.54	**Core i9-7900X** 10 | 4.0GHz	64GB DDR4 quad | 2400MHz	CentOS 7.5
S3	**Titan XP** Pascal | 10.1 | 418.56	**Core i7-4770K** 4 | 3.5GHz	32GB DDR3 dual | 1333MHz	CentOS 7.6
S4	**Titan X** Maxwell 2.0 | 8.0 | 375.26	**Core i7-5960X** 8 | 3.3GHz	32GB DDR4 quad | 2133MHz	Fedora 21
S5	**2×GeForce 980** Maxwell 2.0 | 8.0 | 410.48	**Core i7-6700K** 4 | 4.2GHz	32GB DDR4 dual | 2133MHz	CentOS 7.3

In Volta (compute capability 7.0) and in Turing (compute capability 7.5), each Streaming Multiprocessor (SM), the most basic building block of NVIDIA GPUs, has four processing blocks. Each processing block has one instruction scheduling and dispatch unit, 64 KBytes of register file space, 16 IEE754 32-bit floating point scalar Arithmetic Logic Units (ALUs) (i.e., Floating-Point Units (FPUs)), 16 32-bit integer scalar ALUs, four load/store units and four Special Function Units (SFUs). In addition, each SM has 96 KBytes (Turing) or 128 KBytes (Volta) of L1 configurable cache/shared memory, shared between the four processing blocks. In comparison, in Maxwell 2.0 (compute capability 5.2) and Pascal (compute capability 6.1), each processing block has double the amount of ALUs, FPUs, SFUs and load/store units. All four GPU architectures use a quadrant-based design, therefore the amount of units per SM in Maxwell 2.0 and Pascal is double the amount in Volta and Turing. There are 96 KB of shared memory per SM on the two former architectures.

The GPU configurations considered have each a total of 2560 (GeForce 2070S), 5120 (Titan V), 3840 (Titan Xp), 3072 (Titan X) and 4096 (2 × GeForce 980) CUDA cores. The advertised boost frequencies are 1770, 1455, 1582, 1089 and 1216 MHz, respectively. An important factor in the execution of the proposal is given by the throughputs of AND and POPC instructions. The considered GPU configurations are capable of executing 4.5 (GeForce 2070S) and 7.4 (Titan V), 6.1 (Titan Xp), 3.3 (Titan X) and 5 (2× GeForce 980) tera 32-bit bitwise AND instructions per second at their respective boost clocks. The rate of 32-bit POPC instructions per second is a quarter that of AND instructions for all GPUs.

---

[1] The experiments targeting the Titan V system that are concerned with comparing the proposal with MPI3SNP were conducted using a more up-to-date driver (440.64).

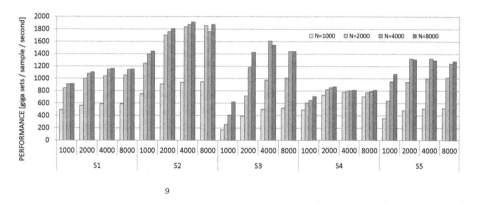

9

Fig. 5. Number of giga ($\times 10^9$) sets processed per second normalized to the number of patient samples (N) for the proposal on five different systems (S1, S2, S3, S4 and S5) and considering different numbers of SNPs (represented at the bottom) and patients (the different chart bars).

In order to fully exercise the capabilities of the proposal, taking into account that real datasets can vary substantialy in regard to size and shape, we have examined synthetic datasets with different numbers of SNPs and patient samples. Notice that the specific values pertaining SNP data of cases or controls in the dataset do not affect the efficiency of the algorithm, thus the achieved performance is representative of what would be achieved with real datasets. A total of 16 datasets were generated, each having a combination of 1000, 2000, 4000 or 8000 SNPs with 1000, 2000, 4000 or 8000 patient records (half cases/controls). Considering 3-way epistasis detection scenarios, the numbers of unique sets of SNPs to be evaluated per problem instance are the following: 166167000 (1000 SNPs), 1331334000 (2000 SNPs) and 10658668000 (4000 SNPs) and 85301336000 (8000 SNPs). Each doubling of the number of SNPs results in a growth of about $8\times$ regarding the total number of combinations of SNPs to evaluate. We rely on the same datasets in the experiments performed to examine the effect in performance of the number of sets to process per scheduling round, setting it to 10000, 20000, 40000, 80000, 160000 or 320000, combined with using 1, 2, 4 or 8 concurrently executing CPU threads. Finally, for the experiments comparing the proposal with MPI3SNP we rely on the two datasets available on the MPI3SNP source code repository[2]. These datasets represent 10000 SNPs from 1600 patients and 40000 SNPs from 6400 patients, half cases and half controls. The number of SNPs in these datasets results in 166616670000 and 10665866680000 combinations of SNPs to evaluate, respectively.

---

[2] https://github.com/chponte/mpi3snp/wiki/Sample-files.

4.2   Performance Analysis Across Different Datasets and Platforms

Figure 5 depicts the performance achieved by the proposal on the different systems employed in the experimentation. Overall, performance tends to increase with the number of patient records. This is especially the case when going from a dataset with 1000 patients to a dataset with 2000 patients. Certain costs associated with execution of the GPU kernel implemented in the proposal are independent from the number of samples in the input dataset. In addition to the cost of initializing the GPU kernel execution on the host in a given round, there are other operations with cost invariant to the number of patient records, such as the calculation of the score on top of the contingency table and the score reduction operations, first between GPU threads in shared memory and then between thread blocks in global memory. After a certain number of patients, which depends on the system targeted, the potential for exploitation of resources gets saturated. Thus, considering more patients makes the wall-clock time increase close to linearly, resulting in similar performance levels. The number of SNPs also impacts performance, which increases considerably from 1000 to 2000 SNPs.

Overall, the attained results suggest that the main performance limiting factor, provided that the input dataset saturates the implementation of the proposal (i.e., sufficient ammount of SNPs and patient records), is the throughput of the CUDA cores, and not that of memory bandwidth. Performing the population counts, which uses the POPC instruction, is the operation that imposes the main restrictions on the maximum performance achievable in this problem for the considered GPU architectures. POPC is more challenging than bitwise AND as, although two instructions of the latter type have to be executed per a single instruction of the former type, POPC instructions execute at a quarter the rate of AND instructions. Even when considering a simplified performance model where only the execution of the POPC instruction is taken into account, it can be observed from the achieved results that the performance of the proposal on all GPUs is close to their compute capabilities. Using such simplified model, one can estimate the performance for evaluation of a given dataset from the total number of CUDA cores and boost frequency of each GPU configuration. The different GPU configurations are capable of executing POPC instructions at different rates (see subsection above). Given that each POPC instruction processes 32 patient records for a given genotype out of the 27 allowed genotypes (for a given triplet of SNPs), each GPU configuration has the potential to achieve $1.185\times$ (from $\frac{32}{27}$) the sets of SNPs per patient record processed per second in relation to the rate of POPC instructions executed per second. Therefore, the maximum performance at advertised boost clocks considering only the POPC instruction would be 1343 (GeForce 2070S), 2207 (Titan V), 1800 (Titan Xp), 991 (Titan X) and 1476 ($2\times$ GeForce 980) giga ($\times 10^9$) triplets of SNPs per sample processed per second. For the largest dataset (8000 SNPs and 8000 patients), the proposal achieved 86, 85, 80, 82 and 87 percent of those estimated values, respectively. One can infer from this analysis, which in fact is not even taking into account the cost of executing the AND instructions, that the implementation of the proposal is able to efficiently use the targeted GPUs.

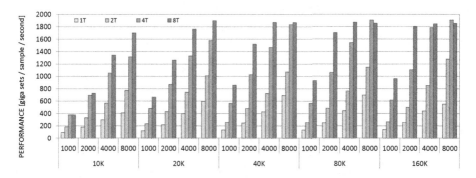

Fig. 6. Effect of the number of combinations to process per round (between 10000 and 160000) and the number of CPU threads (between 1 and 8) on the performance achieved by the proposal on system S2 (Titan V and i9-7900X) considering 4000 SNPs and different numbers of patients (between 1000 and 8000).

Overall, the system with the Titan V (S2) is the fastest at executing the proposal. For the largest dataset, the system S2 achieved 1.63×, 1.30×, 2.31× and 1.12× higher performance than systems S1 (GeForce 2070S), S3 (Titan Xp), S4 (Titan X) and S5 (2× GeForce 980), respectively. The experimentally achieved performance ratios, calculated from comparing performance on all other systems with system S2 (Titan V), are very close to the values that can be predicted based on GPU compute resources and clock frequency. This points to the fact that the execution of the proposal is not being limited by CPU performance.

4.3 Performance Impact of the Number of Combinations per Round and CPU Threads

The number of concurrently executing CPU threads and the number of combinations of SNPs processed per round can have a significant impact on the performance achieved by the proposed approach. Figure 6 depicts the impact, on the system with the Titan V (S2), of setting these parameters, when processing datasets with different numbers of patients. Since datasets with 4000 SNPs have been shown to be sufficient to achieve the maximum performance (see Sect. 4.2), this analysis is focused on examining results for that number of SNPs. System S2 has the CPU with the most cores out of the ones considered in the experiments and the overall most capable GPU. Thus, we will rely on results obtained on that system to demonstrate the importance of the selection of suitable values for these parameters.

The impact on performance of adding more patients observed in the experiments across multiple systems is also observed here. For a given chunk size and number of CPU threads, increasing the amount of patients to process tends to improve performance, as there is more data to process per GPU kernel execution. This allows to better use the available GPU resources. As expected, the increase in performance only happens up to a point. For example, when using

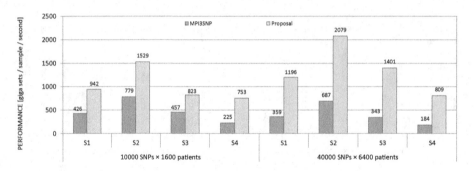

Fig. 7. Number of giga ($\times 10^9$) sets processed per second normalized to the number of patients in the dataset for MPI3SNP and the proposal on different systems.

8 CPU threads and a chunk size of 40000 combinations, going from 4000 patients to 8000 patients did not improve performance. This happens because the GPU kernel is already fully saturated processing the dataset with 4000 patients.

For datasets with the same amount of patients, and for the same chunk size, using more CPU threads tends to result in improved performance, as there are more rounds being concurrently executed. Thus, there is more opportunity to more efficiently utilize the CPU (for generating combination vectors) and the GPU resources (for evaluating combinations) by overlapping execution between the different phases of the proposal, including overlapping computation with memory transfers concerned with the combination vectors from the CPU to the GPU. The few existing outliers where using 8 CPU threads (e.g., 80000 combinations per chunk and 8000 patients) resulted in a small decrease in performance compared with using 4 threads might be explained by additional (or more aggressive) instances of reduction of GPU frequency under heavy load due to power, voltage, and thermal specifications.

For the same number of threads and number of patient records, relying on processing larger chunks (i.e., number of combinations processed per round) tends to result in increased performance for the configurations herein evaluated. More combinations to process per round can help to make each individual kernel execution better use the GPU compute resources. However, saturation is achieved at some point, depending on the number of patients and the number of threads. Note that this does not mean that chunk size can simply be set to an arbitrarily large value. Processing too many combinations per round, in relation to the total amount of combinations to process can result in the number of rounds being too small, at which point parallelism, achieved by concurrently executing rounds, can get severely restricted.

4.4   Comparing Performance with MPI3SNP

Figure 7 depicts results for the systems S1, S2, S3 and S4, comparing the performance archived with the one with MPI3SNP [12]. The performance improvement achieved is 2.21×, 1.96×, 1.80× and 3.35× in comparison with

MPI3SNP, for a dataset with 10000 SNPs and 1600 patients, and 3.33×, 3.03×, 4.09× and 4.39× for a dataset with 40000 SNPs and 6400 patients, on the systems S1 (Xeon E3-1245 V3 + GeForce 2070S), S2 (i9-7900X + Titan V), S3 (i7-4770K + Titan Xp) and S4 (i7-5960X + Titan X). This makes the proposal, on average 2.71×, 2.44×, 2.72× and 3.83× faster on those systems. These experimental results reveal that the proposed approach shows improved behaviour from a performance-wise perspective in comparison to MPI3SNP.

The performance improvement of the proposal in relation to MPI3SNP is higher on the largest dataset. This is consistent with the results of the performance evaluation presented in the previous section, where it is shown that datasets with more patients are more adequately handled by the proposal by better exploiting the available computing resources. Moreover, the system S2 has achieved slightly higher performance when processing the dataset with 4000 SNPs and 6400 samples in comparison with the highest performance achieved in the experiments presented in the previous subsections for other datasets. The Titan V accelerator has achieved higher core clock frequencies on the epistasis detection runs performed in the context of comparing the proposed approach to MPI3SNP due to the use of a clocking strategy (supported from driver version 415.25 onwards) that makes the GPU boosting behavior on the Titan V system similar to that of the other considered CPU+GPU systems.

The wall-clock time required for the evaluation of the dataset with 40000 SNPs and 6400 patients helps at showing the importance of efficiently using all available computing resources. For that dataset, MPI3SNP takes 4 days and 7 hours to completion on the system with the less resourceful CPU+GPU configuration (S4). In contrast, processing that dataset on system S4, by using the proposed approach takes slightly less than a full day.

5   Related Work

Given the combinatorial characteristics and the data-parallel nature of epistasis detection, the methods proposed in the literature can be classified into different categories depending on the targeted computing systems and device architectures. There are approaches aimed at using multicore CPUs [5,7], Intel Xeon Phi accelerators [3,9], GPUs [3–6,12,17–19] and specialized architectures in FPGAs [18]. These approaches can also be categorized based on the interaction order they tackle in the context of epistasis detection. The majority of these state-of-the-art approaches focus on 2-way detection [3,5,7,9,17,17–19], while only rare attempts are made on performing 3-way detection [4,6,12]. Given a set of SNPs to analyze, the evaluation of SNP triplets results in an enormous growth in the number of combinations to be considered when compared to the pairwise evaluation. As such, it is of utmost importance to efficiently leverage the capabilities of computation and memory resources of a given system in order to perform 3-way epistasis detection.

In this paper, the performance of the herein proposed approach is compared with MPI3SNP [12] (a recently published GPU-based approach for 3-way epistasis detection using mutual information as scoring function), achieving considerably higher parallel performance for different datasets. In fact, the performance of the proposal is close to the theoretical maximum across all the GPU architectures considered. This is mainly due to the efficient workload distribution across multi-core CPU and GPU devices, as well as due to the highly optimized nature of the proposed algorithms for data-parallel processing of different SNP combinations on GPU cores. It is also worth to emphasize that significant efforts were made in order to ensure the high-performance calculation of the K2 Bayesian score (the objective function), which is computationally more demanding than the mutual information scoring used in MPI3SNP [12].

Another distinctive aspect lies in the way the workload is scheduled/distributed between the different processors and/or accelerators. For instance, the herein proposed approach differs from related work that employs matrix operations to combine SNP data, such as [6] or [11], which may attain high performance for certain dataset types by relying on General Matrix Multiply (GEMM) or similar matrix operations. However, these approaches require sufficiently large datasets to achieve efficiency, in order to ensure near-maximum performance of the GEMM kernels, as well as to minimize the impact of inefficient resource utilization when evaluating non-unique combinations.

6   Conclusions

Epistasis detection is a computationally challenging problem that has been attracting increased research efforts in recent years. In order to deal with this problem, this paper introduced a high-performance GPU+CPU hybrid approach for exhaustively identifying 3-way epistatic interactions according to the Bayesian K2 criterion. The proposed approach relies on the exploitation of architectural differences between CPU and GPU to orchestrate the key tasks involved in these biological analyses, defining the scope of the execution according to the properties of each operation and the characteristics of the underlying hardware.

The results of an experimental campaign covering different possible dataset shapes (i.e., more SNPs than patients, and vice versa) and sizes are presented. The achieved results show that the proposal is very close at extracting maximum performance out of all five targeted GPU+CPU configurations. The proposed method achieves high performance on 3-way searches in relation to other approaches that do the same amount of core computations for calculating the genotype frequency tables regarding all-to-all combinations of SNPs and which do not rely on specialized cores (e.g., tensor cores or specialized hardware in FPGAs). Compared with MPI3SNP [12], a recently published GPU-based approach, the proposal has been evaluated to be on average $3.83\times$, $2.72\times$, $2.44\times$ and $2.71\times$ faster at evaluating all unique combinations of SNPs, on systems with Xeon, i7 and i9 CPU architectures paired with a Titan X (Maxwell 2.0), a Titan Xp (Pascal), a Titan V (Volta) and a GeForce 2070S (Turing), respectively.

Ongoing work includes an extension of the proposed approach to support multiple nodes in a cluster configuration. Using as a baseline the method herein presented, inter-node processing and load balancing strategies will be integrated to exploit the characteristics of these systems, in the pursuit of highly efficient, higher-order epistasis detection.

References

1. Buckles, B.P., Lybanon, M.: Algorithm 515: Generation of a vector from the lexicographical index [g6]. ACM Trans. Math. Softw. **3**(2), 180–182 (1977). https://doi.org/10.1145/355732.355739
2. Cooper, G.F., Herskovits, E.: A bayesian method for the induction of probabilistic networks from data. Mach. Learn. **9**, 309–347 (1992). https://doi.org/10.1007/BF00994110
3. González-Domínguez, J., Ramos, S., Touriño, J., Schmidt, B.: Parallel pairwise epistasis detection on heterogeneous computing architectures. IEEE Trans. Parallel Dist. Syst. **27**, 2329–2340 (2016). https://doi.org/10.1109/TPDS.2015.2460247
4. González-Domínguez, J., Schmidt, B.: GPU-accelerated exhaustive search for third-order epistatic interactions in case-control studies. J. Comput. Sci. **8**, 93–100 (2015). https://doi.org/10.1016/j.jocs.2015.04.001
5. Goudey, B., et al.: High performance computing enabling exhaustive analysis of higher order single nucleotide polymorphism interaction in genome wide association studies. Health Inf. Sci. Syst. **3**, S3 (2015). https://doi.org/10.1186/2047-2501-3-S1-S3
6. Joubert, W., et al.: Attacking the opioid epidemic: Determining the epistatic and pleiotropic genetic architectures for chronic pain and opioid addiction. In: Proceedings of the International Conference for High Performance Computing, Networking, Storage, and Analysis. pp. 57:1–57:14. SC 2018, IEEE Press, Piscataway, NJ, USA (2018). https://doi.org/10.1109/SC.2018.00060
7. Kässens, J.C., González-Domínguez, J., Wienbrandt, L., Schmidt, B.: UPC++ for bioinformatics: A case study using genome-wide association studies. In: 2014 IEEE International Conference on Cluster Computing (CLUSTER). pp. 248–256 (2014). https://doi.org/10.1109/CLUSTER.2014.6968770
8. Lin, Z., et al.: Genetic association and epistatic interaction of the interleukin-10 signaling pathway in pediatric inflammatory bowel disease. World J. Gastroenterol. **23**(27), 4897–4909 (2017). https://doi.org/10.3748/wjg.v23.i27.4897
9. Luecke, G.R., et al.: Fast epistasis detection in large-scale GWAS for Intel Xeon Phi clusters. In: 2015 IEEE Trustcom/BigDataSE/ISPA. pp. 228–235 (2015). https://doi.org/10.1109/Trustcom.2015.637
10. Niel, C., et al.: A survey about methods dedicated to epistasis detection. Front. Genetics **6**(285), 1–19 (2015). https://doi.org/10.3389/fgene.2015.00285
11. Nobre, R., Ilic, A., Santander-Jiménez, S., Sousa, L.: Exploring the binary precision capabilities of tensor cores for epistasis detection. In: 2020 IEEE International Parallel and Distributed Processing Symposium (IPDPS). pp. 338–347 (2020). https://doi.org/10.1109/IPDPS47924.2020.00043
12. Ponte-Fernández, C., González-DomíÂnguez, J., MartíÂn, M.J.: Fast search of third-order epistatic interactions on cpu and gpu clusters. Int. J. High Perform. Comput. Appl. **34**(1), 20–29 (2020). https://doi.org/10.1177/1094342019852128
13. Ritchie, M.D.: Finding the epistasis needles in the genome-wide haystack. In: Moore, J.H., Williams, S.M. (eds.) Epistasis. MMB, vol. 1253, pp. 19–33. Springer, New York (2015). https://doi.org/10.1007/978-1-4939-2155-3_2

14. Ritchie, H., et al.: Multifactor-dimensionality reduction reveals high-order inter-actions among estrogen-metabolism genes in sporadic breast cancer. Am. J. Hum. Genet. **69**(1), 138–147 (2001). https://doi.org/10.1086/321276

15. Sun, Y., et al.: epiACO - a method for identifying epistasis based on ant colony opti-mization algorithm. BioData mining **10**, 23–23 (2017). https://doi.org/10.1186/s13040-017-0143-7

16. Wan, X., et al.: BOOST: a fast approach to detecting gene-gene interactions in genome-wide case-control studies. Am. J. Hum. Genet. **87**, 325–340 (2010). https://doi.org/10.1016/j.ajhg.2010.07.021

17. Wang, Q., et al.: GWISFI: A universal GPU interface for exhaustive search of pairwise interactions in case-control GWAS in minutes. In: 2014 IEEE Interna-tional Conference on Bioinformatics and Biomedicine (BIBM). pp. 403–409 (2014). https://doi.org/10.1109/BIBM.2014.6999192

18. Wienbrandt, L., Kässens, J.C., Hübenthal, M., Ellinghaus, D.: 1000x faster than PLINK: Combined FPGA and GPU accelerators for logistic regression-based detec-tion of epistasis. J. Comput. Sci. **30**, 183–193 (2019). https://doi.org/10.1016/j.jocs.2018.12.013

19. Yung, L.S., Yang, C., Wan, X., Yu, W.: GBOOST. Bioinf. **27**, 1309–1310 (2011). https://doi.org/10.1093/bioinformatics/btr114

20. Zubenko, G.S., Hughes, H.B.R., Zubenko, W.N.:: D10s1423 identifies a susceptibil-ity locus for alzheimer's disease (ad7) in a prospective, longitudinal, double-blind study of asymptomatic individuals: results at 14 years. Am. J. Med. Genet. Part B Neuropsychiatric Genet. **153**(2), 359–364 (2010). https://doi.org/10.1002/ajmg.b.31017

Walltime Prediction and Its Impact on Job Scheduling Performance and Predictability

Dalibor Klusáček[1(✉)] and Mehmet Soysal[2]

[1] CESNET a.l.e., Brno, Czech Republic
klusacek@cesnet.cz
[2] Steinbuch Centre for Computing, Karlsruhe Institute of Technology,
Karlsruhe, Germany
mehmet.soysal@kit.edu

Abstract. For more than two decades researchers have been analyzing the impact of inaccurate job walltime (runtime) estimates on the performance of job scheduling algorithms, especially the backfilling. In this paper, we extend these existing works by focusing on the overall impact that improved walltime estimates have both on *job scheduling performance* and *predictability*. For this purpose, we evaluate such impact in several steps. First, we present a simple walltime predictor and analyze its accuracy with respect to original user walltime estimates captured in real-life workload traces. Next, we use these traces and a simulator to see what is the impact of improved estimates on general performance (backfilling ratio and wait time) as well as predictability. We show that even a simple predictor can significantly decrease user-based errors in runtime estimates, while also slightly improving job wait times and backfilling ratio. Concerning predictions, we show that walltime predictor significantly decreases errors in job wait time forecasting while having little effect on the ability of the scheduler to provide solid advance predictions about which nodes will be used by a given waiting job.

Keywords: Job · Scheduling · Backfilling · Walltime estimate · Prediction

1 Introduction

This paper is focusing on the problem of inaccurate job runtime estimates as provided by users. We use existing results [6,10,13] and we try to understand the impact that inaccuracy has on various aspects of job scheduling performance. Importantly, we study whether a technique improving runtime estimates has some significant impact on system's behavior. For this purpose, we use a simple runtime predictor which we have developed on our own. This predictor uses historic data to generate runtime estimates for newly arriving jobs. Althought it has been developed on our own in 2018, we have learned recently that our predictor uses similar idea to the predictor used in the past [12].

© Springer Nature Switzerland AG 2020
D. Klusáček et al. (Eds.): JSSPP 2020, LNCS 12326, pp. 127–144, 2020.
https://doi.org/10.1007/978-3-030-63171-0_7

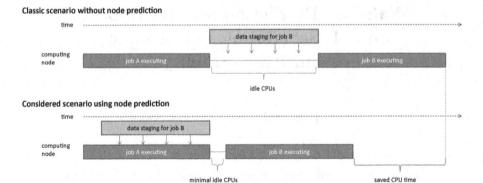

Fig. 1. Normal scenario for data staging is wasting CPU cycles during data staging (top). Considered solution relying on accurate node predictions uses advance data staging onto compute node(s) before job start, reducing idle CPU time (bottom).

The main contribution of this paper is as follows. First, we demonstrate that even simple predictor can significantly improve inaccurate job runtime estimates (Sect. 2). Second, we use detailed simulations to analyze the impact of refined estimates on the job scheduling performance. We analyze how the improved estimates impact the number of backfilled jobs and job wait times (Sect. 3). Last but not least, in Sect. 4 we analyze deeply if refined runtime estimates can improve predictability of system behavior. To achieve this goal we use two different scenarios. In the first one, we analyze the accuracy of job waiting time predictions (Sect. 4.1). This scenario obviously focuses on system users that naturally want to know how long their jobs will have to wait before being processed by the system, i.e., here the question is "when will a job start?". In the second scenario (Sect. 4.2) we analyze the ability of the scheduler to correctly predict (in advance) which node(s) will be selected for each waiting job. In this case, instead of focusing on the question "when?" we rather try to answer the question "where?".

The motivation here is related to jobs requiring either large amount of data and/or jobs requiring special pre-processing, e.g., an ad hoc and independent local file system. In both cases, the time needed to either stage the data and/or setup the file system can cause temporarily low CPU utilization. Our goal is to determine whether it is possible to stage the data and/or deploy the local file system in advance, thus limiting idle CPU time. Obviously, to make this advance staging/setup possible, the scheduler must provide rather accurate advance job allocations (ahead of actual job start). We illustrate the benefit of this approach in Fig. 1 and later describe in full detail in Sect. 4.2.

2 Job Walltimes, User Estimates and Predictor

In this paper, job walltime (or job runtime) denotes the time it takes to execute the job on a computing node(s). This time is not known in advance. Instead, user is requested to provide an estimate for each job. This walltime estimate is used as an upper bound by the resource manager, i.e., job is killed when its actual runtime exceeds the walltime estimate. It is not surprising that in practice these walltime estimates are therefore very inaccurate and overestimated in order to prevent jobs from being killed [3,8]. This causes the relatively high overestimation. Second, scheduling systems also frequently classify jobs according to some default runtime limits. For example, there can be different job queues with different maximum job runtime defaults. Frequently, these default runtime values are then used by many jobs due to users laziness. As a result, most jobs in the system use only few common estimates and therefore "look similar" to the scheduling algorithm (e.g., backfilling).

2.1   Workload Traces

In the remainder of this paper we will be using four different real-life workload traces that come from the Karlsruhe Institue of Technology in Germany (FH1 and FH2), Cornell Theory Center (CTC SP2) and San Diego Supercomputer Center (SDSC SP2). These traces can be obtained at Parallel Workloads Archive [2]. We begin our analysis by showing how user-based estimates are inaccurate and overestimated in all four considered workloads.

This is captured in Fig. 2, which shows the cumulative distribution functions (CDF) of actual runtimes and user estimated job walltimes (blue and red line, respectively). Clearly, user-provided walltime estimates are (very) inaccurate and overestimated. Therefore, we introduce a simple walltime predictor, which tries to refine these overly long estimates by more accurate values.

2.2   Walltime Predictor and Its Performance

The considered walltime predictor is working on a per-user basis, i.e., a new runtime estimate for a given job of a user is computed using information about previous jobs of that user.

The predictor is an extended version of the predictor used in our previous work [4]. It measures the fraction of job's actual runtime and user's estimate (see $usage_{wall}$ in Formula 1), i.e., it measures to what extent the estimated walltime ($est\_walltime$) was actually used. Since the user's estimate is the upper bound of job runtime, $usage_{wall}$ falls between 0.0 and 1.0 representing the relative usage of requested walltime. In other words, the technique measures by how much a user overestimates job's runtime, which is similar to what has been used in [12].

$$usage_{wall}(job_i) = \frac{runtime(job_i)}{est\_walltime(job_i)} \tag{1}$$

$$predicted\_wall(job_i) = est\_walltime(job_i) \cdot \max_{i-5 \le k \le i-1} usage_{wall}(job_k) \tag{2}$$

Once the $usage_{wall}$ is computed, it is stored to be used in the future, i.e., once a new job of this user arrives in the system. When this happens, the

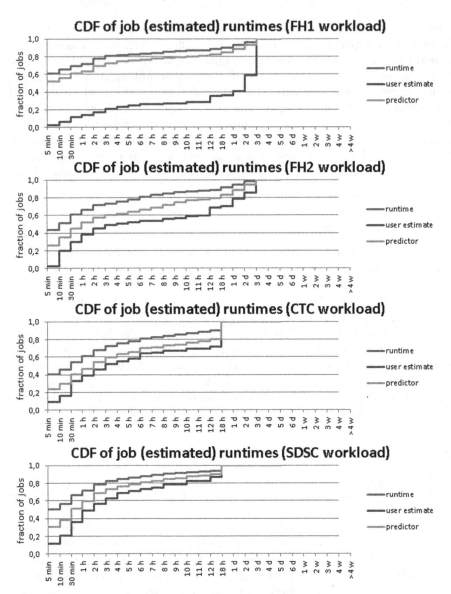

Fig. 2. Cumulative distribution functions (CDF) of actual runtimes, user estimated walltimes and predicted job walltimes for all four workloads (Color figure online).

five most recent $usage_{wall}$ values are considered and their maximum is chosen[1]. The job's walltime estimate is then multiplied by this maximum (see Formula 2) and the resulting $predicted\_wall$ is the predictor's output. It represents

---

[1] In case that a given user has either no or less than five completed jobs then we use the user-provided estimate or those few already completed jobs, respectively.

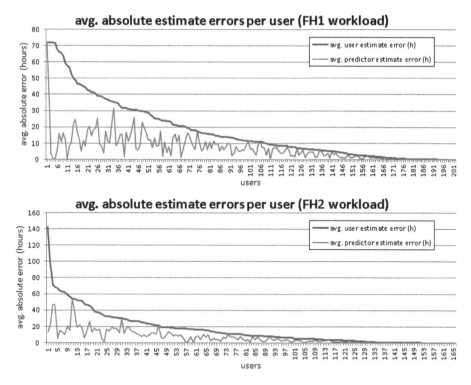

Fig. 3. Avg. absolute errors of runtime predictions (per user) with respect to the walltime being used (user estimate, predictor).

a conservative strategy, where the predicted walltime is calculated using the known relative accuracy of user's recent estimates. By choosing the maximum $usage_{wall}$ (i.e., choosing a job where the difference between actual and estimated runtime was minimal), this technique aims to minimize the number of cases where the new predicted walltime will be underestimated. At the same time, by ignoring older jobs it reflects aging and orients itself more on the recent user's workload characteristics. When a job turns out to be underestimated ($predicted\_wall(job_i) < runtime(job_i)$) the predictor increases its initial estimate by a factor of two. It does so (over the time) until the estimate is sufficient (and job completes) or until the estimate meets the original user estimate (this is still a hard limit which cannot be exceeded).

The impact of the predictor can be observed in Fig. 2 (green line). Clearly, the over-estimated user-based walltimes are now distributed closely to what is the real distribution of actual runtimes (blue line). The improving effect is especially visible when the user-based estimates are very bad, which is the case for the FH1 and also FH2 workloads.

We also analyzed, how our simple predictor performs with respect to *individual users*. Therefore, we have computed the average absolute errors of both

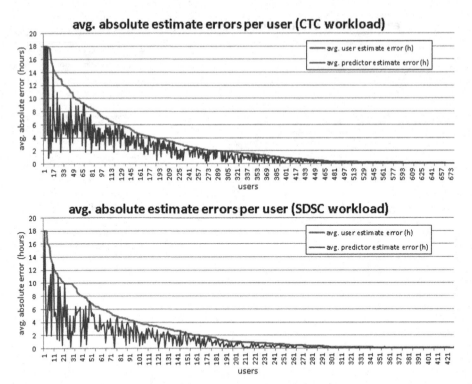

Fig. 4. Avg. absolute errors of runtime predictions (per user) with respect to the walltime being used (user estimate, predictor).

user-based estimates and predictor-based walltimes per each user in the system and plotted these pairs in a line chart which we show in Figs. 3–4 (users on the x-axis are ordered according to the average user estimate error).

These figures illustrate that for some users our simple predictor is not able to reduce the average error very well. Still, it decreases the errors compared to those user-based walltimes quite successfully. Clearly, some users are really poor in judging the duration of their jobs, providing estimates that are (on average) several hours or even days longer than necessary. From this point of view, even a simple predictor like the one we presented makes a good sense to use.

3   Impact on Job Scheduling Performance

So far, we have demonstrated using several existing workload traces that predictor can improve the accuracy of walltime estimates. This section uses detailed simulations to analyze the impact of walltime predictor on the performance of the system. For this purpose, each of those four systems is modeled in Alea simulator [5] and the workload is replayed. For comparison, simulations use either perfect estimates (i.e., exact job runtimes are used), user-provided or predictor-generated estimates to build the job schedule, respectively.

3.1   Scheduling Policy

In all experiments we use *conservative backfilling* [8] as it heavily relies on provided estimates. The schedule is built using available runtime estimates (perfect, user-provided or predictor-based, respectively). In case a job finishes earlier than expected, the schedule is updated using schedule compression algorithm [8]. During the update, jobs are checked one by one and a start time of each job is adjusted, i.e., it is moved into the earliest possible time slot with respect to previously adjusted jobs (compression phase). Similarly, if a job's runtime is underestimated, it is first prolonged (see the discussion in Sect. 2.2) and then the existing schedule is updated, i.e., jobs are reinserted using same mechanism as during the aforementioned compression phase.

3.2   Metrics and Results

As our performance indicators we measure the percentage of *backfilled jobs* and the distribution of job *wait times*. Let us first discuss the impact of improved estimates on the backfilling ratio. The intuition suggests that with more accurate estimates (and even more with perfectly known runtimes) the ratio of backfilled jobs should increase. Conversely, when using inaccurate, user-provided and overestimated walltimes, the backfilling ratio should be significantly lower since most jobs "appear to be too long" for existing gaps. The results we obtained (see Fig. 5) seem to follow this expectation but the differences are not very dramatic.

Figure 5 shows the percentage of backfilled jobs with respect to the accuracy of estimates being used. With the exception of FH1 workload, there is only slight improvement in the backfilling ratio when accurate or predictor-based walltimes are used. The difference between FH1 and remaining workloads is most likely caused by the very bad original user-based estimates available in FH1. As can be seen in Fig. 2 (top), FH1 has the worst user-based estimates among all workloads. It is important to understand that improved walltimes do not guarantee higher backfill ratio. In fact, with better walltime estimates, not only individual jobs

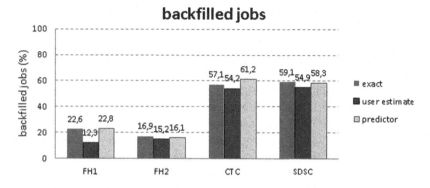

Fig. 5. The percentage of backfilled jobs with respect to the walltime being used (exact runtime, user estimate, predictor).

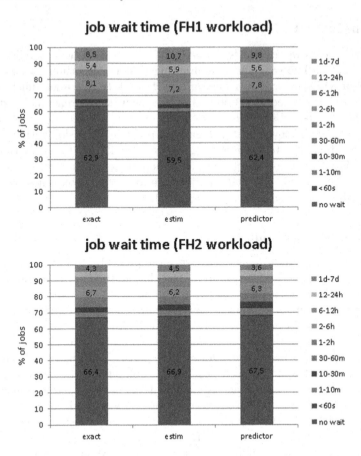

Fig. 6. Distribution of job wait times with respect to the walltime being used (exact runtime, user estimate, predictor).

"look shorter" but also all available holes in the schedule become "shorter" as job runtimes are less overestimated. Therefore, the probability that a job will be backfilled within existing holes is only slightly higher when estimates are better[2].

We also measured the impact of improved walltime estimates on the distribution of job wait times which is captured in Figs. 6 and 7. The main general difference between these two figures is the large amount of jobs that start immediately (see Fig. 6). This is caused by the relatively smaller backlog of waiting jobs compared to the CTC and SDCS workloads (see Fig. 7). Other than that, most of the workloads show that user-based inaccurate estimates are associated with worse distribution of job wait times, i.e., more jobs fall into categories representing long waiting. As soon as the predictor is used, we see a common tendency where job wait times are decreased.

---

[2] With the exception of poor user-based estimates as shown in case of FH1 workload.

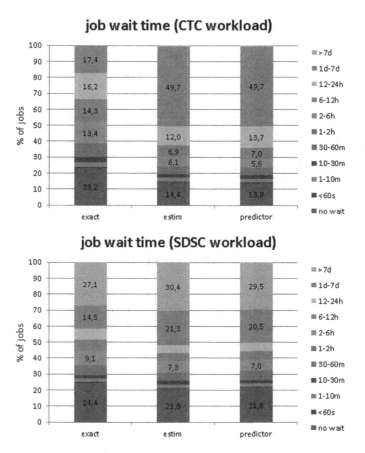

Fig. 7. Distribution of job wait times with respect to the walltime being used (exact runtime, user estimate, predictor).

The only exception is the CTC workload (see Fig. 7 (top)), where the use of predictor does not produce better distribution of job wait times, instead it stays very close to the one dictated by user-provided estimates. This phenomenon has been observed in the past, e.g., in [1,3] and deeply explained in [13] (using the same CTC workload trace). Apart from the explanation provided in [13], we would like to add that metrics like wait time can be easily influenced by even subtle changes in the job processing ordering. Job execution order can be easily manipulated either purposely (e.g., via fair-sharing mechanism) or "accidentally", e.g., as a side effect of using the predictor. Predictor's estimates may shuffle the order in which jobs are executed as backfilling tends to prefer shorter jobs. Clearly, this *shortest job first*-like scheduling reduces average wait time.

Figure 8 shows a hypothetical example of three different schedules that are however composed of the same set of jobs. All three schedules have the same makespan ($C_{max} = 10$ time units) but exhibit very different job wait times.

This figure illustrates the impact of job ordering in a somewhat extreme scale, yet we believe it illustrates nicely that metrics like wait time may oscillate quite wildly.

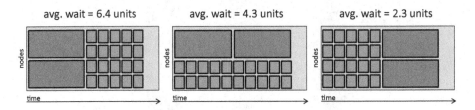

Fig. 8. The impact of job execution ordering on job wait times.

4   Impact on Accuracy of Predictions

This section is focusing on the ability of the scheduling system to provide predictions concerning job wait times and future job-to-node allocations. First, we analyze the accuracy of wait time predictions in Sect. 4.1. Next, Sect. 4.2 focuses on the impact that (in) accurate walltime estimates have on the capability of the job scheduler to provide advance node predictions for waiting jobs, i.e., the ability to correctly predict where a waiting job will be executed.

4.1   Wait Time Predictions

It is quite convenient when the scheduling system is able to provide information when a given job is likely to start executing. This is especially useful for interactive jobs. Although the system can use a scheduler-independent solution like QBETS [9], we use this section to analyze the accuracy of predictions that the scheduler can provide on its own. In this case, the scheduler is using the schedule (built by conservative backfilling) to estimate how long a job will wait before its execution will start. Since these wait times can be continuously refined (shortened) as jobs are completing earlier and the schedule is compressed, we use the initial estimate returned by the scheduler at the moment of job arrival. This can be seen as the first "response" the user gets when he or she submits the job. The accuracy of predictions is measured by computing the absolute error of predicted wait time with respect to the actual job wait time.

Figure 9 shows the absolute errors in predicted job wait times when using either user-provided walltime estimates or the predictor-based estimates. It nicely illustrates the ability of the predictor to decrease the prediction error. This is mostly visible in case of FH1 and FH2 workloads which have the worst user-based estimates (see Fig. 2 and related discussion). From this point of view, predictor-based estimates can deliver much better predictions of job waiting times, thus giving the users more optimistic responses concerning when their workloads will be executed.

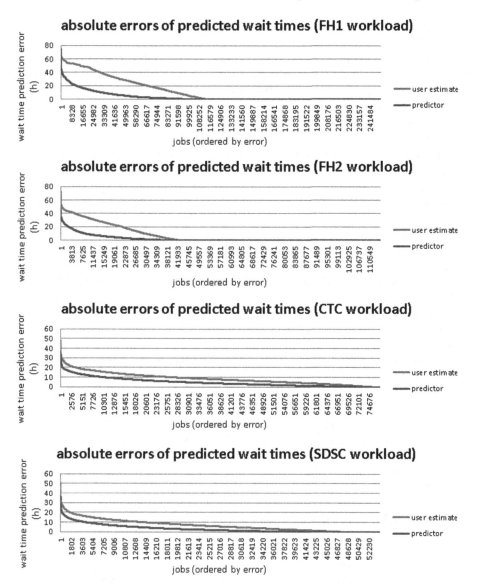

Fig. 9. Absolute errors in predicted wait times of jobs when using either user-estimated walltimes or predictor.

4.2   Node Allocation Predictions

The ability to predict node(s) for waiting job in advance can be very useful. If the target node(s) is known for reasonably long time (e.g., at least a few minutes ahead) this time can be used to stage all job-related data in advance, thus saving

CPU cycles. Also, if needed, local ad hoc file system can be setup for a waiting job in advance. We have illustrated this approach in Fig. 1.

This section analyzes whether it is feasible to predict the target node(s) ahead. More specifically, we measure for how long the target node has been known prior job start. We called this time period *Valid Node Allocation Time Period* and denote it as T_{node}. To sum up, for each job the T_{node} is computed as the difference between job start time and the time when the final accurate prediction has been made (i.e., the one that was correct). In case a job starts immediately after its submission, T_{node} is equal to zero. Otherwise, the job is waiting and the scheduler is adding that job into the schedule. If perfect walltime estimates (exact runtimes) are used, the schedule being built is accurate and can be used to correctly predict target node(s) for jobs in advance. However, since job walltime estimates are inaccurate, the schedule is constantly adapting to jobs finishing at different times than previously predicted. This impedes the effort of the scheduler to provide reasonably accurate node predictions as planned node and time allocations can change virtually at any time. As we have shown in our earlier work [11], with inaccurate estimates only a small portion of jobs can achieve accurate predictions, i.e., only a fraction of jobs gets a reasonably high (useful) T_{node}.

T_{node} is also negatively influenced (reduced) by backfilling approach [11]. As demonstrated in Fig. 10, jobs being backfilled can distort previous node allocations, thus decreasing T_{node} for those jobs being affected. Therefore, instead of backfilling, we use simple First Come First Served (FCFS) policy to built the job schedule in this use case. This means that existing holes in the schedule are not being filled with later arriving jobs in order to reduce the negative effect observed in backfilling. FCFS policy simply finds the earliest available free slot *at the end of the schedule*, without searching for possible gaps within the existing schedule. For example, if FCFS was used in the scenario presented in Fig. 10 instead of backfilling, FCFS would place *new job* behind job #5 leaving all preceding gaps unused.

Moreover, we have extended the approach used in our previous paper [11] and developed a significant extension to the scheduling policy, which allows us to "pin" jobs to their planned nodes if their predicted start time is near enough.

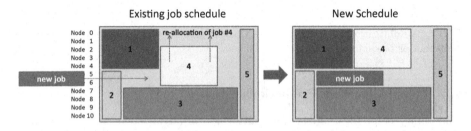

Fig. 10. An example of backfilling distorting previous node allocations for job #4 as a result of its "gap filling" approach.

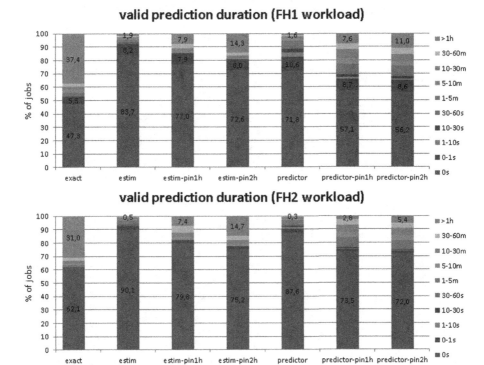

Fig. 11. Distribution of durations of valid node predictions (T_{node}) with respect to the pinning interval (none, 1 h, 2 h) and walltime being used (exact runtime, user estimate, predictor).

In other words, if a job is about to start soon (e.g., during 1 h) we do not allow the scheduler to change the planned nodes for this job. Thus this job's node allocation is fixed and its T_{node} cannot decrease. Without node-pinning, jobs can be shifted to different nodes — e.g., as a result of early job completion and the following schedule compression procedure. This reshuffling of the whole schedule then destroys existing predictions while reseting all corresponding T_{node} values to zero. Therefore, pinning helps to keep predictions valid subject to inaccuracies in the job schedule. In our implementation, node-pinning is only activated when the planned job's start time is within a given "pinning interval" x, i.e., that job is planned to be executed within next x minutes.

In the following text, using a series of experiments, we analyze how the T_{node} values are distributed with respect to varying accuracies of walltime estimates (exact, user-estimated, predictor). We also measure what is the effect of the newly developed node-pinning functionality. For this purpose, we analyze the effect of either no node-pinning or pinning with short interval ($x = 1$ h) or pinning with long interval ($x = 2$ h). Since the absence of backfilling and the use

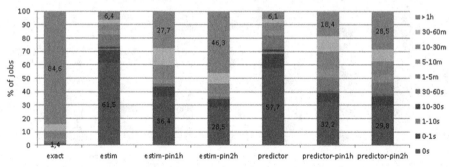

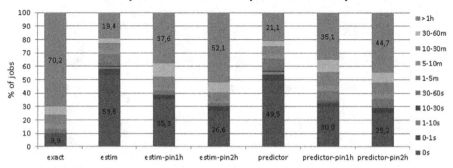

Fig. 12. Distribution of durations of valid node predictions (T_{node}) with respect to the pinning interval (none, 1h, 2h) and walltime being used (exact runtime, user estimate, predictor)

of node-pinning can potentially lead to poor performance, we also measure this impact by comparing job wait times of all considered scenarios.

Figures 11–12 shows the durations of valid node predictions (distribution of T_{node} values) with respect to the pinning interval (none, 1 h, 2 h) and walltime being used (exact runtime, user estimate, predictor). From these distributions we can quickly identify the positive effect that node-pinning has on the ability of the scheduler to provide reasonable advance node predictions. On the other hand, the effect of predictor is rather moderate. It does show positive effect in case of FH1 workload (the one having worst user-based estimates) as it significantly increases the fraction of jobs that have $T_{node} > 0$ s. Moderate positive effect can be seen for FH2, CTC and SDSC workloads (comparing estim vs. predictor). However, in most cases the largest benefit is evidently achieved through node-pinning rather than through improved walltime estimates.

The node-pinning functionality developed in this work sadly has some obvious drawbacks. Since we do not use backfilling, nodes can easily become underutilized when waiting jobs are already pinned to different (busy) CPUs. To measure the

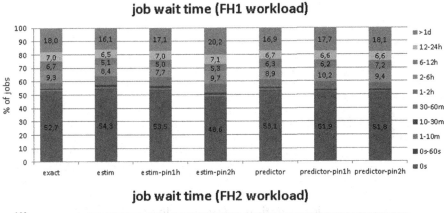

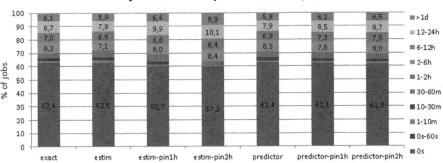

Fig. 13. Distribution of job wait times with respect to the pinning interval and wall-time being used.

impact, we provide Figs. 13–14 that show wait time distributions corresponding to the experiments focusing on node predictability.

Clearly, the effect of FCFS policy (even increased by node-pinning) is heavily influencing the wait time distributions as can be seen by comparing these distributions to those observed for "pure" backfilling in Figs. 6–7. FCFS worsened waiting times while node-pinning added even more delays. Also, it is worth noticing that the accuracy of estimates plays smaller role in this use case since the FCFS policy is less dependent on the quality of estimates than conservative backfilling used in Sect. 3.

4.3   Summary

To sum this use case, we have shown that proposed node-pinning extensions of the FCFS policy along with the predictor help to increase node predictability (higher T_{node} values) but at the expense of deteriorated wait times and poorer utilization. This clearly is not a desirable outcome and it leaves the problem open for further research. At the same time, we have seen that when using accurate walltimes reasonable node predictions are achievable and for many jobs their

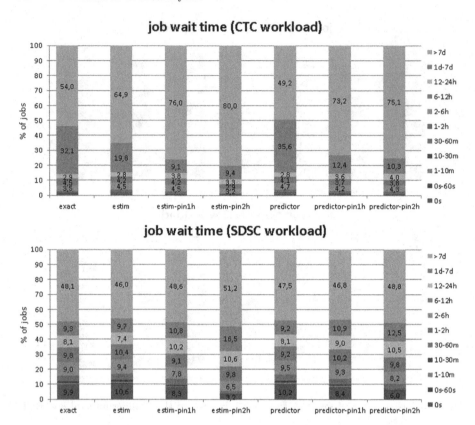

Fig. 14. Distribution of job wait times with respect to the pinning interval and walltime being used.

T_{node} is sufficiently long to allow for advance data staging. There are several classes of computations where job runtimes can be predicted very accurately and advance data staging is very useful due to the large size of input data. One such type of computation represents, e.g., the processing (converting) of raw video data.

Also, not all jobs probably require such a special treatment, i.e., only truly data-demanding jobs benefit from advance data staging. Therefore, it would be interesting to pin only these data-heavy jobs and use the remaining jobs to efficiently "fill the holes", i.e., use selective backfilling. Our results show that the benefits of FCFS does not overweight its poorer performance.

5   Conclusion and Future Work

In this work we have studied walltime estimates and the use of a simple walltime predictor with respect to their impact on several different aspects of job scheduling. This analysis focused on the predictor's accuracy and the effect it has on system performance and predictability. Our main findings are summarized in the following list:

- Even simple predictor improves the accuracy of walltimes
- Better accuracy improves backfilling opportunities but the effect is not dramatic
- Wait time can be slightly reduced with better estimates (but other effects play role)
- Significant improvement can be achieved in wait time predictions
- With the existing predictor, node allocations cannot be predicted very well
- Better node predictions can be achieved by using heavily modified FCFS-based scheduler using "node-pinning", however job waiting times then deteriorate heavily.

In the future, we want to implement more advanced predictors as well as test them in practice using the PBS Pro system being used in the Czech national computing infrastructure *MetaCentrum* [7]. Also, we would like to further improve our node-pinning policy and introduce selective backfilling which should reduce the negative impact on job wait times and utilization. Another promising, yet more demanding, way is to design "node-aware" scheduling algorithm, which takes node prediction into account. For example, the new algorithm can try to place each job so as to overlap with the minimal number of previous jobs, thus limiting constant job re-allocations upon early job completions. In the example of Fig. 10, this would suggest placing job #4 as continuing job #1 from the outset, instead of having it use nodes that had previously been assigned to both job #1 and job #2.

Acknowledgments. We acknowledge the support and computational resources supplied by the project "e-Infrastruktura CZ" (e-INFRA LM2018140) provided within the program Projects of Large Research, Development and Innovations Infrastructures, and the project Reg. No. CZ.02.1.01/0.0/0.0/16_013/0001797 co-funded by the Ministry of Education, Youth and Sports of the Czech Republic. We also highly appreciate the access to the workload traces provided by the Parallel Workloads Archive and the Karlsruhe Institute of Technology.

References

1. Chiang, S.-H., Arpaci-Dusseau, A., Vernon, M.K.: The impact of more accurate requested runtimes on production job scheduling performance. In: Feitelson, D.G., Rudolph, L., Schwiegelshohn, U. (eds.) JSSPP 2002. LNCS, vol. 2537, pp. 103–127. Springer, Heidelberg (2002). https://doi.org/10.1007/3-540-36180-4_7
2. Feitelson, D.G.: Parallel workloads archive, February 2018. http://www.cs.huji.ac.il/labs/parallel/workload/
3. Feitelson, D.G., Weil, A.M.: Utilization and predictability in scheduling the IBM SP2 with backfilling. In: 12th International Parallel Processing Symposium, pp. 542–546. IEEE (1998)

4. Klusáček, D., Chlumský, V.: Evaluating the impact of soft walltimes on job scheduling performance. In: Dalibor Klusáček, N.D., Walfredo C., (eds.) Job Scheduling Strategies for Parallel Processing, vol. 11332, pp. 15–38. Springer (2018). https://doi.org/10.1007/978-3-030-10632-4_2

5. Klusáček, D., Tóth, V., Podolníková, G.: Complex job scheduling simulations with Alea 4. In: Ninth EAI International Conference on Simulation Tools and Techniques (SimuTools 2016), pp. 124–129. ACM (2016)

6. Bailey Lee, C., Schwartzman, Y., Hardy, J., Snavely, A.: Are user runtime estimates inherently inaccurate? In: Feitelson, D.G., Rudolph, L., Schwiegelshohn, U. (eds.) JSSPP 2004. LNCS, vol. 3277, pp. 253–263. Springer, Heidelberg (2005). https://doi.org/10.1007/11407522_14

7. MetaCentrum, September 2020. http://www.metacentrum.cz/

8. Mu'alem, A.W., Feitelson, D.G.: Utilization, predictability, workloads, and user runtime estimates in scheduling the IBM SP2 with backfilling. IEEE Trans. Parallel Distrib. Syst. **12**(6), 529–543 (2001)

9. Nurmi, D., Brevik, J., Wolski, R.: QBETS: queue bounds estimation from time series. In: Frachtenberg, E., Schwiegelshohn, U. (eds.) JSSPP 2007. LNCS, vol. 4942, pp. 76–101. Springer, Heidelberg (2008). https://doi.org/10.1007/978-3-540-78699-3_5

10. Smith, W., Taylor, V., Foster, I.: Using run-time predictions to estimate queue wait times and improve scheduler performance. In: Feitelson, D.G., Rudolph, L. (eds.) JSSPP 1999. LNCS, vol. 1659, pp. 202–219. Springer, Heidelberg (1999). https://doi.org/10.1007/3-540-47954-6_11

11. Soysal, M., Berghoff, M., Klusáček, M., Streit, A.: On the quality of wall time estimates for resource allocation prediction. In: ICPP 2019: 48th International Conference on Parallel Processing: Workshops (2019)

12. Tang, W., Desai, N., Buettner, D., Lan, Z.: Analyzing and adjusting user runtime estimates to improve job scheduling on the Blue Gene/P. In: IEEE International Symposium on Parallel and Distributed Processing (IPDPS), pp. 1–11. IEEE (2010)

13. Tsafrir, D.: Using inaccurate estimates accurately. In: Frachtenberg, E., Schwiegelshohn, U. (eds.) JSSPP 2010. LNCS, vol. 6253, pp. 208–221. Springer, Heidelberg (2010). https://doi.org/10.1007/978-3-642-16505-4_12

PDAWL: Profile-Based Iterative Dynamic Adaptive WorkLoad Balance on Heterogeneous Architectures

Tongsheng Geng[1(✉)], Marcos Amaris[2], Stéphane Zuckerman[3], Alfredo Goldman[2], Guang R. Gao[4], and Jean-Luc Gaudiot[1]

[1] University of California, Irvine, CA, USA
{tgeng,gaudiot}@uci.edu
[2] University of São Paulo, São Paulo, Brazil
{amaris,gold}@ime.usp.br
[3] Laboratoire ETIS, CY Paris Universités, ENSEA, CNRS, Paris, France
stephane.zuckerman@ensea.fr
[4] University of Delaware, Delaware, USA
ggao.capsl@gmail.com

Abstract. While High Performance Computing systems are increasingly based on heterogeneous cores, their effectiveness depends on how well the scheduler can allocate workloads onto appropriate computing devices and how communication and computation can be overlapped. With different types of resources integrated into one system, the complexity of the scheduler correspondingly increases. Moreover, for applications with varying problem sizes on different heterogeneous resources, the optimal scheduling approach may vary accordingly. We thus present PDAWL, an event-driven profile-based Iterative Dynamic Adaptive Work-Load balance scheduling approach to dynamically and adaptively adjust workload to efficiently utilize heterogeneous resources. It combines online scheduling (DAWL), which can adaptively adjust workload based on available real time heterogeneous resources, with an offline machine learning (profile-based estimation model) which can build a device-specific communication computation estimation model. Our scheduling approach is tested on control-regular applications, Stencil kernel (based on a Jacobi Algorithm) and Sparse Matrix-Vector Multiplication (SpMV) in an event-driven runtime system. Experimental results show that PDAWL is either on-par or far outperforms whichever yields the best results (CPU or GPU).

Keywords: Heterogeneous many-core computing · Workload balance · Adaptive modeling · Ml assisted scheduling

1 Introduction and Motivation

As the current TOP500 rankings show, most High-Performance Computing platforms feature heterogeneous hardware resources (CPUs, GPUs, FPGAs, *etc.*) [11].

© Springer Nature Switzerland AG 2020
D. Klusáček et al. (Eds.): JSSPP 2020, LNCS 12326, pp. 145–162, 2020.
https://doi.org/10.1007/978-3-030-63171-0_8

In the future, the nodes of such platforms are expected to be even more heterogeneous and they will feature side-by-side, fast and slow computing units mixed with accelerators, I/O nodes, *etc.* Heterogeneous platforms offer the promise of both better energy efficiency and performance. However, this comes at a cost in terms of code development and resource management.

Meanwhile, whole sectors of scientific computing continue to rely on iterative algorithms. In particular, Stencil-based computations are at the core of many essential scientific applications: Stencils are used in image processing algorithms, *e.g.,* convolutions; partial differential equation solvers, Laplacian transforms, or computational fluid dynamics, linear algebra, *etc.* More specifically, the Jacobi iteration method [19] has been proposed to solve sparse triangular systems arising from incomplete Cholesky preconditioning. A diverse set of realistic symmetric positive definite test problems have proved that Jacobi iterations are effective for a large range of problems [4], while block techniques can further help improve the performance. Other kernels are also used in iterative algorithms, such as sparse matrix-vector multiplications (SpMV). As opposed to Stencil (regular computing per row/column), the individual work-items of SpMV exhibit a different computational load profile since the numbers of non-zero elements per row may vary significantly. However, both Stencil and SpMV are control-regular, and the accelerator and host regularly synchronize until the computation is finished. Finding the right workload balance between accelerator and host for both Stencil and SpMV is the challenge.

Our research is based on the following observations: with a few exceptions (detailed in Sect. 5), most work dealing with accelerators—GPUs—has followed one of two paths: (1) fully offload the most compute-intensive parts of a given application to a GPU, or (2) statically partition the "hot" parts of an application between "CPU-friendly" and "GPU-friendly," *i.e.,* running solely on (respectively) the CPU or the GPU.

This paper presents a novel approach to dynamic scheduling of tasks on heterogeneous systems. It is based on a profile-based machine-learning approach and explores the concept of *co-running*, as defined by Zhang *et al.* [25]: a system has enabled co-running if it runs applications decomposed into tasks capable of running simultaneously on both CPUs and general-purpose accelerators. Our approach, PDAWL, offers the following characteristics:

1. PDAWL is a Profile-based Iterative Dynamic Adaptive WorkLoad balancing algorithm for heterogeneous systems. It can dynamically and adaptively adjust the workload based on the run time situation (dynamic) and hardware platform (static) information. An offline machine learning approach is employed to build the heterogeneous resources performance-workload (communication vs. computation) estimation model based on the analysis of the performance of pure CPUs and GPU. The online scheduler adaptively adjusts the workload allocation based on the run time situation. Combining online and offline information improves flexibility and accuracy.
2. The event-driven characteristics of PDAWL increase flexibility: Multiple levels of parallelism can be employed to improve the flexibility of scheduling.

3. The efficiency of PDAWL is evaluated with control-regular applications: Stencil-based kernels (Jacobi algorithm), featuring regular data process and SpMV-CSR kernels, featuring irregular data process.

The rest of the paper is organized as follows: Sect. 2 reviews the main concepts of this work; Sect. 3 describes our methodology; Sect. 4 focuses on our main experimental results; Sect. 5, reviews the state of the art Finally, Sect. 6 concludes this work and presents the planned future work.

2   Background

PDAWL leverages data-driven execution models and their implementation in large-scale heterogeneous machines at the runtime system level.

Runtime System: We extended DARTS [1,18], an implementation of the Codelet Model [26], to include GPU-aware scheduling capabilities. DARTS relies on dataflow-inspired event-driven parallelism. It can implement fine, coarse, or hybrid-grain parallelism as demanded by the scheduling algorithm.

Heterogeneous Computing: This work considers CPU-GPU heterogeneous systems where GPUs are connected to a host machine via a PCI Express (PCIe) bus. Both have different memory address spaces, and data must be explicitly copied back and forth between the two memory pools.

Concurrent Streams on GPUs: CUDA has been augmented with stream-based constructs starting with CUDA v7. This allows the accelerator to efficiently overlap computation and communication with the host.

3   Methodology

In this section, we present the two ways with which we spread the workload between the host and the accelerator. Dynamic adaptive work-load scheduling is discussed in Sect. 3.1; Sect. 3.2 presents our complementary profile-based approach. As will be discussed in Sect. 4.1, we will target two types of control-regular kernels: Stencil, and a sparse matrix-vector product.

3.1   Dynamic Adaptive Work-Load Scheduler

We aim at finding the right load balance that will maximize throughput when CPUs and GPUs execute. Different factors [9] should be taken into account: the accelerator's memory size, the throughput of PCIe, the structure of the memory hierarchy, the utilization of the cache, the respective computing capabilities of CPUs and GPUs *etc.*

Data-regular Computations. The workload can be decomposed into multiple instances of the same tasks and run on both CPUs and GPU.

$$GPU_{naive} = \text{memcpy}_{Host \to Device} + \frac{\text{Compute}_{Device}}{\text{NumThreads}_{Device}} + \text{memcpy}_{Device \to Host} \tag{1}$$

Eq. 1 models the total GPU execution time. However, it is overly simple. For example, when the various DMA engines are available on modern GPUs, as well as the `Stream` type in CUDA, it is possible to overlap communications and computations. This means that Eq. 1 is a pessimistic/worst-case view of a single GPU's performance. Conversely, it guarantees performance will be maximal if GPU_{naive} is "not too high."

$$CPU_{naive} = \frac{\text{Compute}_{Host}}{\text{NumThreads}_{Host}} \tag{2}$$

Eq. 2 models the CPUs execution time. This model is also rather naïve; While data transfers with the DRAM are not negligible, they take orders of magnitude less time than data transfers on a PCIe bus: they can be neglected. Further more, the performance does not always scale well over multiple cores and nodes. The memory/cache conflicts and synchronization issues incur quite a large overhead. Moreover, HPC processors tend to have a very efficient and aggressive way of prefetching data, which tends to fully hide the latency related to DRAM transfers—especially in the case of consecutive reads or writes. The overlapping data transfers (due to caches and prefetching operations) are included in the execution time.

$$r = \frac{CPU_{naive}}{GPU_{naive}} \tag{3}$$

In Eq. 3, r is the ratio between two quantities, GPU_{naive} and CPU_{naive}, computed in Eq. 1 and 2. If $r \gg 1$, then the workload will execute much faster if it is on an accelerator. Hence, most if not all of the computation will be carried on the GPU. On the contrary, if $r \ll 1$, then the amount of data transfers is saturating the PCIe bus when running it on a GPU, and in general, the overall computation is much faster using general-purpose processing elements. When $r \approx 1$, task scheduling must enable co-running, so that both the host and the accelerator are allocated their fair share of the work in order to complete the computation as fast as possible.

Data-irregular Computations. Irregular computations can lower GPU performance dramatically. To counter this effect, we can extract the irregular parts and assign them to CPUs. The remaining regular workload can then follow the same methodology as with data-regular computations.

The Dynamic Adaptive WorkLoad (DAWL) Scheduler. DAWL was created to decide what tasks should be scheduled and where to schedule workload to minimize the load imbalance between heterogeneous processing elements. It adjusts

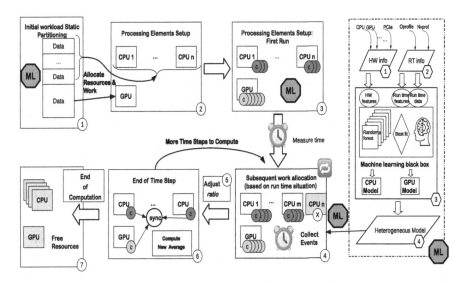

Fig. 1. PDAWL – The Dynamic Adaptive Work-Load scheduling algorithm coupled with Machine Learning. Machine learning occurs in steps 1, 3, and 4 (see the bold polygon ML).

the workload distribution on different computing resources based on real-time information and the knowledge we have derived from Eq. 1, 2, and 3. It consists of seven main steps, outlined in Fig. 1.

1. Set up the initial workload on all the Processing Elements (PEs), namely CPUs and GPU.
2. Configure PEs according to the given workload. This includes how many CPUs will be put to work, whether the GPU will be also used, how much shared memory (for the host) and global memory (for the accelerator) must be allocated, the number of streams on the GPU, *etc.*
3. Simultaneously run tasks on both CPUs and GPUs, and time each execution for their specific workloads.
4. Check the status of the PEs, estimate the completion time of other devices based on the history timing measurements. Then allocate and run the next workload on available PEs. Repeat until the remaining workload is within 10% of the total workload.
5. Calculate the value of *ratio*, where $ratio = \text{CPU}_{cur}/(\text{CPU}_{cur} + \text{GPU}_{cur})$. CPU_{cur} and GPU_{cur} are the amount of all work finished on CPUs and GPU, respectively. The corresponding GPU ratio is obtained using the same method. The CPUs or the GPU only take $\lfloor ratio \times \text{remaining workload} \rfloor$ amount of work. The remaining workload is dynamically allocated to whichever (set of) PE(s) is available after completing early.
6. Evaluate the load-balance metrics collected during the time step execution, in particular the execution time. Adjust (coarsen) the task granularity based on available PEs and the metrics.
7. Free all resources: PEs and memory.

3.2   Profile-Based Machine Learning Estimation Model

Eq. 1 and Eq. 2 are too naïve to model complex situations. The growing variety of hardware devices as well as their combinations, increases the difficulty of building accurate mathematical estimation models. Furthermore, *any* change in the hardware configuration may cause great performance variations and result in a need to rebuild the mathematical model. Moreover, the mathematical model cannot capture the run time situation which is another important factor that affects the accuracy of the performance estimation model.

Considering these factors, we designed a profile-based Machine Learning (ML) approach to reduce the complexity of establishing an estimation model while promoting its accuracy. We call the resulting algorithm PDAWL, short for Profile-based DAWL. It follows four phases, as shown in Fig. 1's dotted box:

1. Collect hardware information. Table 1 lists some parameters. In addition to these, the host's cache related and more GPU parameters have also been collected.
2. Collect the application's profile information at run time as training data. The pure CPU and pure GPU performance model are used to predict the heterogeneous (co-running) performance model.
   - CPU: We collect cache and branch related events using Oprofile [10]
   - GPU: We used the gpu-trace and api-trace APIs to collect CUDA run time information and events.
3. Normalize the collected data to a common scale
4. Cluster features: a hierarchical agglomerative clustering algorithm (HAC) is utilized to group similarity features, collected from Oprofile and Nvprof, and finally obtain 4 to 12 features.
5. Build a pure CPU and pure GPU profile-based estimation model.
   - Run a set of ML algorithms such as linear regression, support vector machine (SVM) and random forest model. Specifically, the linear regression model can be shown in the form: $ln(F(X)) = \sum_{i=1}^{n} w_i \phi_i(x_i)$. Where $\phi_i(x)$ are functions from the set of $x, x^2, x^3, x^4, e^x, lnx, x \cdot lnx$; x_i are features from last cluster step. The logarithmic scale is used to fit the final data $F(X)$. It provides reasonable approximations with the target variable and reduce the non-linearity factors [2]. For SVM, we try the polynomial and Gaussian kernels.
   - Overfitting: we use 10-fold cross validation and L2 regulatity to reduce the overfitting problems.
   - Evaluate models: To evaluate how well the model fits the data, a coefficient of determination, $R_{squared}$, is used. $R_{squared} = \frac{\text{Explained variation}}{\text{Total variation}}$, with $0\% \leq R_{squared} \leq 100\%$. 0% indicates the model explains none of the variability of the response data around its mean while 100% says that the model explains all the variability of the response data around its mean.
   - Build an estimation model with the best matched ML algorithm to predict an application's performance on this specific heterogeneous platform.

6. Build a heterogeneous prediction model based on the pure CPU and GPU model. Based on Sects. 2 and 3.1, and Eq. 1 and 3, the concurrent streams technique will be utilized when the workload is far larger than the GPU's global memory. Then, the huge workload will be split into relatively small concurrent workload tasks. In this case, we can use the small workloads performance information, obtained from the GPU model, to predict the large workload allocation and execution on GPU.

PDAWL results from the combination of the heterogeneous prediction model and DAWL. DAWL can dynamically adjust the workload allocation depending on the run time execution situation. It monitors the actual execution time and compares it with the ML-provided baseline. It then increases the confidence interval for the next tasks and can further compensate for the insufficient offline ML method. The ML model remains suitable or provides some guidance when the software or the hardware changes. This approach is suitable for all iterative algorithms, as they often require some form of global synchronization. The reason why we combine offline ML with online scheduling methods together is to expect the test applications can satisfy the real-time requirements. If there is no real-time requirement, we can use the online ML (such as stochastic gradient algorithm) to replace offline ML to build prediction model.

4 Algorithm Implementation and Experiment Results

4.1 Experimental Testbed

Table 1. Hardware platforms

Machines	Param.									
	CPU parameters					GPU parameters				PCIe
	Cores	Clock	Socket	L3 Size	Mem	SM	Clock	L2 Size	Mem	
Machine1 (K20)	32	2.6 GHz	2	20 MB	64 GB	13	0.71 GHz	1.25 MB	4.8 GB	6.1 GB/s
Machine2 (K20)	40	3 GHz	2	25 MB	256 GB	13	0.71 GHz	1.25 MB	4.8 GB	6.1 GB/s
Machine3 (k40)	8	3.4 GHz	1	8 MB	16 GB	15	0.75 GHz	1.5 MB	12 GB	10.3 GB/s
Machine4 (Titan)	12	3.4 GHz	1	12 MB	31 GB	14	0.88 GHz	1.5 MB	6 GB	11.5 GB/s

We ran the experiments on four heterogeneous systems, as shown in Table 1 and 2. Stencil-based computations and Compressed Row SpMV (SpMV-CSR) were selected to evaluate our DAWL and PDAWL.

Target Applications: Stencil Computation To emphasize a worst-case scenario, we used the Stencil kernels described in [8], without ghost cells, which enhances the need for synchronization. Specifically, we focused on kernel: a 5-point 2D Stencil, double precision. We fixed the number of time steps to 30, removing the convergence test at the end of each time step for simplification

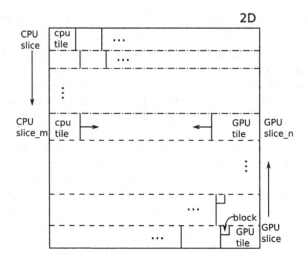

Fig. 2. GPU/CPU hybrid: 2D Stencil slicing and tiling

and to make it more deterministic. Note that the CPU tasks and GPU tasks within one time step were totally independent and that a global barrier was inserted at the end of each iteration. Each experiment was repeated 20 times. There are no confidence intervals as the standard deviations were small, the larger one being 5% and the average smaller than 1%.

The partitioning approach we employed for CPU/GPU tasks entails two steps named "Slicing" and "Tiling," respectively, as shown in Fig. 2. A static Blocks-Tile size was selected for DAWL. As mentioned in Sect. 3, different systems architecture can yield different parameters for our ML model. Hence, it tries to find the right match between a given Blocks-Tile size and the number of concurrent streams to issue. This results in near-optimal compute-communication overlap.

Target Applications: SpMV Computation We reuse the SHOC benchmark suite's implementation of SpMV-CSR [5], for both the CUDA and CPP sequential versions. We convert the sequential code to parallel code where every CPU core can calculate one or multiple rows. Considering that the number of non-zero elements per row in a sparse matrix may make a significant difference, we call the denser rows (with many more non-zero elements) "irregular rows," whereas the others are deemed "regular rows." Once the irregular rows can be processed separately, the majority regular rows that are left over can be considered at regular computing and can run with our DAWL and PDAWL. To split regular and irregular rows, we build up a co-running model on SHOC SPMV-CSR. More specific steps will be shown in the following:

1. Analyze and evaluate statistic information (see Table 3) to estimate the sparsity degree of the matrix. NNZ is the number of total non-zero elements; μ

is the average number of non-zero elements per row; σ is the variance of the number of non-zero elements per row; CV is the coefficient of variation per row; MAX is the maximum number of non-zero elements per row.

2. Build priority groups based on the information. The highest priority level contains the maximum non-zero number per row(s). The majority regular rows construct of the lowest level. In the same level, group members have similar non-zero numbers so they can run parallel. To simplify the model, we statically set the ratio (30%) as the threshold. Top 30% maximum non-zero number per row(s) will be extracted from the matrix and added to CPUs priority groups. The ratio can be learned using ML model, but it will increase training cases and time.

3. Run irregular and regular computations on CPUs and GPU, in parallel. CPUs will proceed from the higher to the lower level and GPU will proceed from the lowest level. Concurrent streams are leveraged here.

4. Synchronize all the computations at the end.

Parameter Space of Our Experiments. We used `numactl` to allocate memory in a round-robin fashion and avoid NUMA-related issues. We configure the GPU memory to 2 GB as an example to explain our methodology. We will not show experiments with other GPU memory configuration since the overall trend is the same for all of them.

Table 2. Software Environment

Machines	GCC	CUDA
Machine1	v6.2/v8.1	v8.0
Machine2	v4.85/v6.2	v8.0
Machine3	v5.4	v9.0
Machine4	v4.92	v9.1

Table 3. Matrices for SpMV

Name	Dimension	NNZ	μ	σ	CV	MAX
circuit5M	5.56 M	59.52 M	10.71	1356.62	126.68	1290501
eu-2005	0.86 M	19.24 M	22.30	29.33	1.32	6985
in-2004	1.38 M	16.92 M	12.23	37.23	3.04	7753
FullChip	2.99 M	26.62 M	8.91	1806.80	202.73	2312481
kmer_U1a	67.7 M	138.8 M	2.05	0.37	0.18	35

Matrices Used for our Experiments. We use 50 sparse matrices from the University of Florida Sparse Matrix Collection (UFSMC) [6] to train and 5 matrices 3 to evaluate our DAWL/PDAWL.

4.2 DAWL: Performance Analysis

To comprehensively characterize DAWL, we performed a series of workload performance analysis. We compared the DARTS-DAWL performance with GPU-Only, CPU-Seq, DARTS-CPU, and DARTS-GPU (see Table 4 for details). DARTS-DAWL is the implementation of DAWL on DARTS. Based on the parameters mentioned in Sect. 3.1, DARTS-DAWL may run on multiple CPUs or GPU, or be co-running on both CPUs and GPU.

Figure 3 shows the speedup of different variants for the Stencil. DARTS-GPU use concurrent streams all time. while, GPU-Only use a one-stream method when

Table 4. Stencil kernel implementation

Implementation	Illustration
CPU-Seq	Sequential c++ code
GPU-Only	CUDA code
DARTS-CPU	Multi-threads c++ code
DARTS-GPU	CUDA code on DARTS (concurrent streams)
DARTS-DAWL	DAWL hybrid code on DARTS

the problem size is smaller than the GPU memory capacity. This is to avoid superfluous synchronizations between the host and device. Concurrent streams are utilized when the problem size is larger than the GPU's memory capacity to overlap communication and computation.

Figure 3 demonstrates the validity of our model. With 30 iterations constraints on Stencil kernels, when the workload is less than the available device memory, r from Eq. 3 is far larger than 1, and the application allocates all the workload to the device so as to yield maximum performance. When the workload is larger than the available device memory, it is allocated to both the host and the device. Adding the communication & synchronization costs between two resources types ultimately causes the total performance to drop. The speedup ratios are quite different on different systems, which is due to the differences in hardware. *e.g.*, the GPU of machine 3 is a Tesla-K40, which has a higher clock and memory frequency than Tesla-K20.

DARTS-DAWL on machine 3 should run in pure GPU mode based on the analytic model. Here, DARTS-DAWL is hard coded to co-running to show our ML approach will improve performance even in the worst case which chooses the wrong target device as shown in Fig. 5.

4.3   Profile-Based Estimation Model and Result

Section 3.2 shows how we use the performance of pure CPU or GPU to predict that of concurrent CPU-GPU. Our training/validation/test set is split into two, CPU and GPU. The "CPU set" is to build a CPU performance-resource estimation model which can provide the "best" scheduler using minimum computing resources to obtain the maximum performance (shortest execution time) for a specific workload. combining spread and compact mapping policies, we run experiments with different active CPU threads number (*e.g.* 2, 4, 8, 16...) to obtain the necessary run time information by using Oprofile. PDAWL utilizes this information to provide an accurate prediction model even when (for example) some PEs are suddenly turned off because of power issues.

The "GPU set" is used to build a GPU communication-computation overlap model, to estimate data transfer and execution time. In particular, the right Block-Tile size can perfectly overlap communication and computation on a system; and yet, the overlap ratio may be very low on other systems since the

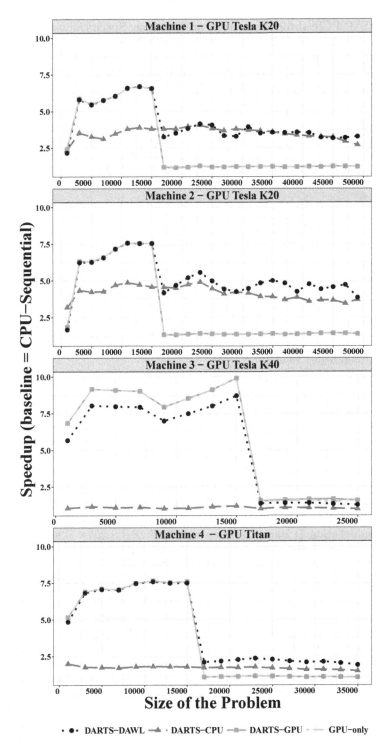

Fig. 3. Stencil: Speedup of the different versions

available SM, PCIe throughput, *etc.* are different. Specifically, the estimation model consists of: API launching, data transfer between host and device and device computation parts. We run the two version of GPU code, with or without concurrent streams, combining with different Block-Tile size.

The information collected by the runtime helps gather more than two hundreds features for each type of device. HAC was employed to group features. Figure 4 shows one dendrogram aiming at grouping the features in five clusters. One feature with the maximum variance is selected from each cluster. We then selected different group of features running the dendrogram algorithm with different numbers of cluster groups (*e.g.,* 4, 5, 6, $\cdots$, 12).

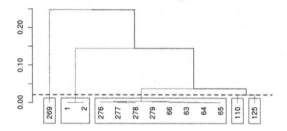

Fig. 4. Stencil: Dendrogram with 5 clusters from features with correlation between the execution times higher than $|0.75|$

Table 5. Stencil : Mean Absolute Percentage Error

Machines	#1	#2	#3	#4
MAPE	6.43%	7.41%	3.45%	1.68%

After running various ML algorithms, as described in Sect. 3.2, it turns out that the model that finds the majority of the best matches both for Stencil and SpMV computation is *linear regression:* $0.93 \leq R_{squared} \leq 0.94$. The chosen model may change with different types of applications and hardware configurations. To measure the progress of the learning algorithm the Mean Absolute Percentage Error (MAPE) was used. Table 5 shows the MAPE of the linear model for each machine in the Stencil experiments. The important factors vary with the hardware configuration and cluster group numbers.

Figures 5 show the results for PDAWL. Compared to `DARTS-CPU`, the number of PEs changes with runtime. Our scheduler can reach up to 6× speedups compared to sequential runs, 1.6× speedup compared to the multiple core version, and 4.8× speedup compared to the pure GPU version in the Stencil. Figures 5 shows that one cannot always obtain significant speedups using profiling. This is especially true around *drop points* (drop points are unstable points and are affected by multiple co-running hardware/software conflicts parameters, which our machine learning estimation model did not take into consideration).

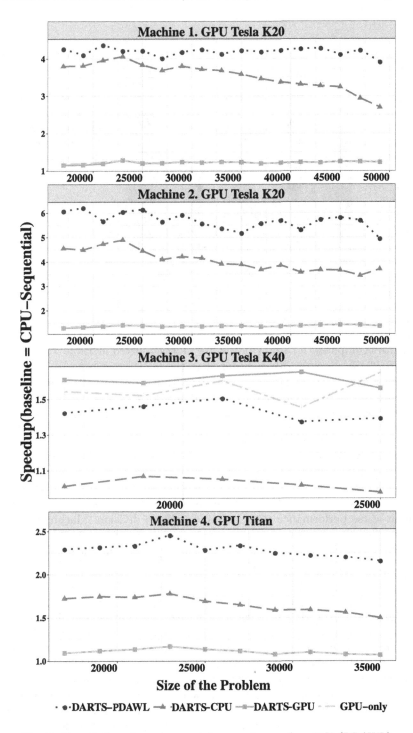

Fig. 5. Stencil: Speedup when matrices are larger than 17K (PDAWL)

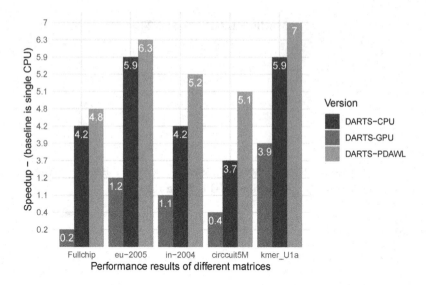

Fig. 6. SpMV Performance(SpeedUP)

Figure 6 compares the SpMV of the five Matrices listed in Table 3 on Machine 1. `DARTS-PDAWL` executes 30.5× faster than the GPU version and 1.37× better than the multi CPU version. Our ML algorithm can be further improved by combining online learning Algorithms and neural-networks with our learning estimation model.

5   Related Work

The main challenge of the load-balancing mechanism is to precisely divide workload on processing units. A simple heuristics division approach may actually result in worse performance than a simple uniform division. Machine-learning-based prediction mechanism or/and online profiling-based scheduling algorithms have been deployed to determine the workload partitioning decision on many-core homogeneous/heterogeneous systems.

[12] proposes an empirical adaptive mapping, a fully automatic technique to map computations to processing elements on heterogeneous multiprocessors. [21] utilizes an ML approach to decide whether to parallelize a loop and how to schedule candidates on multi-core platforms. [16,17] proposed two profile-based scheduling algorithms for data-parallel applications in heterogeneous CPU-GPU clusters.The ML approach is utilized to predict the best distribution of data block size among different processing units. [25] performs a series of workload characterization analysis to understand the co-running behaviors on integrated CPU/GPU architecture. The main factors affecting the co-running performance: the architectural differences between CPUs and GPUs and the limited shared memory bandwidth. Based on this information, an ML model can be built to

predict coarse-grain workload partitioning on a co-running device before porting the program. [24] proposes a fine-grain workload reshaping approach which combines performance prediction, from an ML model, and partitioning threshold, from an online-turning model, to partition the workload between CPU and GPU on integrated architectures. When the workload is lower than the threshold, it is executed on GPUs. Otherwise, CPUs are employed. [14] and [15] focus on the accelerator sharing control for multiple kernels and propose to use ML to determine whether to run OpenCL code on GPU or OpenMP code on multi-core CPUs. [22] uses ML to decide whether to merge or separate multi-user OpenCL tasks running on the most suitable devices in a CPU-GPU systems.

Except for architectural differences, communication between CPUs, GPUs, and the memory has a pivotal role. [3,7,20,23,25] propose an analytical performance model that includes PCIe transfers and overlapping computation and communication. [13] proposes PARTANS, an autotuning framework for CPUs and GPUs to execute Stencil computations over two nodes with multiple GPUs. Data transfer on the PCIe bus play a crucial role to determine the number of GPUs to be utilized. To handle the communication-synchronization problem between CPUs and GPUs,

Most of these are aimed at coarse-grain workload partitioning and loosely synchronized parallel workloads where specific tasks are often run only a specific type of processing element (*e.g.*, CPU or GPU). [24] works for fine-grain partitioning, but static workload partition is inherently rigid. Furthermore, the precision of the ML model determines the efficiency of workload partitioning approach. The hardware change during runtime may have a catastrophic effect on the performance. At the same time, hardware changes during runtime may happen frequently, and as much as half of the CPU cores may be turned off because of power issues.

Our work focuses on synchronization between CPUs and GPUs. Further, the communication between CPUs and GPUs plays a central role in our dynamic scheduling approach. Finally, our approach is neither purely static nor dynamic. We combine the two models: an offline ML model provides us with workload allocation, while DAWL dynamically balances the workload to compensate offline-ML inaccuracies.

6 Conclusions and Future Work

We have presented PDAWL, an iterative event-driven scheduling algorithm designed to better load balance tasks in a heterogeneous system. It leverages a profile-based approach based on offline machine learning and an online scheduling approach. The Machine-Learning estimation model can help build an estimation model in a heterogeneous resource context. It consists of a CPU model and a GPU model. We used ML to find the best workload-resource match to improve the CPUs' utilization rate as well as the optimal estimation model to improve GPU performance since building an accurate mathematical general-purpose GPU performance model is nigh-impossible, as the search space is too large. Online event-driven scheduling can make up for the inflexibility of offline machine learning and increase accuracy of scheduling.

Two applications, Stencil and SpMV, have been chosen to evaluate our approach. Experiments with Stencil and SpMV show that PDAWL yields speedups up to 1.6× and 1.37× for a multi-core baseline, 4.8× and 30.5× for pure GPU execution.

Future work includes augmenting our model with power consumption parameters to enrich PDAWL and determining good trade-offs between performance and power on heterogeneous architectures. We plan on adding Deep Learning algorithms to PDAWL. We will also employ meta learning to reduce training time when run our PDAWL on other configuration Hardware environment.

References

1. Arteaga, J., Zuckerman, S., Gao, G.R.: Generating fine-grain multithreaded applications using a multigrain approach. ACM Trans. Archit. Code Optim. **14**(4), 1–47 (2017). https://doi.org/10.1145/3155288
2. Barnes, B.J., Rountree, B., Lowenthal, D.K., Reeves, J., de Supinski, B., Schulz, M.: A regression-based approach to scalability prediction. In: Proceedings of the 22Nd Annual International Conference on Supercomputing, pp. 368–377. ICS 2008, ACM, New York, USA (2008). https://doi.org/10.1145/1375527.1375580
3. Chen, Q., Guo, M.: Contention and locality-aware work-stealing for iterative applications in multi-socket computers. IEEE Trans. Comput. **67**(6), 784–798 (2018). https://doi.org/10.1109/TC.2017.2783932
4. Chow, E., Anzt, H., Scott, J., Dongarra, J.: Using jacobi iterations and blocking for solving sparse triangular systems in incomplete factorization preconditioning. J. Parallel Distrib. Comput. **119**, 219–230 (2018)
5. Danalis, A., et al.: The scalable heterogeneous computing (SHOC) benchmark suite. In: Proceedings of the 3rd Workshop on General-Purpose Computation on Graphics Processing Units, pp. 63–74. GPGPU-3, ACM, New York, USA (2010). https://doi.org/10.1145/1735688.1735702, http://doi.acm.org/10.1145/1735688.1735702
6. Davis, T.A., Hu, Y.: The university of florida sparse matrix collection. ACM Trans. Math. Softw. **38**(1), 1:1–1:25 December 2011. https://doi.org/10.1145/2049662.2049663, http://doi.acm.org/10.1145/2049662.2049663
7. García, V., Gomez-Luna, J., Grass, T., Rico, A., Ayguade, E., Pena, A.J.: Evaluating the effect of last-level cache sharing on integrated GPU-CPU systems with heterogeneous applications. In: 2016 IEEE International Symposium on Workload Characterization (IISWC), pp. 1–10 September 2016. https://doi.org/10.1109/IISWC.2016.7581277
8. Geng, T., et al.: The importance of efficient fine-grain synchronization for manycore systems. In: Ding, C., Criswell, J., Wu, P. (eds.) LCPC 2016. LNCS, vol. 10136, pp. 203–217. Springer, Cham (2017). https://doi.org/10.1007/978-3-319-52709-3_16
9. Lee, V.W., et al.: Debunking the 100x gpu vs. cpu myth: An evaluation of throughput computing on CPU and GPU. In: Proceedings of the 37th Annual International Symposium on Computer Architecture, pp. 451–460. ISCA 2010, ACM, New York, USA (2010). https://doi.org/10.1145/1815961.1816021, http://doi.acm.org/10.1145/1815961.1816021

10. Levon, J., Elie, P.: Oprofile: A system profiler for linux (2004)
11. List, T.S.: November 2017. http://www.top500.org
12. Luk, C.K., Hong, S., Kim, H.: Qilin: exploiting parallelism on heterogeneous multiprocessors with adaptive mapping. In: Proceedings of the 42Nd Annual IEEE/ACM International Symposium on Microarchitecture, pp. 45–55. MICRO 42, ACM, New York, USA (2009). https://doi.org/10.1145/1669112.1669121, http://doi.acm.org/10.1145/1669112.1669121
13. Lutz, T., Fensch, C., Cole, M.: Partans: an autotuning framework for stencil computation on multi-GPU systems. ACM Trans. Arch. Code Optim. (TACO) 9(4), 59 (2013)
14. Margiolas, C., O'Boyle, M.F.P.: Portable and transparent software managed scheduling on accelerators for fair resource sharing. In: 2016 IEEE/ACM International Symposium on Code Generation and Optimization (CGO), pp. 82–93, March 2016
15. O'Boyle, M.F.P., Wang, Z., Grewe, D.: Portable mapping of data parallel programs to opencl for heterogeneous systems. In: Proceedings of the 2013 IEEE/ACM International Symposium on Code Generation and Optimization (CGO). pp. 1–10. CGO 2013, IEEE Computer Society, Washington, DC, USA (2013). https://doi.org/10.1109/CGO.2013.6494993, http://dx.doi.org/10.1109/CGO.2013.6494993
16. Sant'Ana, L., Cordeiro, D., Camargo, R.: PLB-HeC: a profile-based load-balancing algorithm for heterogeneous CPU-GPU clusters. In: 2015 IEEE International Conference on Cluster Computing, pp. 96–105, September 2015. https://doi.org/10.1109/CLUSTER.2015.24
17. San'Ana, L., Cordeiro, D., de Camargo, R.Y.: PLB-HAC: dynamic load-balancing for heterogeneous accelerator clusters. In: Yahyapour, R. (ed.) Euro-Par 2019. LNCS, vol. 11725, pp. 197–209. Springer, Cham (2019). https://doi.org/10.1007/978-3-030-29400-7_15
18. Suettlerlein, J., Zuckerman, S., Gao, G.R.: An implementation of the codelet model. In: Wolf, F., Mohr, B., an Mey, D. (eds.) Euro-Par 2013. LNCS, vol. 8097, pp. 633–644. Springer, Heidelberg (2013). https://doi.org/10.1007/978-3-642-40047-6_63
19. Tribbey, W.: Modern database systems. In: Kim, W. (ed.) Modern Database Systems, chap. Numerical Recipes: The Art of Scientific Computing (3rd Edition) is Written by William H. Press, Saul A. Teukolsky, William T. Vetterling, and Brian P. Flannery, and Published by Cambridge University Press, 2007, Hardback, pp. 30–31, ISBN 978-0-521-88068-8, 1235 Pp. ACM Press/Addison-Wesley Publishing Co., New York, USA (1995). https://doi.org/10.1145/1874391.187410, http://dx.doi.org/10.1145/1874391.187410
20. Van Craeynest, K., Jaleel, A., Eeckhout, L., Narvaez, P., Emer, J.: Scheduling heterogeneous multi-cores through performance impact estimation (pie). SIGARCH Comput. Archit. News 40(3), 213–224 (2012). https://doi.org/10.1145/2366231.2337184, http://doi.acm.org/10.1145/2366231.2337184
21. Wang, Z., Tournavitis, G., Franke, B., O'boyle, M.F.P.: Integrating profile-driven parallelism detection and machine-learning-based mapping. ACM Trans. Archit. Code Optim. 11(1), 1–26 (2014). https://doi.org/10.1145/2579561, http://doi.acm.org/10.1145/2579561
22. Wen, Y., O'Boyle, M.F.: Merge or separate?: multi-job scheduling for opencl kernels on CPU/GPU platforms. In: Proceedings of the General Purpose GPUs, pp. 22–31. GPGPU-10, ACM, New York, USA (2017). https://doi.org/10.1145/3038228.3038235, http://doi.acm.org/10.1145/3038228.3038235

23. Yang, C., et al.: Adaptive optimization for petascale heterogeneous CPU/GPU computing. In: IEEE International Conference on Cluster Computing, pp. 19–28, September 2010). https://doi.org/10.1109/CLUSTER.2010.12

24. Zhang, F., Wu, B., Zhai, J., He, B., Chen, W.: Finepar: irregularity-aware fine-grained workload partitioning on integrated architectures. In: 2017 IEEE/ACM International Symposium on Code Generation and Optimization (CGO), pp. 27–38, Febuary 2017. https://doi.org/10.1109/CGO.2017.7863726

25. Zhang, F., Zhai, J., He, B., Zhang, S., Chen, W.: Understanding co-running behaviors on integrated CPU/GPU architectures. IEEE TPDS **28**(3), 905–918 (2017). https://doi.org/10.1109/TPDS.2016.2586074

26. Zuckerman, S., Suetterlein, J., Knauerhase, R., Gao, G.R.: Using a "codelet" program execution model for exascale machines: position paper. In: Proceedings of the 1st International Workshop on Adaptive Self-Tuning Computing Systems for the Exaflop Era. EXADAPT 2011, ACM, New York, USA (2011)

Author Index

Printed in the United States
By Bookmasters